Hands Open

•Leslie Powles the author

Hands Open

Twice round the world single handed
east-to-west and west-to-east

Leslie Powles

KENNETH MASON

Published by Kenneth Mason
The Old Harbourmaster's, Emsworth,
Hampshire PO10 7DD
Designed by Articulate Studio

British Library Cataloguing in Publication Data

Powles, Leslie
    Hands open, twice around the world single-handed:
    east to west and west to east.
    1. Voyages around the world—1951-
    I. Title
    910.4'1   G440

    ISBN 0-85937-338-X

Contents

PART ONE/FIRST TIME ROUND

Chapter 1
A mobile home to carry self, suitcase and a set of golf clubs.
Realising the dream   *page 7*

Chapter 2
The start of the journey. Losing the Caribbean and finding
Brazil!   *page 25*

Chapter 3
From Brazil to the Panama Canal and mugging in Colon.
The paradise of Hiva Oa   *page 53*

Chapter 4
Tahiti and Australia. Through the Great Barrier Reef and on
to South Africa, St Helena, Ascension and home. What kept
you?   *page 77*

PART TWO/SECOND TIME ROUND

Round the world non-stop, the first single-handed circumnavigation both ways. Where the hell have you been?   *page 107*

Postscript and a tribute   *page 215*

• Solitaire the boat

PART ONE   First time round

1

FROM A DEEP SLEEP to panic: Christ, she's aground on the reef again! Struggling from my bunk on legs that will not respond, I hear a baby's cry and a man's soothing voice, speaking in a language I cannot understand. Trying to pierce the gloom through sweat-filled eyes, I realise I am no longer aboard my sinking boat, but bed-bound in a small white room. Moonlight through a window touches wall-mounted posters about pregnancy before outlining rafters that disappear into blackness. Then memory floods back.

The population of Tutoia, a small fishing village on the Brazilian coast had increased that day with the birth of a child howling its first protest at the moment that a wreck of a man lay near to gasping his last. I had been half carried, half dragged from my boat and into their hospital, blister-faced with feet infected and groin swollen. Sailing, I had once read, was a peaceful pastime punctuated by moments of extreme excitement but after my experience on the reef a week earlier 'extreme excitement' seemed the ultimate in understatement. As to those pregnancy posters on my wall the only thing I'd given birth to was a yacht called *Solitaire* or, as she was registered, *Solitaire of Hamble*.

She was conceived in South Africa towards the end of 1968; before this I had spent two years working as a radio engineer in South Yemen where I had taken to golf. But knocking little white balls over the desert held no future and I had flown to South Africa to practise my newly-acquired skills on grass, which led first to employment by an electronics company and then, indirectly, to sailing. One morning I wandered along Point Yacht Club's jetty in Durban where cruising yachts from all over the world had come to rest, colour splashing from their fluttering flags, and was struck by their freedom. They were not shackled to land by chains whose links were forged by careers, mortgages and fashion; their mooring lines were but spiders' webs so fragile that they could be broken on a whim or a wind's whisper. Suddenly I wanted to throw my arms wide and scream at the heavens, YaaaaaaaaHoooooooo. But an Englishman of course doesn't do that sort of thing, not at ten o'clock on a Sunday morning, not in Durban.

I gave thought neither to sailing nor to the vessel itself, simply appreciating that a boat could be both home and transport for self, suitcase and a set of golf clubs from A to B at minimal cost. Conception then you might say was by rape rather than seduction – a rape whose resultant fertilisation would entail a four-year pregnancy thanks to inflation, financial rather than physical. Early 1969 found me back in England with only £2,000 to my name; a sum that was hopelessly inadequate for the sort of boat I coveted. So I took a contract in Saudi Arabia as an aircraft radio engineer and pushed my savings up to £4,500, only to return home to yet more inflation. At this stage I met a young English couple just back from two years' sailing in the Mediterranean, who were now off around the world in a beautiful 45ft sloop. Believing them to be experienced I considered myself lucky when asked to act as crew, but we motored most of the way to Gibraltar and I can recollect no single incident or experience that proved useful on subsequent voyages, unless it was a strong desire to sail alone. I would make blunders but they would be mine rather than someone else's; they were certainly not the yacht's and never the sea's whose roar can burst an eardrum but, when it comes to excuses, is profoundly deaf. No, I would sail single-handed. Alone.

After another stint in Saudi Arabia the beginning of 1973 found me possessed of the respectable sum of £8,500, by which time the price of the type of boat I wanted had jumped to more than £12,000. Then I chanced on an advertisement in a yachting magazine, 'come to Liverpool and build your own Nor-West 34, hull and deck, £1,300'. I promptly made an appointment, and one cold morning in January drove through Liverpool's leaning dock gates, easing the throttle to prevent tyreslip on the oily cobblestones. The dock's stagnant waters housed a waste of pans, cans and blackened bottles and on the adjacent rusty railway lines weeds flourished. A mouldering brick building, about 900ft x 90ft, with a high sloping roof showing gaping holes, was the boatbuilders' headquarters where two modern cars, parked by high sliding doors, hinted of better things to come inside.

I edged mine alongside, wondering whether to brave the drizzle that was turning to rain; then making a dash for the doors, I grabbed the padlock and heaved. Nothing happened. Minutes later I'm still attempting to get in; only now I am being tried out for Arsenal and taking running kicks at the door. All I want is to force my way inside and tell them what they can do with their stupid boat. A polite cough as an immaculately-dressed man emerges from a side door. 'Mr Powles? We've been expecting you. My name is Keith Johnson, managing director. This way, please.' And he escorts me into this derelict slum as if it's a Hilton Hotel. Inside are two enormous plastic tents. 'This is where we lay off the hulls; the plastic prevents dust falling onto the resin'. All is spoken in a serious voice, despite the heavy rain still soaking us. We move further into the building in search of a dryer spot where, in Nelson's time, the floor might have been of stone and is now, after centuries of dust, but a puddled dirt surface. The managing director still rattles on. 'We have two plugs for building the hulls, one used by the company, the other for do-it-yourself people. The company can build a hull and deck for £2,500. Have a look, as it happens a couple of our self-building customers are just about to remove the plug from their hull.' With that he points to the far end of the shed where a crane hovers over the vague outline of a boat.

It was love at first sight. Instinctively I knew this I had to have. 'What's the specification, Keith?'
'She's a bermudan sloop in foam sandwich and glassfibre designed by an Australian, Bruce Roberts. She's 33ft 6ins long, 24ft 6ins on her waterline, with a beam of 10ft 6ins and a draft of 5ft 6ins. Classed as a cruiser racer she can sleep up to seven people'. She would have more room than the Contessa 32 which I had seen at the London Boat Show but could not afford and had the same clean lines as the Contessa with a fine entry, keel and skeg, but I could not see my wanting ever to sleep seven people aboard her.
'What will she cost complete?'
'Around £4,000 to £5,000, but that's up to the individual. We charge a basic £1,300, which includes the use of the plug for a month, a female mould for the deck and all building materials, a set of plans and fitting-out instructions and free rent for a month. After that there's a small charge if you remain longer.'

I would need a place to live. 'If I bought a small caravan could I keep it alongside the hull?' I asked. A quick nod to that. 'If I gave you a cheque for a deposit today, when could I start?'

There was a pause. 'It's short notice but you could start in a month's time. ' I wrote a cheque for £400.

The womb that was to develop *Solitaire*'s embryo would not be safe and warm, but she could still be a beautiful baby and with my £8,500 I would give her the best start I could in life. On the 80 mile drive back to my home town of Birmingham I considered two priorities: first I had to buy a caravan, second I would need help for a few days.

Having bought a secondhand caravan for £200 I arranged for a school-leaver to spend a week with me, contracting to feed him, to take him to the cinema once, and to pay him £10 in wages. A couple of hometown mates agreed to spend a long weekend helping me to fibreglass in return for a slap-up meal and all the beer they could drink. Ken Mudd and Tony Marshall were both quality control engineers, Ken with British Leyland, Tony with Lucas Electronics. The first I had met when I worked on guided missiles after returning from Canada in 1956 following the break-up of my first marriage. Tony came on to my scene in 1970 together with his wife Irene and their two lovely blonde daughters: their home was to become a workshop and a haven where I was always welcome.

The plug, or former, looked like an inverted hull built of wooden laths with half-inch gaps. While upside down, sheets of polyurethane foam (up to three feet by four feet and half an inch thick) are sewn onto it, using a forked 'bogger'. String is forced through the foam and between the laths, forming a loop into which nails are placed. When tension is applied the nails prevent the string pulling out, forcing the foam hard against the plug, much like a bobbin in a sewing machine.

The building of *Solitaire*, as I had already named her, went to schedule. After nine days, thanks to the help from one boy and two friends, the hull was covered with rough fibreglass, which left three weeks of my month for the miserable part – screening and sanding. Talcum powder and resin are mixed to form a paste, then a catalyst (hardener) is added with which to plaster the rough hull. For smoothing I hired heavy industrial sanders with vacuum attachments but white dust flew everywhere. I had to dress in overalls, taping the cuffs and trouser bottoms, and wear a face mask and hat. By night ghost-like figures would move as if they had fallen into flour vats, self-raising puffs for their feet or shimmering haloes round their heads, careful never to leave the building in their disguise by night lest the local population be diminished by heart arrest.

As the weeks passed the weather warmed, and more people started building. The shed became a village community with its own characters; some, like driftwood, bumped alongside briefly, leaving but a faint impression before disappearing. Others would weave themselves into the fabric of my life with acts of kindness and consideration. I would make my voyages and have my moments of glory but without such friends it is difficult in retrospect to see how.

Stan turned up one morning in a 20-ton tipper to build his hull. Until then there had been no facility for removing the mountain of rubbish in the middle of the floor. The rats that infested it grew tame, no longer scurrying away at the approach of a human but stopping to clean their whiskers, lift a paw to their forelocks and give an apologetic half smile, as much as to say, 'morning, govner'. This always started my day well for I would nod and even consider raising a hand in the weak-wristed wave favoured by royalty.

The yacht builders arranged for a tractor to load our mountain onto Stan's truck, to be carted away when he left. From then on we threw our waste directly into his lorry. At the end of ten days Stan's hull looked great. He and his father had worked hard and had benefited from the experiences of previous builders, even using steel rollers to smooth out the raw fibreglass. Glittering it stood there still wet, waiting for the catalyst to dry and harden it. Next morning it was still golden, gleaming and wet, but streams of yellow syrup were falling from its edges into gooey pools. After a week of trying everything including heat and nearly pure hardener, it was finally agreed that the resin was faulty. Since Stan had already lost three weeks' work with his truck, he asked for a replacement hull brought to the same stage as his own. The company offered to supply a man and materials, whereupon Stan rebelled. Next day his tipper had gone, having upended our mountain on the floor, bigger than ever. Only the rats were smiling.

Bing, a scientist, was helped by two teenage daughters. His keel had been formed along with the hull and was a box section some eight feet long, three feet deep and nine inches in the middle, tapering to rounded ends. This box took two tons of ballast which would prevent the yacht, with sails raised, from flopping onto its side. In theory you could stand the boat on its nose, roll it upside down, or simply drop it from an aircraft to bob right side up. There was a disadvantage: if you ever put a large hole in the bottom of your craft,

11

your life savings would go down like a brick.

At this time we could use two materials for the keel, iron or lead. The first to build a hull (Berny and Vic) had made a plaster mould of the inside of the keel from which a local foundry would make a two-ton iron casting for £90. Lead, which took up less room and gave a lower centre of gravity thus making for a stiffer boat, would have been preferable, but the price was more than double – £250.

Bing called a meeting and described how we might use non-active atomic waste, heavier than lead, which the British Government were dumping in the North Atlantic. Bing thought we might get a load cheap. We were all keen on the idea until someone asked, 'since we will be walking over the stuff, what would happen if it became active?' Without hesitation Bing replied, 'it would have the same effect on your sex life as the loss of your testicles.'

As I hurried away I said to a newcomer, Rome Ryott, 'I don't mind risking one but not both.' 'I'm risking neither!' said he. Rome had arrived in my life with dash and style, driving directly into the building in a sporty red Capri, complete with beautiful blonde passenger. He was tall, broad-shouldered, narrow-hipped and as he walked in with quick, bouncing steps, full of purpose I fully expected to hear James Bond theme music. His first words were not 'anyone for tennis?' as I had anticipated, but enquiries about the boat he was due to start building the following week. His soft, educated voice had a Wodehouse stutter assumed to give him time to choose his words. He became my closest friend.

The yacht's deck was made from a female mould, a process that took only a few days. The principle was much the same as housewives have used for years to turn out fancy jellies. First you coated the mould with wax (release agent) which in turn was given a heavy coat of paint (gel coat). The laying up, as for the hull, started with very fine lengths of fibreglass, looking much like tissue paper, and built up to heavier grades, with a layer of woven rovings. Water was then forced between the deck and mould to break it loose, and there was your completed deck, already smoothed and painted.

One Sunday night at the end of his month Rome, packed and ready to set off, called at my caravan. 'I have to be at work tomorrow morning,' he said. 'Since I've just had one leave I'll only manage to get here for long weekends to build the deck I . . . I . . . was wondering if I gave you a hand to build your deck would you help me to get mine finished?'

'Sure, Rome.' I replied. 'By the way what *do* you do for a living?'

● Flight Lieutenant Rome Ryott, top acrobatic pilot, alongside his Jet Provost

'I'm a pilot in the RAF,' he answered.

From that moment I knew Rome would not figure as one of my pieces of driftwood; it was perhaps because I had always wanted to be a pilot but more, I suspect, because with his quiet unassuming manner Rome accepted me for what I was, ignoring my background, lack of education, working class accent and financial standing. Rome was someone I could always look up to, yet he never once looked down on me. His father had been a silent movie actor (hence

13

the son's exotic name) who had died leaving his widow Grace with two young children, Rome and his sister Terry, to bring up. After a short period in the merchant navy, Rome joined the RAF, where he learned to fly first helicopters then jets. Interested in sailing since an early age he had already owned several boats which he changed regularly along with sporty cars and even sportier girl friends.

I was born in Birmingham which, for an Englishman, is about as far from the sea as you can get, on October 24, 1925 and was brought up there, living in a small terraced house with parents and young brother Royston. We were a normal working class family, never well off, my father employed as a foreman at the Rover car factory. During the depression the rentman would bang on the door while we cringed inside; they were terrible years for my father, a proud man who stood on his own two feet and never failed to pay his debts.

The second world war broke out when I was 13, and the following year I went to work in an aircraft factory as a machinist on Pegasus aero engines. But my ambition was to be a pilot. As a boy I had spent hours at the local airfield watching Tiger Moths, Hawker Hinds and Gloster Gladiators drop over the boundary fence. Aged 17 I joined the RAF not as a pilot, but as a wireless operator/air gunner. Having completed the training I became a sergeant, but the war was over before I could join an operational squadron. My service career ended running a station laundry in Italy, with 12 lovely young women to look after – an occupation in which I upheld the finest traditions of the British Empire but for which, unfortunately, no medals were awarded. Since then I had had many different jobs, in many countries. In my time I belonged to four skilled unions, only because I had to in order to work. I had had my own businesses including a garage, a haulage firm and shops; I was always a loner, never feeling I belonged.

My introduction to the opposite sex started with Nancy in Crewe, courtesy of two American Eighth Airforce bomber wings. As I had just been promoted sergeant Nancy came in the form of a celebration and I shall always remember her with gratitude for her understanding, kindness and tuition. 'Navigator to pilot, left, left a bit. Hang in there old buddy . . . bombs awaaaaaaaay.'

I married two charming ladies and was divorced from two charming ladies. No children came from these associations, only cocker spaniels whose custody was fought over with more bitterness than the D-day beaches of Normandy· the battles were always lost when it was pointed out that I was a wandering soul, unable even to

14

provide a proper home for them.

Brian Gibbons reached Liverpool to build his boat – by Jaguar. He owned a factory in the midlands (not far from my home town), a boss who was not frightened to get his hands dirty and without doubt the finest all-round engineer I have ever met. Married, in his mid-thirties, his friendly, rugged face was topped by a mop of unruly hair. His clothes, like his hands, were likely to show oil or grease stains and he spoke with assurance and authority in a mid-land accent. Brian had bought a finished hull and deck and would turn up with lumps prefabricated in his garage or works which slotted precisely. He overtook us all: I was for ever seeking his advice which he seemed to encourage, milling over prob-lems with the same sort of concentration

● **Sergeant Leslie Powles 7725023 trained as air crew, ended up running a laundry**

some people show for *The Times* crossword. It was never long before he would return, a stub of pencil and a scrap of paper in his hand. 'This is what you do, our kid.' And you had your answer.

Once the plug was removed, the hull was placed in its cradle. Then three-inch channels were chiselled out of the foam to form stringers and bulkhead recesses. The plans called for three layers of two-ounce fibreglass to be laid up inside the hull but I went way above this specification, trying to build more strength into the boat. As bulkheads were fitted and glassed into position we started to use new terminology: we would be working in the forward compart-ment, the heads, or main cabin.

After completion the decks would be lowered into position with a two-inch lip running around the outer edge until it came flush with the top of the hull. It was then through-bolted, and later capped with wood to make the toerail. The inside corner would be glassed in to give more strength and make it watertight.

Brian had asked for layers of fibreglass to be left out as he wanted a lighter, faster yacht; but he put strength back by running two Iroka beams along each side of the boat, under the deck, which were then glassed in position. He also put a third beam across the rear cabin bulkhead. Through-deck U-bolts took the standing rigging.

I followed Brian's example despite the fact that I had been adding weight instead of reducing it. By this time people were saying I was

15

over-building *Solitaire*, using back-up systems to back-up systems but I knew she would have to look after both of us until I could learn the ways of the sea and sailing.

If you asked the driftwood what they remembered about me, they would probably reply, 'Leslie? Oh yes, he was the one who cut a blooming great hole in the bottom of his boat'. In fact it was nine inches wide and four feet long. I had never liked the skeg which was hollow, and, when banged with a fist, would vibrate. I spent a weekend in Tony Marshall's garage building a replacement of Iroka, a modification which one day was to save *Solitaire* – and me. The size was increased to allow 10 inches to extend into the hull for bracing with a hole drilled ready to take the stern tube and propeller shaft. For a few days the boat sat with a gaping hole in her bottom. To lifted eyebrows and inquiring looks, I would merely say, 'mice'.

In June my mother was taken to hospital which meant that I had to return home. I managed to find a good position with Ken Mudd, as a quality assurance engineer for British Leyland. *Solitaire* was moved 80 miles overland into a field where I fitted her out, buying unplaned planks of Iroka for her interior. Most of the work was carried out with the help of an old friend, Tony Marshall, who had started out as a carpenter. Len Westwood, a foreman motor mechanic at British Leyland, helped to fit a new 18hp Saab diesel engine. When the time came to instal *Solitaire*'s ballast I bought two tons of scrap lead but could not decide how to pour the casting. I considered using an old bath as a melting pot, but the snag was manoeuvring this lump into the boat now that her deck had been fitted. When in doubt I did what I always did . . . phoned Brian Gibbons who had got over this problem by building an adjustable die with which you could make ingots to suit the shape of the keel. Having borrowed it I spent two days in Tony Marshall's back garden where we cut a 32lb gas bottle in half for use as a cauldron. For heat we used coke with a couple of car air blowers. The resultant 80 castings fitted to perfection and with a few gallons of encapsulating resin the job was completed. *Solitaire* began to show her beauty and was ready to be christened in sea water. A government agent had visited and presented her with a British birth certificate. She was painted and anti-fouled, mast, boom, and rigging ready for fitting.

Although Rome had been stationed up north we had kept in contact with weekly letters and the odd visit. He already had a berth in Lymington, his home town on the south coast. In March 1975 he took his yacht there, so I went along to lend a hand and learn the

• Boat yard view of Solitaire in final stage of construction in 1975.
She starts to show her beauty

ropes. There I was introduced to his mother Grace, a fitting name
for such a lady with her easy smile and quick laugh. Born in South
Africa, she still had tinges of the accent. I met her lovely daughter
Terry and Terry's husband Martin Maudling, the former Chancellor
of the Exchequer's son, which started another lasting friendship.

By now I had reached the stage where people began to say, 'it
must be great to own your own yacht and sail around the world. I'd
love to do the same but . . .' 'But' is always the crunch. Invariably it
would be followed by, 'I'm still paying the mortgage' . . . the wife's
not keen . . . the cats have had kittens'. If people were honest with
themselves, they would admit they led a contented life and had
no reason to change it.

As for me I was 49 years old, had a well paid, secure job, with no
possible chance of finding another if I gave it up, but I had no buts.
The dream I had had in South Africa six years earlier was stronger
than ever so I surrendered my safe future and moved *Solitaire* to
Lymington where she was immersed in sea water and baptised. The
launch went without a hitch, *Solitaire* bouncing like a beautiful baby,
just above her waterline. The father, however, was to find himself in
embarrassing situations over the next few months in trying to
understand his child. John, the dockside foreman, and his lads had
gently lowered her into the water and stepped the mast. Only one

end of the rigging wires had connectors which had to be secured to the tangs on the mast. Everything was held in position by the halyards. Later I would cut the stainless rigging wires to length and fit Norseman connectors . . . I had been telling John how I had built *Solitaire,* impressing everyone with my plans to sail around the world single-handed. Then I asked where I could park my boat. John pointed to a berth less than 50 yards away.

'Would you please take us over?' I asked.

He was busy, he replied, and since there was no wind or current I would have no problem. Slack water was what he actually said. I then explained that I had to check the engine, change my socks and look for leaks. When I finally ran out of excuses I admitted I had never berthed a boat or tied one up in my life. We chugged over at a third of a knot to catcalls, cheers, and cries of 'bon voyage' and 'send us a card from Cape Horn'.

Two days later I was in trouble again. I had completed the work on the rigging and had fitted the boom when a stranger asked, 'when are you fitting your kicking strap?' What on earth was he talking about? Suspecting that he was pulling my leg, I gave a vague wave of my hand and said, 'maybe tomorrow'. The solution seemed easy: go to the chandlery and buy one. Next morning I was waiting for them to open.

'Good morning, I'd like to buy a kicking strap, please.'

'We don't have any made up.'

'When will you have some made up?'

'Well, we never make them up, we sell the parts.'

'Fine, I'll buy the parts.'

'What size, sir?'

'What do you mean? I'll take average.'

'How much rope do you need, sir?'

'Oh a few feet.'

'Don't you think you should measure the length you require . . . sir?'

'Right, I'll be back.' As I left the shop I had a brain-storm. Back in the marina I found the first yacht with someone aboard who looked intelligent.

'Hello, that's a fine craft you have there. And a nice kicking strap.' A puzzled look. 'What are you on about? Mine's in the locker.'

Rome arrived to help me buy the necessary pulleys and ropes to put tension on the boom, the kicking strap. After that he took *Solitaire* into the Solent to supervise my first faltering steps. She handled better than his own yacht, he said, with less weather helm, which might be due to my using lead ballast instead of iron. My sailing, however, was less impressive. I had taken over after Rome had shown me how to set the sails for different points of sailing. An hour went by with Rome becoming very quiet. Fine, I thought, he's taught me all I need to know. Now I can pop off round the world.

'Nice day, Rome.'

'Not bad, we could do with a bit more wind.' (We were becalmed at the time.)

'Er, that's it, then my old mate. I'm all set to go, ah?'

'Well, Les, I'd give it a bit longer.'

'How much longer Rome? A couple of days?'

'Maybe a year.'

Later, when he had jumped in the dinghy to take pictures of my sailing by, 'Rome, just one quick question before you paddle off. How do I stop the bloody thing?'

'Les.'

'Yes, Rome?'

'Make it two years.'

The following week I took *Solitaire* out alone, a single-hander for the first time. I had given much thought to this, deciding that the cautious approach would be best with the engine on slow tick over so that if I bumped into other boats only small pieces would be removed. I realised my mistake soon after leaving the pontoon when wind and current revealed how quickly *Solitaire* could move sideways. Craft that minutes before had seemed deserted became festooned with happy, smiling yachtees . . . joyously waving fenders, old truck tyres . . . and boathooks. Out in the less restricted Solent things went better until I hoisted the mainsail and genoa. There was a tangle on the genoa winch due to my failure to feed its sheet through the deck block; and the mainsail was not filling properly as I had forgotten to slacken the topping lift. Thereafter there were no other problems. She would sail close to the wind unattended, even allowing me to make a cup of tea!

The mechanics of sailing were never to trouble me, but I deeply regretted not having had the opportunity to start in dinghies as a boy, to learn to do things correctly from the start. Bad habits take years to break, whether swinging a golf club, driving a car or sailing a yacht. I had some help in that I had been born a coward. I disliked arguing and would always walk around people when possible. As a boy I had stood in my school playground with blood streaming from my nose and soaking a torn shirt, hands open by my side. The bully

19

had continued to slap my face, egged on by the jeers of the other children. It wasn't that I was afraid, just that there seemed no point in fighting. Only when I realised I was trapped did my hands become fists.

I approached the sea in the same way, hands open. I had no wish to fight the sea, to claim false achievements, to feel anger. At the first sign of the sea's disapproval I would lower my colours and drop sail; only when *Solitaire*'s life was threatened would I fight back. The sea was far stronger than any ship so I must always try to live with it, hands open.

I stayed out a couple of hours, anxious now to return to the marina to try out a new theory. My approach to berthing had been quite wrong, far too slow it allowed outside elements to take over. The marina berths consisted of long pontoons, both sides of which had fingers, to form an H, each U-portion taking two yachts. Should you fail to stop when entering your berth, the bow of your boat slowly rises up the pontoon before sliding gently back into the water.

I went down the long line of boats at approximately five knots in a graceful curve, sweeping round at the last moment to line up on our berth. A boat's length away, I pulled back on the pitch control lever which provides forward, stationary and reverse drives – and it jammed. In the next few seconds I broke several world speed records, none recorded. When I opened my eyes it was to find *Solitaire* lying alongside her berth docilely, indignant at the delay in having her lines made fast. Later a twit arrived. 'I say, old boy, everyone was concerned by your departure, but jolly impressed by your return.' I would spend much time wondering whether he was serious or sarcastic.

The main hold-up to our departure now was the lack of self-steering gear. This had been a long drawn-out affair starting in Birmingham a year before. Three leading manufacturers had quoted roughly £250. After Rome's remarks about *Solitaire*'s lack of weather helm, I felt she could be steered by any of these gears, and settled for one that was compact and neat with a direct drive onto a balanced rudder. This was the beginning of a long association with Hydrovane, one I have never regretted. Indeed, the independent rudder one day would save *Solitaire*.

Group Captain Rex Wardman turned up at crack of dawn one morning soon after my arrival in Lymington and banged loudly on *Solitaire*'s side.

'Come on, Rome, you lazy devil, time to get up.'

I stuck my head out of the hatch. 'It's not Rome, it's Les and you've got the wrong bloody yacht.' Rex was a little shorter than me, a little older, having joined the RAF in the 1930s to fly many of the aircraft I had watched and admired as a boy. A jolly man, he lived life to the full, brushing problems aside with logic and a flick of the hand. As an experienced sailor Rex had been one of the first to take a berth at Lymington; over the coming years it would be hard to count the number of times he and his wife Edith had been around when I most needed them.

On this occcasion, after inspecting *Solitaire*, Rex muttered, 'it seems hardly fair to keep buying yachts when some people go into a field with a bucket of resin, a roll of fibreglass and build their own'. The final insult, on seeing the piece of old wood I was using as a tiller, was 'I don't think much of that'. He enforced the point by taking a kick at it and left me thinking that that was the last I would see of him. Minutes later he staggered down the jetty with two beautifully laminated tillers on his shoulders. 'I've changed my yacht to wheel steering. Give one of these to Rome and keep the other for *Solitaire*.'

Without even waiting for thanks he was off again.

Rex took me racing in the Solent a couple of times, not that I really enjoyed it. I found the sport a bit hair-raising, especially the starts, watching all that money being thrown about with seeming abandonment. On one occasion Rex had a beautiful crew member whom I assisted in the galley, and by the end of the day felt I had made a fair impression. Helping her ashore she belched in my face. 'Leslie, how could you?' she said and stalked off with another crew member, which just about summed up yacht racing for me . . . expensive, attractive and often with nothing but a belch at the end.

By August, 1975 time was running out; and so were funds with berthing fees of £10 a week only £300 remained in the kitty. *Solitaire* was still uninsured and the risk of damaging another yacht due to my lack of experience was worrying. Soon it would be autumn with a bleak English winter not far behind, making sailing difficult. Although I had a reasonable amount of food on board I had no accurate timepiece, liferaft, flares or transmitter. Charts, too, were in short supply, along with navigational books.

Rome was still insisting I wait another year, while Rex Wardman was threatening to break both my legs if I started on a world cruise so ill-prepared. But despite shortages I wanted off, to have *Solitaire* to myself away from prying eyes and to learn our lessons together in solitude, listening to sounds we had not heard before, riding on

21

waves, skirting their edges, gliding over peaks, surfing down valleys, seeing over horizons, controlling our own destinies.

I had no desire to be one of tomorrow's people: we're off tomorrow when we've bought our new sail, we're off tomorrow when we've painted the topsides, we're off tomorrow when we've bought a bigger boat. I foresaw the final excuse, 'we're off in a hearse. We ran out of tomorrows.'

I had wanted to start six years before, not tomorrow but yesterday. Whenever asked about my first port of call, I would say, 'Barbados'. To avoid technical or navigational questions I would become flippant. 'I'll potter down the middle of the English Channel and when 300 miles into the Atlantic I'll turn sharp left and sail between the Azores and Portugal. Then I'll fork right onto Barbados' latitude of 13°20' and I'll stay on it until the island appears over the horizon.'

At that time I believed celestial navigation to be beyond my limited education, a belief which goes back to the early days of sailing when captains hugged the secrets of navigation to themselves fearing that mutinous crews might take over their ships. The fact that the young couple with whom I sailed to Gibraltar took no sights, despite having a first class sextant on board, did nothing to rid me of my apprehension. Rome showed me how to correct for sextant error but then I made the mistake of asking him to explain the formula. There is no need to know this any more than there is to grasp the working of a car's gearbox: simply accept that it works and try to understand the rules. To learn to use a sextant takes less than an hour, a noon sight for latitude no more than a day. Yet I was foolish enough to sail without this basic background.

I had neither accurate timepiece nor navigation tables, so there was no possibility of my carrying out sights for longitude. I possessed a small portable receiver but this had only long and medium waves with limited range and was unable to pick up BBC overseas broadcasts for time checks. My navigational equipment consisted of charts, compass, Walker trailing log (to register distance covered), Seafarer depth sounder, and a Seafix radio direction finder (one of my main hopes for safe navigation since I remembered my morse code from RAF days). A major mistake was not to carry the *Admiralty Book of Radio Signals* which gives the stations around the world; instead I had *Reed's Almanac* which prints European call signs only. However *Reed's*, with a £10 plastic sextant, would give the information for sights for latitude. With my limited sailing experience it would have been more sensible to have studied two or three English ports, using daylight, tides and weather to coastal hop.

Ken Mudd and his family came down to spend the last week with me. Ken, a born do-it-yourselfer, fitted gas bottles, radar reflector, hatches, battery and goodness knows what else. At the end it seemed only fair to take him and his family for a sail, as in any case I wanted to try out the newly-fitted self-steering gear. However Ken gave me no chance of doing this, seizing the tiller as soon as we were under way and refusing to give it back, glaring down at me from his six feet two inches at any intrusion on his new-found pleasure. He managed to chalk up one first with *Solitaire* when he ran us aground.

We had dropped sail and were motoring back to our berth. 'Stay just this side of the black markers,' I had instructed. 'Watch out for the ferry.' I was fiddling with the self-steering gear again, leaning over the stern, when . . . 'Les, we seem to have stopped.'

'You stupid clot, Mudd. You've put us *on* the mud. Where's the marker?' He pointed to a blackbird sitting on a post. Too late I remembered the day I had first met him. We were standing a few feet from a works clock as big as a barn when he asked me the time. Ah well, no one's perfect. With a bit of jumping about we soon got off. Ken and his family returned to Birmingham that night, not out of embarrassment but simply because it was the end of a holiday. It would be nearly three years before I saw him again.

I was passing the point of no return; my old banger was sold, there were last-minute calls to my parents, to Tony Marshall, Irene and their children, Tracy and Sally, with a few belated words of thanks for all their kindness.

By the night of August 17, 1975 *Solitaire* was just about ready to sail. Covers were off, and the number one genoa and working jib hanked onto the twin forestays, the Avon dinghy half-inflated on deck ready to act as a liferaft. Grace Ryott came down to wish me well with a box of chocolate bars. Ann and her daughter Susan invited me aboard their boat for a late supper, as they had done so often before. This time there was too much to do, but I was grateful for their help in turning *Solitaire* so that she was pointing in the right direction. (I didn't want her kissing the other yachts goodbye!)

Monday, August 18, 1975 I shower and mail a dozen postcards. A kiss on the cheek from Anne and Susan, a final wave. We're off around the world, not to fame and fortune but to laughter, pointing fingers and cries of 'you're the one who finished up in a maternity hospital.'

2

AS THE BOAT MOVED SLOWLY down river that Monday and into the Solent I hoisted the sails at nine o'clock to start a voyage that would take us 34,000 miles around the world and last more than two-and-a-half years. It was a beautiful morning with south-westerly winds in a blue sky patched with a few scattered clouds. I had some anxious moments when the self-steering failed until I discovered I had repeated an early mistake and had set a reciprocal course. I streamed the Walker trailing log to start registering *Solitaire's* journey.

Half an hour later we were sweeping past the Needles in company with another boat, both close on the wind, neck and neck, red ensign saluting red ensign. Then I showed off, leaving the cockpit to sit on the pulpit forward as if to say, 'look no hands'. *Solitaire* surged ahead while I yearned to climb the mast to look down at the arrowhead her bow was making, to watch her long white wake, longing to run alongside to see her hull in graceful flight. God, it was marvellous. I turned on the radio full blast and made entries in the log. 'Yipeee,' I concluded, 'Yipppeee!'

I decided to come about and follow the coast at which *Solitaire* hesitated for a second, wondering why we were separating from her new playmate. Then she saw the distant headland and was off again, heeling for more speed, like a puppy seeking a new interest. The wind blew free with no bills to pay at the end of the month for that! Oceans lay ahead like orchards of succulent fruit: we could gorge ourselves and feast all free, free, free.

The rentman called that evening, first with a light tapping on the door, followed by a more insistent banging and whistling. Initially I paid no attention then, growing nervous and weary, became too exhausted to care. By six that evening we had problems. The wind was increasing, the sea becoming choppy as I reduced the headsail to working jib. With darkness, the lighthouse on Portland Bill started flashing but *Solitaire* was much too close inshore to clear the headland and its race, so I came about and headed south. France was 60 miles away, with plenty of sea room in that direction. Then a fog descended, thick, grey banks obliterating the lighthouse which prompted me to start the engine in order to maintain a compass course. The outlines of large ships waltzed by, partnering *Solitaire* in a dance of disaster, faint shapes towering above us, their unfamiliar lights confusing me. Sometimes I turned away, sometimes circled back, sails aflap. Terror!

During one these panics I managed to tangle the trailing log line around the skeg so that now I would have no idea how far *Solitaire* travelled on her manic course. Tuesday morning saw us still beating into angry seas, completely lost. I tried to keep heading west, confused and logless. My radio direction finder would certainly have supplied the answers had I not managed to leave it switched on with the result that the batteries were now flat. Turning *Solitaire* off the wind I headed north-west to bring us back to the English coast. Late that night shore lights showed faintly through the murk so I dropped sail and stayed on watch until morning when the fog lifted. Land! We were sitting in the western end of a vast bay, in the far distance, a harbour. From the chart Falmouth was shown to the west of a large bay. Full of confidence *Solitaire* motored over to a young lady in a rubber dinghy and in what I thought to be a swashbuckling manner I shouted, 'ahoy there, missy. Could you please tell me where you anchor in Falmouth Harbour?' A look of horror crossed her face. Ye gods, I thought, my flies are open. The poor creature's legs seemed to give way and she collapsed in the bottom of her craft, whence weird sounds emerged followed by a tear-stained face.

'Miss, I only want to know where you anchor in Falmouth Harbour.'

'About 100 miles westwards,' came a shrieked reply.

Brixham is a delightful place. For a while *Solitaire* circled its harbour like a cat looking for a comfortable place to settle, this my first attempt at anchoring. Exhausted, I used my remaining strength to tie a length of rope onto a 25lb CQR anchor and throw it over the side. With that I sat on deck, head in hand, until a man in a dinghy appeared alongside.

'Are you all right?' he asked. I nodded whereupon he suggested that it would be advisable to put a length of chain on the anchor before the rope. I fetched up about 20 feet and after helping me to re-anchor he invited me to dinner with him and his wife. Next morning they were gone. I forget their names, even their faces, but I will always remember their kindness. I stayed only a few days in Brixham, using the yacht club's showers but not daring to enter the bar as I could still hear the girl's laughter ringing in my ears. Perhaps the word had gone around: we have a fool in the harbour.

The sail to Falmouth, starting at dawn one morning, arriving early the next, proved easy. Close on the wind all the way we made a fair course without overmuch tacking, sailing with main and number two genoa in a reasonable force three to four. I managed to pick up all the headlands by day and identify the lighthouses by night and having replaced the RDF batteries I could now confirm my position with radio fixes. *Solitaire* and I enjoyed this part of the voyage, arriving fresh and slightly more confident. As Falmouth seemed crowded we moved to the other side of the river and the picturesque village of St Mawes. *Solitaire* has no fitted tanks, she carries her water in six five-gallon containers. When these were filled, I bought a roasted chicken, some vegetables, and prepared for our first long voyage together across the Atlantic.

On August 28, 1975 I hauled up anchor at the start of a lovely English summer's day with the dew still wet on *Solitaire*'s deck, motored out of the sleeping harbour and raised sail. A faint breeze from the north-west seemed reluctant to speed us from our homeland so *Solitaire* drifted south, her self-steering debating whether to hold her on a course or give up and go back to bed. By afternoon we were only 12 miles south of Falmouth when a large ketch headed towards us, passing down our side under full sail. I could hear shouting, see its crew waving their arms as though in distress. Quickly dropping the headsail I started the engine, turned into wind and made after them. It turned out their motor had broken down and they were lost.

'Which way Falmouth?' they called, 'and how far?'

That I could give them this information amused me and for the rest of the day I kept chuckling to myself. Had they but known! Good humour came to an abrupt end that night when I managed to rip the mainsail. Soon after the ketch had left us, the wind started to pick up so I hoisted a smaller genoa, then, just before dark with heavy clouds forming and the wind increasing, I reduced to working jib. That stormy night, still on a broad reach, I tried to drop the main without turning into the wind but the sail caught on the crosstrees and ripped. When it was finally down and lashed I was violently sick. I was to be sick at sea only twice, due to my idiocy rather than an upset stomach. On this occasion I was concerned about the sail repair, having previously sewn together nothing more complicated than an old pair of socks. What bothered me most was removing the sail from the mast as Rome had fitted it for me when I had been elsewhere. Did you take it from the mast first or from the boom? It was only a passing fear. I tied the sailbag onto the mast and fed the sail directly into it – successfully.

When next I went below I had my first experience of the different worlds of sailing. On deck it was cold with a screeching wind, breaking waves and glowing phosphorus. Below it was peaceful and warm. *Solitaire* broad-reached comfortably, delighted to be off the wind and the pounding sea. The rip proved to be only a few inches long and easily repaired so *Solitaire* and I learned another lesson. There's an old saying of the sea, 'when you think of reefing (shortening sail), that's the time to reef'. I have always taken this to extremes.

The number two genoa and working jib were permanently fixed to twin forestays and I invariably changed down to the smaller working jib at the slightest excuse such as increasing wind, heavy swell, unusual clouds . . . and, after many months at sea, on instinct that all was not right. I liked to clear shipping lanes as soon as possible. Once in open sea I would switch off lights to preserve the batteries and sleep through the night, relying on intuition to wake me for weather changes, deviation from course or ships in the vicinity. That way of thinking would have been different if there had been other people on board when I would have been responsible to them for keeping a good watch at all times. Besides, there is no way you can develop this intuition when other people are around.

After leaving the English channel I stopped using the number one genoa. It provided insufficient extra speed for its size and, hard on the wind, with the foot running along the deck inside the stanchions, it restricted my forward vision. I was to become lazy at sea. If I could make 100 miles a day I would be content and, should I fail to achieve this distance, who cared? When I found *Solitaire* slamming into heavy seas, I would drop all sail, batten myself below and read or sleep. If the winds turned into storms and they were aft of the mast I would simply run with them on a broad reach under working jib. I was never frightened and indeed found comfort in gales by thinking either of Chay Blyth who had rowed the Atlantic, or Bombard who had crossed it in a rubber dinghy.

28

My boat was strong so why should I worry? I enjoyed the solitude and there were plenty of books to read. I had never to be in a certain place at a given time, the crazy world could wait until I chose to join it again. Meanwhile I had friendly dolphins who entertained me nightly with their ballet dancing. Like a king before his court I sat back applauding, enjoying a last cup of coffee at the end of another halcyon day. Navigation was proving easier than expected. I had stayed as far out of the Bay of Biscay as possible and still received limited RDF signals from England, Spain and Portugal. Two or three such bearings gave me a reasonable fix which was confirmed by dead reckoning using a £20 Bosun's compass and the trailing log for distance travelled.

When I had been at sea for ten days I read the instructions in *Reed's Almanac* and used my Ebco plastic sextant to take my first sight for latitude. It took longer than is normal as I had no accurate timepiece aboard. My old car clock lost 40 seconds or so a day which meant I had to guess when the sun would reach its maximum height, following it on its upwards curve to the top of its arc, and only too relieved when my calculations tied in with the pencilled RDF positions. For a few days I continued this cross-checking until we were 300 miles into the Atlantic when the signals faded. Now we would have to depend on dead reckoning and the sextant. Dropping below the Azores *Solitaire* picked up the beautiful trade winds, constant at force three to four over our stern. There were times when I thought she had stopped: surprised by the silence I would put down my book and go on deck only to find the log spinning merrily away at a steady five knots. In these conditions I started to learn the importance of a varied food supply. Cooking would have given another interest, another pleasure, were it not that nearly all the food onboard was tinned; the fresh food I had bought in Falmouth had been eaten in the first week. One meal I relished, rice and curried chicken, and regretted having no more. In time I would learn to carry the things that would last and were cheap to buy: rice, flour, onions, cabbage, eggs.

The main event of our Atlantic crossing took place on September 23, 1975 at precisely 1400 hours GMT. It would be many weeks before I learned the importance of this day and the changes it would make to my life. All that is recorded in the ship's log for that day is, 'distance travelled 2,442 miles. Latitude 23°41' north.' From now on things would happen that made no sense. I would go over incidents again and again, sometimes believing I was losing my reason as I tried to understand why, after things had gone so well, suddenly I seemed unable to do anything right. I kept pushing *Solitaire* south but the reduction in latitude was too slow and simply would not agree with the compass course or dead reckoning. I checked the compass against that on the RDF set but both gave similar readings. I went over my latitude figures repeatedly, always getting the same answer. It could not be my method of working out sights whose correctness I had confirmed long since. I tried to remember where the fast-flowing Gulf Stream started its journey north; I knew its current sometimes reached five knots but I had no charts to guide me and the sea tells no secrets. Could it be I was under the influence of the Bermudan triangle where ships and aircraft had vanished perhaps, it was suggested, as the result of large compass variations? Day after day we pushed further south into dangers that subsequently would make me shudder at my stupidity.

As the trade winds began to drop we had periods of calm punctuated by vicious squalls, the first of which started at night. Previously there had been light rain squalls but these were something quite different. I would wake up in the night to an eerie silence. Suddenly, screaming winds would start whistling in *Solitaire*'s rigging whereupon she would come off her broad reach and luff up. I would dash on deck naked, stopping only to throw on a life harness, to find sheets of warm water pounding the sea flat. I would drop the mainsail and within a few seconds all would be normal with *Solitaire* back on course under a clear, starry sky, as if nothing had happened. Two days later I saw these squalls for what they were . . . seemingly atom bomb mushrooms, starting at sea level and spreading upwards to blank out the sun. Normally I would drop the mainsail as quickly as possible and free the genoa sheets if it seemed the squall would blow for any length of time. Later I was to question many seamen how they reacted. One said he merely allowed the yacht to luff up, arguing that you were through a squall quicker than trying to run with it. Most of those I spoke to seemed to drop or slacken sail. During this confusion and despondency, I learned a lot about the sea, *Solitaire* and myself.

One day we were beating into a breaking sea with a long swell, *Solitaire*'s bow being thrown high in the air every now and then, for her to fall back, burying her nose, waves streaming up her decks towards the cockpit. I needed to take off the large genoa that was driving her into these seas to slow her down but as I have never been a strong swimmer, a cross between a breast stroker and a dog pad-

30

dler, I did not fancy going forrard for a ducking. In the middle of a sail change *Solitaire* started to lift and just as I thought she was about to take off in flight we started down again. Seas broke over the bows, whirling first around my feet and then my chest. I grabbed the forestay in panic, drawing in breath as though it were my last, before sinking into a green world which sucked me away from *Solitaire*. Water filled my nose and I choked. After what seemed a lifetime I was lifted clear, terrified, trying to draw breath into burning lungs, spitting out mouthfuls of neat sea.

At that moment, strangely, I stopped being afraid. My fear was replaced by anger and I screamed obscenities using every backstreet gutter word I could remember, even managing to invent a few. Within minutes using hand like steel claws I had changed sails and was back in the cockpit, sucking the salt from my lips which I spat over the side.

'You bloody bitch,' I said. It was not until I had towelled myself down, and was sitting with a cup of tea, that my hands stopped shaking. Then I began to think about the strange chap I had met on the foredeck, this Jeckyll and Hyde character. If I could control him and harness his anger to give me the strength to survive I would have learned another valuable lesson which must serve me well.

At ten o'clock that night on October 13, after being at sea for 57 days and having logged 4,340 miles, a lighthouse flashed, which should not have been there as, by dead reckoning, we were still 200 miles from Barbados. Our noon sight that day had put us 14° 40'N, more than 80 miles above the island. My sole chart, which covered the whole Caribbean, reduced Barbados from 20 miles to one inch, and showed two lighthouses but no flashing codes. I decided to sail down the island to pick up the other light but soon thought better of it and headed out to sea to await morning.

Dawn found *Solitaire* sailing on a southerly course parallel to an island with sandy beaches, palm trees and hills in the distance. A few dhow-type vessels about 40ft long with large triangular sails made of odd pieces of material were in sight, each with two or three dark-skinned men on board whose curiosity made them come alarmingly close. By noon, sea and sky had taken on the same shade of blue, the horizon hazy.

Despite problems in getting a decent sight it appeared to confirm the previous day's latitude. Using my RDF set I was surprised to pick up a loud SLI morse signal which indicated I had sailed above the Barbados Islands and was cruising down the coast of Martinique

31

with Saint Lucia to the south. Although I had no radio codes for the area, that would surely account for the SLI call sign. Barbados then was 90 miles to the south-east. Although it meant retracing my steps I decided to sail there because a young girl had once said it was 100 miles to Falmouth and her laughter still rang in my ears.

Since we were sailing into open seas I slept well that night, in fact I even had a lie in, made a leisurely cup of tea and came out of the cabin yawning. A glance at the compass revealed we were still on course with the trailing log behaving satisfactorily and the self-steering working well. To starboard I was surprised to see land about three miles away but, over the bow, *Solitaire* was facing huge breaking seas. The cup scalded my legs as I dropped it scrambling over the hatchboards. I was halfway to the tiller when the air filled with flying spray. As there was no time to tack I fled below, slamming the sliding hatch; for a moment silence endorsed a short-lived sense of relief, then the earth spun out of orbit as *Solitaire* was lifted sideways. Believing this a new game she went willingly, flying in her eagerness to please until struck viciously by a gigantic hammer which stopped her dead, knocking her legs from under her. And I heard a baby howl . . .

In the cabin movement was too fast for the eye to register. As the

LESLIE POWLES' FIRST CIRCUMNAVIGATION, WEST-TO-EAST

boat fell on her side I found myself on the floor: lockers burst open and I was bombarded by books, tins, bottles . . . whatever could fall fell and sea-water gushed in. The seas had her, like a tiger bringing down a fawn, swinging her in a complete circle. She shrieked. I tried to escape through the hatch but solid water flung me back to the floor, the cabin darkened by green shades that covered its windows. Now she was dragged sideways, leaving skin and blood on jagged rocks, and crying in her agony but there was nothing I could do for her.. Trying to restore sanity to this madness I picked up a book from the shambles to blank out her screams. Then her cries changed to defiance, although the sea still pushed her sideways. Now she was riding with the blows, staggering to her feet after each knockdown. She would take stumbling steps, sit down, then quickly push herself upright, complaining the while at such treatment. Again and again she was slammed down but with each knockdown her stubborness increased until after being turned again in a complete circle, she finished up all standing when the noise subsided. She stood there swaying, quietly sobbing, but on her feet and proud.

I slid back the hatch cover and emerged shamefaced, embarrassed by the dangers I had left her to face alone and bitterly repentant of my hope that some small part of her would be found so that my family would not spend years wondering if I were alive or dead. From the cockpit her decks appeared to have been swept clean: dinghy, fuel containers, spray dodgers . . . all had disappeared. Later I found them hanging over the side secured by odd bits of lashing. The mast still stood, heavy spray running off the untorn sails like rivers of tears. The battens in the main had broken and the headsail sheets flew free but were intact.

A glance into the cabin showed the wreck that had been my home. Rubbish floated in deep water, not as bad as I had thought locked below when I would have sworn she was half-full. That had been with *Solitaire* on her side, now that she was upright water ran to her bilges, reducing the level. The boat was held in soft sand, the reef she had survived lay to one side, the distant shore to the other, the sea brown and shallow. After hauling everything back onboard and securing, I started pumping but as it took an age to clear the water in the cabin I feared her hull might be cracked. The tiller was jammed to one side, but by pushing with both feet I managed to centralise it and the plywood weather vane on my self-steering gear had broken but I could soon fit a spare. *Solitaire* started to come alive again and with a little encouragement she might even be away. I thought of using the motor, but after that pounding doubted it would ever start until I turned the key whereupon the engine gave a half-turn and roared into life. *Solitaire* shuddered with pleasure and as I pulled in her sails she leaned, sighed and moved. I felt her sweating forehead on my cheek as she whispered in our secret language, forgiving me my faults and weaknesses. Life was full again . . . the music of Bach, the birth of Christ. It was Christmas, Christmas day in October. We were off to Barbados.

Solitaire edged her way nervously back along the reef where the echo sounder gave no reading. The distant water seemed even shallower, so we stayed close in, eyeing the sea warily lest it brought on fresh assaults. Salt water and spray still showered us but as we rounded the end of the reef the air cleared and I could see again. The first thing I spotted was a green and white sail. 'Americans,' I thought, setting off in hot pursuit. I wanted to inspect for damage and clean up the mess below so, as she was holding a good course, I switched off the motor and let the self-steering take over. Water oozed through the cabin floor and worriedly I started pumping again. We were still in sandy seas that stretched to the horizon, the echo sounder occasionally registering a few feet. Old green sails was even closer inshore. Still trying to catch him we rounded a headland with a lighthouse perched on it but the other craft pulled away and disappeared. Where had this land come from? I tried the RDF again and the SLI signal came through loud and clear as ever. I checked the chart. Martinique had coral banks halfway down its east coast; a lighthouse was shown a few miles north of these. Maybe we had hit these banks and rounded the light so I decided to follow the coast.

At noon the horizon was even hazier with no chance of a sight. Then a second island appeared which, if we were sailing down the west coast of Martinique, had to be St Lucia. I decided to pass between the two and then head for Barbados. A few hours later I realised that these islands were merging and that we were entering the mouth of a river! At that point I realised I badly needed help for there was nothing in the Caribbean that looked like this. *Solitaire* was sailing in shallow waters where the charts showed 50 fathoms or more. The river banks continued to close in on us, now three to four miles apart. Small open fishing boats and canoes appeared with the same patched triangular sails I had noted on the earlier vessels. I closed them, pointing down river, and shouting, 'harbour' which brought only smiles and shrugs. Then I tried shouting, 'porto' at which they waved me on.

Moving through the same dirty brown water the echo sounder read seven to eight feet. Now and again *Solitaire* would hesitate as we touched soft sand but in no way put out she would shake herself and continue on her way. A Spanish-style village began to appear above a bay to starboard, first a church, then white buildings with red-tiled roofs, and finally a jetty with a flat-bottomed canopied boat tied to it. A walled road ran up a hill with people already lining it. I attempted to anchor but such was the current it would not hold and *Solitaire* was swept towards the shore which made me decide to carry on up river and find another haven.

Just before dark the river ended in forest. I dropped anchor and was contemplating inflating the dinghy and rowing ashore when a canoe appeared manned by a negro with a dirty cloth at his waist tucked between hairy legs. He passed with thrusting strokes, muscles bulging and fugitive looks from the whites of his eyes. A forked spear lay in the bottom of the canoe, most likely for fishing. Holy cow, I thought, I wouldn't like to meet that on a black night, so decided to stay where I was.

It had been a long day but there was still much to do. For the first time since the knockdown I dried out *Solitaire*, including her bilges. Water had been coming in pretty fast and I had been pumping her out every two or three hours without tracing its point of entry.

By now it was dark and the sky full of stinging insects. Thinking to eat I went below into an oven where I managed a cup of tea but spent so much time defending myself with flailing arms that food was not worth the effort. Perhaps those tropical marauders fancied some real English roast beef. I closed the hatch and slept so deeply that dragon bites would not have wakened me. When I came to at dawn, my face was puffed and swollen. Having feasted heartily off me through the night, the dragons had limped off home – gorged. Now all I wanted was to get back to sea. The trip up river had taken six hours. Two days later after forcing a way back through thick, brown chocolate I was to remember those few hours as pleasurable!

At first the return was not too bad. In the cool of early morning I hoisted the sails and started the engine. At the end of each tack I would simply turn the self-steering onto its new course and stand with a genoa sheet in each hand, letting go on one, taking up on the other as we came through the wind. The slow-running engine kept her moving as she came about, easing her through any soft sand. Hard-in sails helped her to heel, which lifted the keel slightly. Every now and again I would pump the bilges but progress was slow. The mid-day sun reflected off a burning deck. Standing in the cockpit was uncomfortable even in a minimal shirt and shorts as I sought relief from the hot breeze, quite unconscious of the sun's damage to my skin and eyes. The previous night's bites were now sore and itching and when darkness fell we still had not reached the village. I tried to continue sailing but islands of hard-packed sand constantly delayed *Solitaire*. When we ran hard into one particularly shallow patch, I called it a day, anchored and made tea for again I could not face food. All I wanted was the night's cool comfort. Bliss . . . then the dragons arrived for another feast. I sailed next morning as soon as I could make out the shore line.

The river began to widen and by noon *Solitaire* was a mile or two beyond the village, still running into islands of hard packed sand just below the surface which were impossible to see. Normally they did not cause too much concern: we invariably hit them on their down-river side and the wind soon floated us off again. Then, after running into one soft patch, *Solitaire*'s motor stopped. The engine uses sea water as a coolant but the muck we were sailing in did not agree with its digestion, so it overheated and gave up the fight. Lacking its thrust we drifted astern and finished on the wrong side of a hard-packed island. For the first time since leaving England I inflated the dinghy and stepped off *Solitaire*, dropping our anchor with 200ft of rope in deep water.

A few fishing boats closed to see what was going on. One came alongside with a crew of three whom I invited aboard *Solitaire* and gave them cigarettes, the first people I had spoken to since the lost souls on the ketch off Falmouth. Not that I could understand these men's language. I felt they had originally come from Spain or Brazil, and spoke Portuguese or heavily-accented Spanish. Dark-skinned peasants in rolled-up trousers, secured by string, they wore tattered shirts and, above all, battered straw hats – which I envied. One or two of the words they used I recognised, 'please', 'yes', 'no' with which I tried to obtain my whereabouts. One pointed to me and asked, 'Saint Lucia?' Getting somewhere at last, I thought. I shook my head and said, 'Barbados'. Waving in the general direction of the DF signal, I asked 'Saint Lucia?' To this they all nodded their heads enthusiastically. I fetched my chart of the Caribbean, and pointed to my position. It was as if it had a curse, they would not even look. I kept pushing it under their noses, pleading, 'please señor'. Then I noticed *Solitaire* was leaning further over, a foot of sand showing around her. It could not be happening. The Caribbean has no such tide. My guests sat back smoking and smiled confidently, waiting for *Solitaire* to float. I watched the miracle of the waters rising until she pulled on her anchor line and swung into deep chocolate whereupon I farewelled the fishermen, hauled up the sails, and again started reaching for blue waters. Within an hour it was dark but the river grew wider as we tacked by the stars. I nipped below and made tea, putting marmalade on a cheese biscuit. Next moment I was spread-eagled over the foreward bulkhead. *Solitaire* had hit an island and was on her side. Before I had time to panic a wave had picked her up and gently deposited her in deep water where she continued serenely as though nothing had happened. That would teach me to go below without permission.

Then as I picked up the lighthouse and made towards it I started to hear a strange but familiar sound I could not place. Dropping sails, I put down the anchor and, head on tiller, fell asleep after sailing and pumping for nearly 40 fasting hours. Dawn found us close inshore, a shore covered by bushes. Then I remembered and recognised the sound I had heard, crickets! Once clear of the land, I studied my chart, trying to identify the coast with the compass. Nothing made sense. There was no river that size on Martinique, nothing like it in all the Caribbean, the brown water too shallow, the tides quite wrong, the land too flat. I could not just sit there, we had to sail in some direction. I would sail north, back the way we had come, so I brought *Solitaire* onto that heading. But that could not be right, we must sail south and home in on the RDF to St Lucia. I turned *Solitaire* south. In the end I was changing course every few minutes and circling, circling. I gave up, apologised to *Solitaire*, made tea and ate my marmaladed biscuits. Since first hitting the reef three days ago I had accomplished nothing. The trip down river had ended with me burned by the sun and savagely bitten.

The natives had said St Lucia again and again: my last latitude had been 14°30′N so river or no river I must be on the west coast of Martinique. Nothing else was possible. Finally I headed north. On Sunday, October 19, 1975, *Solitaire* was back on course for Barbados which I believed to be south-east and I followed the coast until clear of land when I found that sailing in clear water had increased the leaks. I was now pumping out *Solitaire* every two hours. Next morning I hallucinated, believing that my brother Royston was sleeping in my bunk. Should I disturb him and ask him to have a go at pumping? Later I made two cups of tea, and took him one in the cockpit. Just before dark, standing in the hatchway, I felt a chest pain. Looking down I saw I was pushing hard against the hatch cover to make room for family and friends standing behind! Of course I saw no one. There was no fear, nothing worse than having too much to drink and making a fool of oneself. Too much worry, too much sun.

Thoughts of sailing direct to Barbados were given up on Tuesday, October 21. Then one of the twin forestay bottle screws, which allow the standing rigging to be adjusted, broke. Later I learned that it failed because there was no universal coupling at its base. With loose rigging I turned *Solitaire* and ran westwards. My condition was deteriorating, my skin so burned that even a light shirt proved painful, yet I had to spend hours in the cockpit pumping and sailing *Solitaire*, the sun ever blazing, the spray stinging. I could no longer see the horizon. There was no mirror aboard, but I knew my eyes were nearly closed and my head was blistering.

Wednesday, October 22. A week had passed since hitting the reef. Sailing back into the brown shallows, I saw a large bay with the same fishing boats and canoes, the same peasant crews. My spirits rose when I saw a large marker buoy, the type used to mark shipping channels. I circled it, but the echo sounder showed only a few bitterly disappointing feet. Ashore were palm trees and several thatched huts. Motoring down I found flat water with no current, so

38

anchored in seven feet or so, backing away to allow the chain to run out. I went below, glad to be out of the flying spray and burning sun, and lay on my bunk for the first time in many long days. I moved my eyelids a fraction to close them. Beautiful, deep soothing sleep. Then a bump on *Solitaire*'s side. I staggered on deck to find a dug-out canoe alongside with a jet-black man and woman, both with broken teeth and flat faces as if they had been in a car accident, and a coloured, handsome man with Spanish features. He made signs indicating the sea would soon leave the lagoon, precisely what I needed to allow me to sleep in safety and, later, inspect *Solitaire*'s hull. To please them I thought I'd move *Solitaire* a few feet. I started her motor, removing its cover to make sure it was not overheating and stumbling, pushed my leg against the revolving flywheel. A quick burning pain . . . I watched the blood run without the slightest interest, switched off the motor, gave my visitors cigarettes and pumped the bilges. Finally lovely sleep.

I awoke spluttering, my face immersed in sea water. *Solitaire* was lying on her side where water had collected into which I had submerged my face when turning in my sleep. On deck I could see we were about 200 yards up the beach, the sun about to make its appearance. Clambering over *Solitaire*'s side, I felt cooling sands on my grilled feet. Ecstasy! A bent old man was examining the beach pools and extracting stranded fish which he belted over the head before dropping them into his sack. I joined in the game for a while, laughing and dancing like a clown until, tiring of the sport, I went to lay out anchors as close as possible to the sea. By now *Solitaire*'s starboard side was completely exposed and I could examine the wounds she had endured on the reef. A large piece missing from the bottom of the skeg accounted for the jammed rudder. Halfway along her hull on the waterline was one area that had been pushed in the depth of a dinner plate, another and larger area simply flattened. Other parts were scratched and gouged, although none an inch deep, the thickness of her skin. In the hot sun *Solitaire* soon dried out. Still searching for the cause of the leak, I saw dampness where the after end of the keel joined the hull which I had reinforced with fibreglass at least an inch-and-a-half thick. When I cleaned it with a file, water trickled out.

Fortunately I carried resin and fibreglass onboard in sealed containers; unfortunately I had no brushes or gloves to protect my hands. Despite making a brush from a rope's end I still managed to cover my hands with resin which I tried to clean with rag and sea

39

water. Then I had the brilliant idea of using sand and finished up looking as if I were wearing brown gloves, which at least stopped me scratching my face. It is inadvisable to glass over a damp surface but, by adding extra hardener, I made a half-decent job.

By the time I had finished a crowd of natives had gathered. The last job was to inspect my stock of 18 bottles of spirits and some 600 English cigarettes which, as I was a non-smoker, were mostly for trade. I came across about 40 sodden yachting magazines and took them on deck, intending to dump them. A girl reached up, so I gave her one. Next minute I was beseiged by fighting, screaming women and out of the newspaper business. I decided the men should also have a treat and dished out half a dozen bottles of whisky and gin and, to add to the party spirit, started handing out cigarettes. While this was going on I tried to hold some kind of a conversation without much luck. Suddenly I heard the name 'Pele'.

'Football,' I shouted, and pretended to dribble a ball. Pointing to myself I said, 'golf'. The best I could get from my fans was, 'goof'. I still had a set of golf clubs onboard, so fetched them, made a round hole in the sand, marched back 150 yards, selected my trusty five iron and asked the admiring public to stand back. With my 'sand-paper' gloves I had a good grip on the club. Making my first back swing as wide and slow as possible, I came down and through what I saw as *two* blurred balls, holding my stance at the end of the applause. A slight titter. Looking down I could still see two balls. On my fourth attempt I managed to move them ten feet. I tried to explain that my first three swings had been practice, not that I minded their laughter even if they were drinking my grog. I looked for revenge. My old fishing partner, rolling about much the worse for wear, seemed a likely victim. Prizing a gin bottle from his shaking hand I gave him the club, pointed to the ball, the general direction of the hole, and stood well back. The poor old man could hardly stand and I started to feel sorry for what I was doing. Encouraged by his mates he finally swung and made solid contact. The ball flew off in a majestic trajectory to land a few feet from the hole. He was carried around on the shoulders of a cheering crowd as though he had just won the British Open. I handed out all the balls, three dozen or so, and the rest of my golf clubs, not particularly caring if I got them back. With that I went to join the only friend I had in the world. From *Solitaire*'s deck the beach took on a festive atmosphere: golf balls were flying like white meteors over sands covered by drying magazine pages while staggering drunks held cigarettes like prize

40

Havana cigars. I had brought havoc to this sleepy village but felt content for the first time since hitting the reef.

Around noon a Land Rover came down the beach with two uniformed men and a civilian who was the first to speak.

'No problem,' he said.

Thank the lord, I thought, for someone who could speak English. Quickly I told him of my adventures since leaving England, finishing up with a question, 'where am I?'

'No problem,' he replied. We went in this circle three times before I realised 'no problem' was the extent of his English. Passport and ships' papers were handed over and for the first time I heard the name Tutoia. It was decided that Maurice, one of the uniformed men, would stay with me to help refloat *Solitaire* and then navigate us to this Tutoia, a fishing village two miles or so away at the other end of the bay. The tide came in just before dark and *Solitaire* stood on her feet again. Some 40 yards offshore Maurice took the tiller while I watched the echo sounder. Then it grew dark which confused Maurice and we hit the mud. In the near vicinity were several canoes using lights. When Maurice called, one came over and without a word he stepped in and was swallowed by the dark. I spent a worried night trying to sleep on deck wrapped in a sail. *Solitaire's* keel was held as though set in concrete and there was no way of getting ashore unless I grew wings.

● **Solitaire at rest off Tutoia**

When Maurice returned at dawn *Solitaire* was again afloat. I started the engine and Maurice navigated us through a winding path of water cut in the forest until I had my first sight of Tutoia, a dirty beach with a single wooden jetty against a background of a few red-roofed modern bungalows among scattered palm trees.

I was given to understand a naval officer wanted to see me and tried to make myself presentable, covering my blisters with light-weight trousers and a long-sleeved shirt. As I could not get shoes on my feet I cut off the bottoms of some old pumps and bandaged them on. A native named Tony came out in his canoe and Maurice indicated that in future this man would look after me, so there would be no need of my rubber dinghy. I was taken to the largest of the bungalows which turned out to be Navy Headquarters and after a short wait was shown into an office sparsely decorated with pictures of ships. Behind a large desk sat a handsome officer wearing American-type light khaki navy uniform, silver bars agleam.

This was the commanding officer, Lieutenant Orland Sapana. Later I was to hear villagers refer to him as a saint and within a few days I was agreeing with them. The only other piece of furniture in the room was the biggest, softest, most luxurious easy chair whose arms reached out to me like those of a beautiful woman. My aching body longed to be engulfed by her and when I became aware Sapana was inviting me to sit I slowly lowered myself with closed eyes only to receive another full-throated belch. The seat had no springs and I was sitting on the floor. Lieutenant Orland had disappeared; all I could see was the underside of his desk. I pulled myself up until my nose rested on its surface from where I tried to carry on an intelligent conversation. Although Orland could speak no English, he used words that were nearly international.

'Military . . . sporta?'

I gathered he wished to know if I was in the services.

'Sport,' I replied.

'English?' he asked.

'Si, yes. English,' I repeated and then pointed at him.

He said he was Brazilian which confused me as I had always thought Saint Lucia was British.

'Saint Lucia? Brazilian?' I queried, shaking my head.

'Si, si.' He stretched his arms wide and said, 'Brazil'. Putting his hands close together, 'England'.

I was not having that, so I bent both arms intending to say 'England stronger' but having let go of the desk I was again swallowed by the

42

armchair. When I re-emerged Orland was rocking back and forth, pretending to hold a baby and smiling. At first I thought he wanted to know if I had any children. He then picked up my papers and pointed first to the date on the calendar then to my birthdate . . . October 24. Today was my birthday!

His face took on a look of concern and pointing to my own spoke the one word I'd been fearing, 'hospital'. I tried to make my way out of the office repeating, '*Solitaire, Solitaire,*' too frightened to leave her however much I needed medical attention. It was like being on the moon with someone suggesting you leave your space craft, your only means of returning to earth, plus the normal concern of entering any hospital wondering when they would release you. Orland understood this because he kept repeating, 'no problem, no problem'.

Maurice then returned and I was told to accompany him to a hotel for a meal. Most of the houses around had been standing for years, their whitewashed walls, two feet thick, broken by heavily shuttered windows as if under siege from the scorching sun. Poorly-dressed peasants offered fish and over-ripe bananas for sale but the village smelt of decay, flies seeming to cover its filth. Whenever Maurice and I came into view all movement would stop. I walked through statues that moved only to watch my stumbling progress. Now and again I would stop to tie the bandages on my feet when, seeing me kneeling on the cobbles, they would move forward to help only to retreat with shy smiles wishing me, 'good morning' as I looked up.

The hotel was another terraced house, larger than its neighbours with a small courtyard in front. Behind its shutters it was cool. The main room had long scrubbed tables, kitchen chairs and sturdy sideboards; the walls were covered with browning family photographs such as I had last seen as a boy, in my grandfather's house. Would I like to shower? I was shown across a dirty yard to what I first thought was a lavatory but inside which was a 40-gallon oil drum filled with water and a pannikin for throwing it over oneself. There was no soap or towel, but it proved the finest shower of my life. I patted myself dry with my shirt and tried to finger comb my hair. As this hurt I simply pushed it back from my forehead and replaced the four-knotted handkerchief I had been using as headgear.

I was given two boiled eggs, some bread, and the worst cup of coffee I had ever tasted. There was another person in the room, a young Castro, with thick black hair and beard. About 30 years of age he could speak a little English and introduced himself as Professor

Maguil, a visiting teacher. He asked if I would visit the local girls' school that evening and give a talk, explaining that although the children would be unable to understand what I was saying nevertheless they were trying to learn English and would welcome an opportunity to meet their first Anglo-Saxon.

A second man entered, Maguil's age, slightly built and beardless, a Dr Benedito Carvino. They talked together awhile, and from their glances clearly they were discussing me. I heard Lieutenant Orland's name mentioned.

Maguil turned 'Leslie, hospital,' he said seriously. Already I felt I had been separated from *Solitaire* too long, so I shook my head and returned to her. Tony took me back to my boat in his canoe and spent the afternoon aboard. Married with six children he lived in a small concrete box containing several beds built from odd pieces of wood, covered with bits of blankets, with a cooking fire in the middle of the dirt floor. Whenever I wanted to go ashore I would blow a whistle; either he, his wife or children would row me.

The youngsters added a touch of drama to this task. With a paddle as big as they and a fast-flowing current they had to drag the canoe well upstream before starting across, timing their meeting with *Solitaire* before being swept past. I showed Tony how to use my gas stove and where the tea and coffee was kept. Considering their poverty Tony and his family were the most honest people it has been my privilege to meet and nothing was ever taken without my say-so.

Just before dark a single-engined aircraft, a Cessna 126 I reckoned, landed close to the village. That night I returned to the hotel for dinner, ready for my solo performance at the girls' school. Seated at the table with eight or ten other men eating prawns and rice, the man opposite me spoke in English. He was Ivan, the pilot of the aircraft I had seen land, and someone with whom I could hold a conversation at last. Alas, he knew only a few phrases and 'words. In fact I was having difficulty myself with sentences, remembering only a few words at a time; if anyone spoke for too long I would forget the earlier part. In fact I found it easier to understand Orland, who spoke no English, than Ivan who in normal circumstances I would have been able to hold in conversation.

What happened that evening frightened me. At the school I was introduced to the teachers and then taken into a classroom with around a hundred females, aged between 14 and 60, all wearing grey skirts and white blouses, a government perk for attending school was the impression I gained. There was a good deal of laugh-

44

ing and shouting and the odd word of English. Since I knew they would not understand if I just talked I drew a chart on the blackboard showing my voyage from England to Martinique, then out to sea and back to Saint Lucia at which the shouting and laughing suddenly stopped and a chill ran up my back. When I turned around my audience stared at me as though I were mad. I had experienced this type of thing before when talking to the fishermen and Orland. I was trying to be friends with these people and I could not understand why they kept trying to frighten me. An attractive girl, aged about 20, was about to leave, her provocative wiggle marking her out as the village flirt. She stopped in front of me, eyeing me up and down with a smouldering look as she said something to Maguil. The silence was broken by roars of laughter. Maguil indicated she wanted to kiss me good night. My answer was to point to my blistered mouth and say, 'problem!' I started to enjoy life again.

Next morning Tony arrived early with a gift from Orland of a plate of toast which we spread with marmalade and shared for breakfast, helped down by coffee. Later Ivan joined us and we sat talking in the cabin for a while. When he said he had flown to many islands and, indeed, Miami I produced my Caribbean chart and pointed to Miami. He nodded, then smiling, pointed to Havana. I tried Barbados and got another 'yes'. Warming to the game I pointed to Saint Lucia and was amazed when he shook his head. I did not appreciate his sense of humour. I had seen him land, he was with me now. Why was he trying to worry me? My head started to ache again and Tony led Ivan away shortly afterwards.

While they were ashore I found a stainless-steel mirror which I cleaned and polished. The reflection surely was not me, not this ugly mass of blisters and yellow, weeping sores? The ginger beard was encrusted with filth, the eyes barely visible, just red swollen lids with slits which started to run as I became sorry . . . not for myself, but for the poor fool in the mirror.

That afternoon Orland, Maguil and Doctor Carvino came onboard. Again I was told I must go to hospital and again I refused. There would be no charge they said, apart from medicines and food. Finally I gave ten dollars to Tony to fetch the antibiotics and disinfectants the doctor prescribed. Professor Maguil was leaving to visit another school and promised to ask the teachers to look after me while he was away. The doctor cleaned my face, gave me some tablets and then they all left.

On October 26 I cut my feet, swollen like glowing balloons, with a razor blade to release the fluid. Later Orland arrived with the doctor and for the first time they saw me in shorts. The condition of my legs seemed to make them angry but lying on my bunk I had the feeling that it had little to do with me. Now and again I tried to explain that there was something wrong inside my head, that I could no longer understand anything. I kept making circular movements by the side of my head saying, 'loco'. I was asked again if I would go to the hospital and again refused. The doctor cleaned me as best he could and angrily pointed to the swarms of flies. 'Englishman loco,' he agreed. They left, none of us happy.

I spent a restless night, my only relief was to keep the blood from my feet by holding them above my head. In the morning I asked Tony to fetch the doctor who inspected my legs. 'Hospital,' he said again, shrugged his shoulders and closed his bag. 'Fini,' he said, which I took to mean the poor man had had enough of me. It was my turn to say 'hospital', and I even managed, 'please, Doctor'. Satisfied he gave me some tablets that seemed to ease the pain. Later he returned with Orland and a stranger. John, who had been in the Merchant Navy and had spent a good deal of time in British ports, spoke excellent English. The fault was mine that it took so long to explain things.

● **The square in Tutoia – from left to right, the church, doctor's house, maternity hospital (arrowed) and post office**

Tony who had been pumping *Solitaire* dry every day would now live aboard and look after her. I was asked to write a brief statement to the Captain of Ports, along with a sketch of *Solitaire*'s damage and a rough chart of my voyage, which I duly did and included a thank-you note for all the kindness and hospitality of the people on Saint Lucia. It was arranged I should enter hospital next morning. I spent those last few hours on *Solitaire* with my feet above my head before being carted off to hospital on October 28, 1975, Tony canoeing me to the jetty to save the long walk. Our trail up the cobbled streets was marked by flapping bandages I could no longer be bothered to tie, the bottom of my pumps dropping off as I staggered into the village square. I went forward bare-footed vaguely aware of a green build-ing on my right, a church in the left-hand corner with two buildings alongside. Tony pointed to the far one and said, 'hospital' towards which I stumbled drunkenly. As I entered I looked up, my embar-rassment at finding myself in Brixham about to be surpassed. Over the door for all the world to see were the words *Hospital Maternidade*. I considered trying to return to *Solitaire* but a light nudge from Tony pushed me into Tutoia's Maternity Hospital!

Maria Da paz Rodrigues, a long name for someone so gentle and pretty, I shortened to Maria that first day. The bed had clean white sheets and since I could not wear pyjamas, because of my weeping sores, I lay on top of them clad only in boxer shorts. Maria started working on my suppurations as soon as I arrived and she had her back to me when I suddenly drew in my breath as though hurt. She looked round, her large brown eyes full of concern, until I started laughing at which she joined in. When she had cleaned my face I made signs I wanted to shave off my beard which she did for me. Already I was feeling much better.

The first week passed quickly. Tony turned up each morning to report on *Solitaire*. Orland would visit and the teachers and girls from the school stayed with me until lights out. After their depar-ture the main entertainment was provided by bats performing acrobatics in the open rafters to the screams and groans of pregnant women, so much better than any late night horror film, with the added spice of finding yourself a blood donor if the bats included you in their act.

During the second week things improved and my head pains eased. I learned a few Portuguese words – and the names of the girls who were visiting me. The doctor's wife would sit with me at night and we would read together from an old English textbook of hers trying to increase her tiny vocabulary. Little old ladies would stay for hours without speaking, just holding my hands. Lovely young ladies would lean over, their black hair cascading down the sides of my cheeks, would slowly moisten luscious red lips and expect me to repeat some stupid Brazilian word after them as they tried to teach me their language.

The night before my release a fisherman, a new patient, came to my room to complain about the noise. Although I thought it a bit of a liberty, I asked the young ladies to take away their tape recorder. I would learn the Bossa Nova another night, I explained.

'What's your next port of call?' the fisherman asked.

'Barbados,' I answered.

'How long will it take?' he queried. When I said two days he told me it was impossible. We argued awhile and he left saying he would give me some charts. Next morning he handed me two of Brazil which I promptly gave back saying I had no intention of going there. He looked at me as though I'd just landed from another planet and pointed to a chart showing Tutoia. 'No,' I said, 'we're on Saint Lucia.'

He pointed to a town 80 miles away called Sao Luis. For a moment I stared at the charts, expecting my head to explode. I was in Brazil, 1,000 miles south of the Caribbean Saint Lucia and had sailed over the equator to hit a reef 100 miles south of the Amazon. How could I have made such an incredible blunder?

On my return to *Solitaire*, I re-read the instructions for taking a noon sight for latitude. 'Declination, north and south. These two elements are additive or subtractive according to the following simple rule. Same names add. Different names (one N and one S) subtract.' On September 23, when halfway across the Atlantic, the declination had changed from north to south (the sun moving south of the equator) and I had added instead of subtracted it.

The day I hit the reef the declination was 8°S, so from 16°S should have been subtracted the assumed latitude 14°40′N for that day. I had hit the Brazilian coast about 1°20′ south of the equator! Eighty miles further south is Sao Luis, the capital and port in that area of Brazil, its call sign SLI. Had I carried the *Admiralty list of Radio Signals* I would have found that Saint Lucia's call sign in the Windward Islands was in fact SLU! But the elementary error that had brought me to this pass I now found difficult to live with. In a sense that second week in hospital saw the start of my wish to make a second, non-stop, voyage around the world.

Before *Solitaire* could continue I had to do something about her broken bottle-screw and loose rigging. As I had no spares I removed one from the twin back-stays, replacing it with four links of anchor chain, and used it on the forestay. Once more *Solitaire* had tight rigging. Feeling pleased with myself I heard a disturbance on the shore where a man in a brightly coloured shirt ran up and down waving his arms and jumping in the air. We watched him awhile until I concluded that it might be a new dance craze and sent Tony over to see if he would like a partner. He was captured and brought out to *Solitaire* where his crew-cut and accent proclaimed him an American. He revealed that he was the aircraft pilot for the Captain of Ports in Sao Luis. When the Port Captain received my letter acknowledging the kindness of the Saint Lucian people he could not read it so passed it on to the American to translate. 'Jesus Chriiiist, this guy doesn't even know which hemisphere he's in,' he had exclaimed, and came to inform me. I thanked him for his trouble claiming that I had now recovered my marbles. After a couple of shots of my whisky and his camera he was gone.

I had just got my breath back when Tony returned with another visitor who looked like Rock Hudson, except that he had thick grey hair and a deeply tanned face and his baritone voice hinted of a French extraction. Lord knows what effect he had on women, but they were out of luck for he was a French-Canadian priest, Father Le Brun, who had heard of my troubles on his aircraft radio and had flown down to see me. I now had visions of the village airport starting to look like Heathrow.

He asked two questions, 'why did I wish to sail around the world alone,' and 'would I go to church that night?' I told him about solitude and contentment; of sailing into setting suns, of shoals of flying fish lifting from the bows, of colours beyond the skills of camera or painter which only God could have created. I had been having trouble finding words so to make him understand I had been using my hands to show fish in flight and dolphins dancing. Yes, I believed in God, but I considered the world to be his church; it was what was in your heart and mind that made you a christian. There was no necessity to go into a stone building to pray. If Father Le Brun did not understand my reasons for avoiding church, nevertheless he seemed content.

Later that afternoon I faced another mystery: jazz music blasting from the sky, over as quickly as a squall. That night I was invited to dine with the doctor and his wife and a few friends whose house adjoined the church. We had been enjoying both food and conversation when the musical earthquake struck and windows started to shake. I looked at the walls expecting to see cracks appear before the house disintegrated, calming down only when I noticed that the other guests ignored this interruption. Conversation continued, but now we were lip reading. Then I solved the mystery of the heavenly music. To call the faithful in a 100-mile area the church was using four loudspeakers instead of bells, one speaker directed into the doctor's window and my left ear.

His wife was trying to persuade me to take her to church that night, pretending she was unable to appreciate my reasons for not going. In the end she employed the normal feminine method of getting her way. Earlier I had refused more food although still hungry. She overcame my objections by saying I did not like her cooking so, not wanting to give offence, I had allowed my plate to be filled again. Now she claimed I was ashamed to be seen with her so I had to agree to accompany her to church.

The village square was crowded and I thankfully turned to go back but mysteriously a path opened up in front of us, people stepping aside as we moved towards the church. Inside it was packed but again the people let us through. For a moment I panicked thinking they were going to marry me off to one of the nurses but finally I found myself in front of the pulpit looking up at Father Le Brun who was smiling at me. He preached in Portuguese but I recognised my own name and *Solitaire*'s, after which the congregation repeated them the way you might say Amen, echoing through the speakers to the crowd in the square. Then he used his hands like flying fish and dipping them like dancing dolphins, having clearly understood what I had told him that morning. The scheme to get me to church had been a well-contrived plan involving Mrs Doctor!

After the service he explained how the villagers wished to bless my voyage but had not anticipated the problem of getting me into church. Had he explained the reason I would have been delighted I replied, adding that he had pinched all my best material for his sermon for which I would forgive him if he would pay another visit to *Solitaire* before he flew off. This perfect day was still not over. Back on the beach I found six of the schoolma'ams waiting for me. Aboard *Solitaire* they produced a guitar and tape recorder and started recording the songs of Brazil, in the intervals one of them reading from some pencilled notes in Portuguese. The performance ran for half-an-hour or so whereafter all gave our christian names just before the tape ran out. I have no idea how long it took them to perfect their timing but it must have been hours. It was a tape I would keep all my life and play a thousand times. I cherish it still.

Next morning Father Le Brun and I discussed my ports of call en route to the Panama Canal. Cayenne in French Guiana – 650 miles to the north – seemed a good prospect, and English was its second language. There I could pick up stores at reasonable prices. Shortly after he left a light aircraft flew over *Solitaire* dipping its wings. A kindly man was off to see if any more of his flock had strayed.

Food in Tutoia was hideously expensive and in short supply but I still had £200 left so I indulged in a couple of tins of spam and sardines and ten pounds of potatoes and bananas to add to my store of three jars of marmalade, six tins of mixed vegetables and a bottle of salad cream and another of mustard. Orland presented me with a sack of oranges and five gallons of diesel while Tony was asked to fill my water containers. Later in the day I watched a football match and, on the way back, was shown a ditch filled with water in which children and dogs were playing. A woman filled a jug from it and Tony made a drinking movement with his hand. It seemed I would be carrying 30 gallons of well-used bath water!

I was delayed for a few days awaiting my papers from Sao Luis, which did nothing to help my nerves. Like being thrown from a horse, the quicker you're back in the saddle the better, although I wasn't keen on coming within a mile of the horse or the sea in case I received another kick in the teeth from sun, sea and reefs.

At first light on Tuesday, November 18, 1975 I switched on the engine, but the diesel grumbled and showed her displeasure at being ignored for so long by emitting clouds of blue smoke before screaming at full pitch to shatter the quiet of the morning. Crickets in the mangroves on the far bank stopped their insistent chattering, and the birds took flight, screeching at the noisy intruder. Pushing the throttle forward the sound reduced to a slow, sexual throb. Tutoia slept on, palm trees lying limp with bowed heads. Over the dew-covered roofs I could see the steeple of the church in which I had received my service of blessing, nearby the maternity hospital in which I'd spent two weeks flat on my back. Would Tony arrive to help lift the anchor or could I play safe for another day?

No such luck! Already he was making his way down the beach, followed by his wife and children. Orland, in full uniform for the occasion, was there too, with his wife and young son, scuttling any chance I had of not sailing. Tony came aboard and quickly pulled up the anchor and, on his return to the cockpit, I gave him the parcel I had made up for his family.

'Adios, Leslie.'

'Adios, Tony,' and he was gone.

As I rounded the bend in the river, I looked back to wave farewell to my friends, a final glance at the kindly village of Tutoia, the home of samaritans.

TONE INDICATES ADDITIONAL STRENGTHENING OF THE BOAT

● **Plans of Leslie Powles' Solitaire of Hamble**

3

SLOWLY WE MOTORED THROUGH the watery forest into a nightmare of shallow brown waters, waves breaking over the sandy islands that threatened our passage. I raised sail, trying to lift the keel by heeling but without success. Ahead I could see the black marker buoy that had greeted our arrival towards which *Solitaire* made her way, picking her steps as though walking through a minefield, with nothing showing on the echo sounder. She lifted and dropped heavily on hard ground, her mast shuddering and I was promptly and violently sick over the stern. Slowly, so very slowly, we struggled to the buoy.

The sea was still brown but Orland had shown me on the chart in his office that if I sailed north I would soon find deep water. Moreover I now had the two charts the fisherman had given me and a list of RDF call signs all the way to Panama. Although I had no harbour charts, the ports I was considering, would be well-buoyed, with Cayenne, 650 miles away in French Guiana, the first.

The first 24 hours were nerve-wracking what with gusting winds, choppy seas, and the bilge pump packing up thanks to a ripped diaphragm. *Solitaire* needed pumping dry twice a day so I made do with a bucket and sponge until I contrived a new diaphragm from some plastic 'rubber' left over from the seat covers. My noon sight on November 19, 1975 put us 22 miles below the equator and as we made our first intentional crossing that night the wind came light from the east enabling *Solitaire* to broad-reach contentedly for Cayenne, dozing along under main and working jib. I should have put up a larger headsail, but relaxed with 80 miles a day, plus another 20 miles or so from the favourable current. My nerves steadied, the cool sea breeze refreshing my scarred skin. To celebrate crossing the equator I dined off spam and chips. As the days slid by the winds continued to decrease but I refused to fly more sail for I was enjoying this voyage too much. I found some flour, in a plastic bag inside a box of sponge mix, and made my first-ever pancakes, spreading them with my favourite marmalade as the radio started to pick up delightful French music. One morning I saw what I first thought was a low flying aircraft coming over the horizon, followed by another and another. As they neared I could see they were modern fishing trawlers with their arms extended. All day, stretching from horizon to horizon, they streamed by *Solitaire*. With darkness they became a blaze of lights making me think I was sitting on a main street. Then, like a body of soldiers, they turned together, headed out to sea and disappeared. A last arrival came scurrying by late for parade. 'Get a move on you hooooooorible little man . . .' I cried in my best sergeant-major voice. When he had gone we had the night to ourselves, and a French woman sang me to sleep with love songs.

On Tuesday, November 25, *Solitaire* lay a couple of miles off Cayenne. I could see trawlers heading inshore but could pick up no RDF signal although Paramaribo in Dutch Surinam was coming in loud and clear from 160 miles away and since it had a lightship to help with the landfall, I decided to sail there instead. We arrived late on Thursday and lay off, keeping the lightship in sight until morning. Although I had tried to hold our position, *Solitaire* had drifted to the north with the current and had to be forced back. Again the waters were chocolate-coloured but a clearly-buoyed shipping lane made navigation easy. A strong outflowing current slowed progress and as ocean-going ships were using the main channel, I pulled to one side, dropped sail and anchored for the night. Food was getting short so dinner consisted of a tin of mixed vegetables, salad cream and an orange, as did breakfast next morning.

We arrived in Paramaribo fairly quickly and rode the broad river on a favourable tide. The port seemed prosperous enough, with clusters of docks housing fleets of shrimp trawlers, the town a mixture of old Dutch buildings and modern stores, a bustling fruit, fish and vegetable market on the dockside. Flags and bunting were everywhere as a week earlier Surinam had gained its independence from the Dutch. The harbour itself was spoilt by a massive cargo ship parked in the middle, upside down, scuttled by the Germans during the last war. I felt *Solitaire* shudder when she caught sight of it but I hastened to disclaim any responsibility.

54

However, I soon managed to get us in trouble again. I dropped the hook about 20 feet from a structure of girders but was suspicious of *Solitaire*'s position in the fast current. If I attempted to lift the anchor again or she started dragging we could find ourselves trying to climb over the top of the sunken German ship. On the girders, wearing green overalls and plastic helmet, stood a black man, looking for all the world as if he had been working on a New York skyscraper when it had sunk. After my experiences in Brazil I knew you could work wonders with the odd packet of English cigarettes, so I waved a pack in his direction, making a diving and swimming action with my arms, shouted 'amigo' and waved him over. His eyebrow merely lifted whereupon I increased my offers to two packs, still without joy. Perhaps he could not swim? The solution was easy: I would throw him a rope which he could tie onto a girder. I would then pull *Solitaire* over and he could lift the anchor while I steered. My throw was perfect, landing plumb at his feet at which he raised the other eyebrow. We both watched with interest as the current slowly snaked the rope back again. After three more perfect throws I grew despondent. 'For Pete's sake will you please tie the rope to the girder,' I cried. To my surprise he picked it up and secured it. Roy turned out to be the dockyard foreman and spoke excellent English, Paramaribo's second language, probably because the Americans run most things there. Roy took me to the Dutch manager who could not do enough. The structure Roy had been standing on was part of a dry dock for lifting prawn trawlers. *Solitaire* could be hauled out at the same time at no expense to me but I turned down the kindly offer, wanting to push on to Panama. The only other cruising yacht in port at the same time belonged to a Frenchman, Stephan, who with his wife and young daughter were preparing to leave on the out-going tide when I arrived. I was invited onboard to share their last meal before they sailed: steak, salad and bread washed down by fresh milk! They put me ashore with the last of the steak in a crusty roll. As I let go their lines Stephan asked what my next port of call would be. 'British Guiana,' I replied. Stephan's mournful plea came back, 'Ooooh, Leslie, don't go there. Very bad people. You will be robbed.'

So I said, 'Right I'll go to Trinidad.'

'Ooooooooh, Leslie, don't go there. You'll be robbed.'

So I asked where they were going.

'Granada in the Caribbean,' they said.

'Right,' I shouted, waving goodbye with my steak sandwich, 'I'll see you there.'

My stay in Paramaribo, thanks to my first real taste of American hospitality, was longer than expected. They were either visiting *Solitaire* or taking me to a barbecue party, the movies or whatever. I bought what tinned food I could afford, always looking for the cheapest buy which did not always pay off as I had to throw away a dozen tins of canned mackerel. The Dutch manager presented me with oranges and a sack of grapefruit. My last day in Paramaribo was spent chiselling through *Solitaire*'s cabin floor and reinforcing the cracked hull with fibreglass.

The 500-miles voyage to Granada took eight weary days. The currents between the islands are strong and as Granada has no RDF station and those available on other islands were weak, dead reckoning became paramount. The last two days brought heavy rain with bad visibility which cleared up at midnight on December 16 when a large black cloud appeared on the horizon with a star in the middle – Granada with a house light high up in the hills.

At dawn I motored to Saint George's main anchorage where I performed my usual party piece of putting *Solitaire* on a reef. To be fair I don't think we should count this one as another yacht was coming out leaving insufficient room for two boats to pass. *Solitaire*, the perfect lady, stepped to one side and we had virtually stopped when there was a grunching sound and *Solitaire* rolled from side to side, shaking her mast as much as to say, 'I don't believe it!'

Instantly a flotilla of small craft, power boats, yachts, gin palaces, even rowing boats tore out as if they had been awaiting our arrival, the air filled with flying ropes and people clambered over our decks attaching them to every conceivable place. Within minutes *Solitaire* was swinging to her anchor, dazed by so much attention. Where, I wanted to know, had they been when I needed them in Brazil?

We had just got shipshape when I heard, 'oooooooh, Leslie,' from a dinghy racing towards me. 'Ooooooh, Leslie, I've been robbed,' said Stephan which had me in stitches. The following night I was laughing on the other side of my face. Blacks would silently raft around the anchored yachts by night intent on robbery so it was unwise to leave craft unattended. New arrivals were quickly made aware of the danger and, in turn, I had already warned another crew that day. I had met David, an American, through his English crew member, and had been invited to his yacht *Rolling Stone* for dinner that night. David had built his boat in England before sailing across the Atlantic to pick up his parents and a girl friend for a holiday. I thought *Solitaire*, anchored no more than 40 yards away, was safe enough since I could still keep an eye on her and for added protection fitted strings to the deck light switch and attached them to the sliding hatches. There was a good crowd on *Rolling Stone* and for a while I sat drinking in the cockpit watching my boat. Finally we disappeared below for a curry meal although every few minutes I would pop my head outside to make sure everything was all right. Then *Solitaire*'s lights came on.

David and another large American, Tom, rowed me over. I thought the thieves might still be aboard but the hatch cover had been ripped off and every locker, drawer and door opened, including the oven's. I would not have thought it possible to wreak so much malicious damage in so short a time. The engine's instrument panel had been uprooted and the spare money I kept there stolen. My portable radio, clothes, tools and two torches had vanished. The ships' papers, my passport and £80 in travellers' cheques should have been at the back of my chart table, but they had gone, too. It was a kick in the crutch. I could sell my outboard motor, WC, even the stove and still continue around the world, but without a passport or ships' papers I was stuck. I told David and Tom the reason for my looking so sick whereupon they started pulling out the charts . . . and found my wallet with the papers and cheques which meant that I could leave for Panama in the morning after all! My visitors had kindly left my RDF, sextant, and compass and had also missed a camera. The police were called but showed perfunctory interest and I was still upset next morning, as if *Solitaire* had been raped. David suggested I hang on for a couple of days and tie alongside *Rolling Stone* for protection and again Americans came to my assistance. Tom and his girlfriend, Karen, presented me with a large bag of food claiming that it had been stored in the bilges too long and was going bad. On inspection I found a recent label from the local supermarket!

Christmas was but a few days away. David and his family were sailing to Prickly Bay, six miles along the coast, where it would be quieter, with less chance of being broken into and *Solitaire* accompanied them, feeling that one rape in a girl's life was one too many. I did not set off for Panama until a fortnight later but in the interim became friendly with more Americans including Bill and his girlfriend Dean who had started on a world voyage but had been forced to give up the idea. Since they couldn't go, they decided to help me on condition I wrote them detailing my progress with pre-addressed envelopes they supplied!

One other thing the Americans in Granada offered was advice: stay at least 20 miles off the Columbian coast and ignore distress rockets. Pirates were using them to attract unsuspecting yachts, then murdering the crews and using the craft for drug trafficking. Finally, take care walking the streets of Colon even in daylight as muggers formed queues to rob tourists.

Solitaire set off on January 10, logged 1,124 miles and arrived on January 23, 1976. Sailing to Panama is like entering the neck of a bottle: trade winds that have swept thousands of miles across the Atlantic can become quite strong and compressed; steep-breaking seas build up but fortunately for us they were from the east and hence over our stern. I left Granada with a comfortable force four from the south-east but by the third day winds had increased and we were down to working jib only, breaking seas speeding behind us. At times *Solitaire* would find herself surfing on them; at others, unable to move fast enough, she would receive a firm pat on her stern, and would turn indignantly as much as to say, 'how dare you, sir'. On one such occasion a wave shot a bucketful of water through the open hatch soaking the cabin carpet again. Thereafter I kept the hatch boards in, closing myself below and emerging only to take noon sights for latitude, obtain fixes, or check sails, rigging and self-

● **Robbed in Grenada – Solitaire alongside Rolling Stone (on the right)**

steering. Most of the time I spent reading the books Bill and Dean had given me and eating strange American foods including stuffed tomatoes of which I had never heard!

The night of my Panama Canal landfall I panicked. As I had been warned to keep 20 miles off the coast I played safe and doubled it then, when it was time to turn towards land, I had the Cayenne problem over again; I could not pick up the Canal's RDF signal. However, callsign TBG came in loud and clear, indicating the island of Taboga lying at the Pacific end of the Panama Canal and since it was in the right direction I set course for it. At about the time I had estimated I saw the loom of a light in the night sky and made for the glow which swung up and became two blooming great headlights. Pirates! Turning off my lights I started the motor to shoot off back the way I had come, only to find another set of headlights blocking *Solitaire*'s escape. At that moment I saw the Canal lighthouse flashing and made for it. Astern were two looms of light in the sky; I'm sure now they were fishing boats using their lights to work by. Maybe I scared them more than they scared me. Maybe.

I waited for daylight before easing through the breakwater where after anchoring on mud flats an American customs launch came over and gave me the good news that I would have enough money to pass through the Canal. It would cost only £30, half of which was a deposit and would be returned later. That was not my only piece of luck: I also received my first letter from Rome who, as an ex-merchant seaman, knew I had to pass through the Canal. I had reported all my blunders and how *Solitaire* kept getting me out of trouble, to which Rome replied that despite so many mistakes at least I was making them only once. I wrote back immediately . . . omitting to mention the reef in Granada! To arrange our transit I moved *Solitaire* into the Colon Yacht Club, one which does not encourage you to linger as they double their prices every three days to make room for new arrivals. You can stay on the mud flats free of charge, but from there it is difficult to arrange for a pilot and crew.

The Colon Muggers must be the world's best and if you haven't been mugged by one of them you haven't been mugged. It's one of the few countries which runs schools for these gentlemen with courses in drug trafficking, kidnapping, and plain everyday murder. After successfully completing their training, many graduates are exported to less well-endowed regions such is the demand for their talents. I made their acquaintance soon after my arrival. Communication between them and the chaps in Granada must have broken down or they would have been informed that I had already been nobbled and there was little left. My partner in this drama, Terrell Adkisson, was not exactly my idea of a Texan, as I had been brought up watching John Wayne and Gary Cooper knock ten kinds of rice pudding out of the Indians. Needing fuel for my trip through the Canal I was hitting the trail along the Old Pontoon when I heard a slow, drawn-out, 'Hoooowdy.' I spun round, dropping my hand to my hip, then quickly removed it in case I conveyed the wrong impression. I was confronted by a scruffy individual wearing checked shirt, glasses and a pair of ex-army trousers four sizes too big. At first the stubble on his face and grey crew-cut hair suggested he was older than I. In fact he was younger, proving again that ageing is a deception practised on people after a long sea voyage and nights without sleep. Adkisson owned *Altair,* a new 28ft glassfibre bermudan sloop, and had recently given up teaching mathematics in Texas to sail around the world with his 22-year-old nephew, Leo, a blonde young man who had spent his previous spare time guitar-playing in a pop group. Terrell needed petrol, or gas as he put it, so we started out on the first of our many adventures together to a garage only a mile away in the Colon district. I had enough money to buy five gallons of diesel; Terrell had his wallet in his back pocket. The garage attendant warned us to be careful, his darting, frightened eyes telling their own story. Groups of blacks were watching us but it was ten o'clock in the morning, broad daylight, so why worry? Half-way back to the yacht club I turned to speak to Terrell and spotted three of the biggest blacks I've ever seen coming up behind us, with

● **The author (left) with Terrell Adkisson**

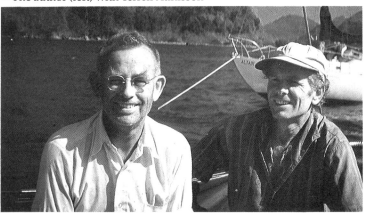

knives. I had dreamed of moments like this. I would push the women and children to one side, take a flying leap, legs drawn to manly chest to shoot out like two murderous pistons, taking the two nearest villains in the throat killing them instantly. The third would be despatched with a karate chop to the head . . .

What I actually did was to shout a warning to Terrell and run in front of a line of oncoming traffic. A screeching of brakes . . . I'm bouncing off a car, the fuel can turning into a tiger that wants to go walkies. It bolts across the intersection dragging me with it, to get clobbered by a truck coming the other way. When I stagger to my feet Terrell has a black on each arm with knives at his chest, while a third is tearing at Terrell's wallet. I shout as loudly as I can to let the blacks know I really mean it, 'hang on, I'm coming.' There's a sound of ripping and Terrell stands in the main street minus trousers – and wallet. He starts running after them with me trying to stop him. If he catches them up they will surely kill him but, outdistanced, he abandons the chase.

Terrell has lost a few travellers' cheques, no cash. Soon his sense of humour returns. 'Just my luck to be arrested for indecent exposure,' he says, looking down at his fancy underpants. He was attacked a second time in Panama City, but this time Leo came up behind with a tin of peaches and started hammering the would-be mugger who ran off. In Colon that could be described as a bad day at the office. It is inadvisable to linger long in Panama.

The 40-mile canal trip is straightforward enough, through pleasant lakes and waterways with three locks at each end. You require a ship's pilot (normally an ex-merchant navy captain), four line handlers and four 100ft lengths of rope. The handlers adjust your lines to keep your craft in the centre of the dock as you rise and fall for which you supply the food and grog for the day and their rail fare back which, in 1976, was just one dollar. Line handlers are not hard to come by. They reckon it's a nice day out.

I arrived at the Balboa Yacht Club on the Pacific side with precisely three dollars so I sold my outboard for 200 to put me back in funds. Again I bought the cheapest food available, unmarked tins of corned beef that turned out to be mostly jelly, tins of tuna that looked and tasted like grey sand, a sack of rice alive with weevils, flour, baking powder and a large tin of treacle as a treat.

For my Pacific crossing (8,000 miles or so) I bought two charts. My first landfall would be Hiva Oa in the Marquesas Islands, a voyage of 3,500 miles or so. Navigation to date had been by dead reckoning with noon sights for latitude and radio direction finding, now I would be sailing into areas of reefs, few lighthouses and fewer navigation aids. Accurate navigation would be essential so I would have to learn how to take sights for longitude. I managed to buy a 1976 Admiralty Almanac and a second-hand set of reduction tables and for accurate timekeeping (one minute in error can put you 15 miles out of position) I helped anti-foul another boat whose owner gave me a small portable receiver in payment. This one had short wave enabling me to pick up the American station WWV which broadcasts time checks 24 hours a day. There was one small problem: the mirrors on my sextant had lost their silvering. A lady presented me with the mirror from her handbag. Cut to size it made my sextant serviceable again. I made one major mistake when, trying to save money, I bought a gallon of cheap anti-fouling. As things worked out it would have been less expensive to have paid more for a better quality.

My custom ashore was to sit on the edge of a group of cruising people, listening to their tales of the sea, trying to pick up tips. *Solitaire* the only craft I knew anything about had now carried me 7,000 miles or more, but I still had not picked up much sailing terminology: talk of schooners, ketches or heavy weather sailing and I was lost. I tried to fade into the background, with the odd 'hear, hear,' and 'dashed good show,' trying to pretend I was one of them. On one such occasion I was with a crowd at the Balboa Yacht Club discussing the particularly bad weather at that time of year in the Caribbean. One American had lost his trimaran. He and his crew, overtired on the trip from Granada, had tried to come through the breakwater at night, missed the lights and hit it but managed to get off before it sank. A Canadian family had tried for ten days to sail in the other direction but after a fierce battle had given up and retraced their steps through the Canal. Another five boats were hoping for an easterly passage, meanwhile waiting for the seas to die down. A Frenchman had ripped the floor out of his yacht to cover the cockpit and give protection from breaking waves. I thoroughly enjoyed their talk; you could virtually taste the salt on your lips.

'Leslie, you've just come through the Caribbean from Granada single-handed,' someone commented.

'Er, yes.' A mass of weather-beaten faces turn towards me.

'How bad was it in your opinion?'

'Pretty bad,' I replied.

'Yes, but how bad?' the voice insisted. I don't want to tell them I spent my time below, reading, while *Solitaire* and the self-steering did the work. I can't talk about wind speed as I had no wind indicator and I would not know a 20ft breaking wave from a ten-footer, yet I desperately want to be accepted by these adventurers. I came out with the incident that made me put in my hatchboards, 'well, my carpets got wet.'

There was a deathly silence.

I escaped next morning to the island of Taboga, six miles away in the Pacific. Terrell and I had heard of a wartime landing barge on the beach there against which it was possible to tie alongside, wait for the tide to ebb and then anti-foul the hull. *Altair* was done on one day, and *Solitaire* the next. Not too keen on the idea, my boat started acting like a spoilt child on bath night until I had tied her up, when she settled. I made a better job of the wound in her side and then applied my cheap anti-fouling which went on like weak whitewash. *Solitaire* deserved better, but with only 60 dollars left in the kitty I had little choice; at least we would be sharing discomforts, I thought, remembering my jellied corn beef and gritty tuna!

Terrell and Leo sailed a week ahead of us, as there were a few jobs still to do on *Solitaire*. I was sorry to see them go, but we would catch up later. I felt I was living in Germany when a knock on the door could mean a call from your local friendly Gestapo inviting you to sample the delights of a lovely concentration camp. Only now in Taboga it would be the army or police searching your yacht for drugs. They paid a visit the day before I left, bringing a dinghy I was supposed to have left on the beach, one I knew belonged to a nearby yacht whose mast had been broken coming through the Panama. A young man with a large dalmatian dog was looking after the parent boat while its owner was away. As I towed the dinghy over to tie it on the yacht's stern I could see the dog running on the beach. Later I heard the full story. The young man had taken it ashore for a walk, the army had tried to shoot it and the boy had put his arms round it for protection. He was now in hospital, half his hand blown away.

I sailed for Hiva Oa on Thursday, February 26, 1976 and for two days *Solitaire* made good time in light winds, gliding along effortlessly on her clean bottom. Conscious of my earlier mistakes I spent hours in *Solitaire's* cockpit listening to WWV for time checks while I took sights for longitude which, in the early days of the voyage, I could easily confirm. As the days passed I began to feel more at home at sea than on land. *Solitaire's* constant movement and my spartan diet kept me slim and fit. As I am blessed with ginger hair and freckles, the sun enjoyed itself colouring my skin anything from brilliant red to deep purple. It was a surprise to find it browning me as well.

No webbed feet or gills yet, but I was metamorphosing into marine life. For instance, storms and calms are treated differently by sea animals. To land life a storm is a personal attack, knocking down a man's chimneys, flattening his crops whereas calms go unnoticed. Sea life however accepts storms which may sink ships but are not malicious and realises that the patient ocean recognises no flags, is not vindictive and far from finding pleasure in rolling you over does not even notice you. But a calm is a personal attack and in early days could mean back-breaking weeks in a longboat towing a square-rigger while searching for life-giving winds, half the crew dying of thirst or hunger.

Solitaire hit her first long calm east of the Galapagos Islands. After the early days at sea progress had slowed with runs of only 30 or 40 miles a day, periods without wind, the self-steering on a knife edge. Now she was about to spend four days in an ocean of thick blue oil below a sky whose solitary, unmoving cloud would retain its shape and position hour after hour leering down on our discomfort. We carried no burgee at the mast top to indicate wind direction but on

● **The first long calm near the Galapagos**

our backstays bore long, red tell-tales which became skirts covering the most beautiful legs in the world, legs that made Betty Grable's look like matchsticks. They would lift slightly, showing trim ankles and then, seeing they had my interest, drop teasingly. Just over the horizon was a Giant bathing in this lake of oil, his movements causing a long swell that swayed *Solitaire* monotonously from side to side. I grew to hate him and the Leering Cloud and the Teasing Skirt. The slapping sails, the rattle of the rigging, the strange sounds that would take hours to find . . . a shifting mug, a loose can. One sound had lasted longer than all the rest, a bruuuuuuph, bruuuuuuph, over and over again. Whenever I moved from my bunk I would alter *Solitaire*'s balance and the noise, hearing me, would stop. Even if I slid along the floor on my belly, holding my breath, I could not catch it. Then the Giant scrubbed his back, and I had it. Bruuuuuph, bruuuuuph. A new drill was rolling back and forth in a drawer. I watched it with pleasure for a few minutes, like a cat with a mouse, then I pounced. Clutching it in my fist I took it to *Solitaire*'s stern, and threw a brand new drill worth a bag of rice 50 yards into the sea. You really should not do that sort of thing. Later I learned the secret of destroying calms. You simply ignore them.

Once the sea was flat I would drop the headsail, and put a reef in the main to reduce chaff which drives the chappie taking the bath bananas. Invariably I would spend my first day on deck busy with odd jobs, always remembering to smile and whistle from time to time for leering clouds hate happy whistling. To attract the teasing skirt I would bring out my secret weapon: a couple of good books and while reading would watch her advances from beneath lowered lids. Red skirts hate being treated in this way and soon show all they have. There are compensations to long calms for at the end you will hear the Hallelujah chorus played by the London Symphony Orchestra. It's like sitting in the Royal Albert Hall, eyes closed, waiting, waiting, waiting. Then a faint cough, a ripple touches *Solitaire*'s side. A flute softly tunes up and the sails stop flapping. The string section play a few bars and her rigging hums. The conductor taps his baton, a slight pause and *Solitaire* is sailing and the most marvellous music in the world is heard. The choir sings Hallelujah, Hallelujah, higher and higher, HHHaaaaaaleeelujah . . .

Solitaire sailed 200 miles to the east of the Galapagos Islands, passing through areas showing six per cent calms on the charts. She had to overcome a north-flowing current of 15 to 20 miles a day as she struggled over the equator for her third crossing to the free-flowing trade winds that started 300 miles to the south. She was sick as she told me but again, because of my inexperience, I took no notice. She lost her will to live, dragging through the sea on legs too tired to move. I assumed the slow progress to be due to the adverse current and light winds, and fought back with every sail arrangement I could possibly manage to contrive.

The first light breezes from the east indicated the start of the trades. *Solitaire* carried no whisker poles for holding out twin head sails simply because I could not afford them. Instead I had made do with two 13ft aluminium poles to which I had fitted eyes at both ends. I tried using these with both the numbers one and two genoas hanked on, plus the full main. Still she would not budge. Seas flowed past her and the self-steering lost control, even the tiller having little effect upon her erratic course. She would broach continually, swinging 180° and backing her sails.

When finally we came into the true trades, constant force three to fours (7 to 16 mph), I sailed on a broad reach, with a quartering wind, the number two genoa poled out, a reef in the main. Yachtsmen would have considered me crazy to have so little sail and in such conditions I would have loved to have set a spinnaker, had I possessed one. Half of the course settings were by sail adjustment as the self-steering was of little practical use.

Unknown to me a cancerous growth was spreading its tentacles around her. *Solitaire's* cries for help quietened as it entered her mouth, silencing her. Now she was wallowing, hardly noticing the winds that entreated her to frolic.

Wednesday March 24, 1976 found us at latitude 6°05'S. We had left the equator 365 miles astern and were 300 miles below the Galapagos Islands. A favourable current gave us an extra 10 to 15 miles a day in south-east winds around force four. In these ideal conditions *Solitaire* should have been romping along covering at least 120 to 140 miles a day. All she produced was a limping 50 miles. Our trailing log clocked only 1,115 miles in 27 days, not a third of the way to Hiva Oa with half our food and water already consumed.

On the self-steering rudder and under the stern I found pink stalks up to an inch and a half in length with a white and grey bud on each top which I cleaned off with a paint scraper. Could these growths be the reason for *Solitaire's* illness? I rejected the idea when I remembered anti-fouling her hull only five weeks earlier; surely that could not be the cause.

During one of those cleaning sessions I found myself in one of

66

those stupid situations that happen only to singlehanders. I had pushed myself through the bars of the pushpit as far as I could, leaning well out and holding on with one hand while scraping with the other. I felt a pull on my hair and threw the scraper into the cockpit, grabbing at my head. My hair had become tangled in the trailing log line! It took me a good half hour to free myself. After that I had a dread of getting stuck up the mast only to be discovered a year later as a swaying skeleton.

Afloat it is difficult to see all of *Solitaire's* hull as it rounds sharply just below the waterline and falls away to the keel, so I decided to lean out as far as possible, using a lifeline and an extra rope for support. I had expected to find someone's old sail or a bunch of rope tangled on the keel; instead I found a swaying pink and white garden completely covering the hull, keel, and skeg. No wonder *Solitaire* had wept. Again I felt as I had when the bruuuph, bruuuuumh drill had come to light. I prepared to pounce then, deflated, realised it had us in thrall, that I had a plague of goose barnacles.

There were three reasons why getting rid of them would cause problems: I'm a poor swimmer, there were sharks in the area, and I'm a confirmed coward. I spent the morning making every conceivable excuse I could think of for not going over the side. *Solitaire* listened in silence except for a muttered slop slop, slurp slurp. I suppose she could have nagged that I had been the one to give her a cheap coat of anti-fouling and thus responsible for her sickness but she didn't, which made the need to be forgiven the more dramatic. I badly needed to hear her whisper and laugh with me again.

In the afternoon I dropped her headsail and under the main brought her onto a reach, allowing her to roll in three- to four-foot waves. The rubber dinghy was inflated and secured to leeward. With two lifelines and armed with a scraper, I dropped into it and then, holding onto the toe rail, reached down the hull as far as I could on each roll. I spent an hour or so on one side, clearing only a foot and a half of barnacles, their rubbery feet still clinging below the water-line.

Hanging onto *Solitaire*, trying to keep a grip with my toes as the dinghy dropped away, made me want to give up and throw up. Oh well, tomorrow it would only be worse so I climbed back onboard, turned *Solitaire* around and worked on her other side. Then we were back on course, broad-reaching with our number two genoa filling with only a slight improvement in her performance. All the thanks I got for my trouble was, slop slop, slurp slurp.

67

For the next few days I lost interest in everything but trying to ease the pain in my arms and stomach. We became a couple of tetchy invalids reluctantly settling for a desperately slow passage. To save water I stopped shaving and started my first intentional beard as we slurped across the Pacific in perfect slurping conditions. I would spend hours in the cockpit marvelling at this sailing paradise with its cool trade winds and clear, blue skies broken only by a few wispy clouds. The transparent waters provided a private aquarium of beautiful tropical fish that would look up, saucer-eyed, to admire our exotic garden of pink stems and nodding white heads which grew larger with each slurping mile.

At night I had an I-hate-barnacles hour. No longer content with merely scraping them off, I wanted to inflict pain and hear their screams, to collect every last one and lay them on *Solitaire*'s decks so that we could both witness their death throes. The day of reckoning was drawing near. On Friday, April 23, after eight weeks or so at sea covering 3,020 miles and with 600 miles still to go to Hiva Oa, we sighted our first ship. To be honest it was not a ship but a yacht and they sighted us, not I them. I had felt like a spot of work that morning and spent half an hour picking the weevils out of my daily cup of rice. Despite this strenuous exercise I still felt pretty active, but could think of nothing that demanded attention until I remembered my golf clubs which were as dirty as old boots. So I spent the morning below cleaning them. Towards noon I heard the sound of a trumpet. If that's Gabriel, I thought, I'm not going and banged my head to clear it. Then it sounded again. On deck, clutching my five iron, I see there's a 40ft boat off our bow manned by an elderly couple and two in their mid-twenties, Canadians by the home port on their stern. Their twin-poled headsails have been eased and they are holding position a few yards off. I walk up to *Solitaire*'s pulpit.

'Ahoy,' they shout, 'we've had you in sight all morning. Seeing no one on deck we became worried.'

'I'm fine,' I said, waving my iron, 'I was cleaning my golf clubs.'

There's a thoughtful silence. 'Do you know if there's a bank in Hiva Oa?' they ask, 'we need to cash a cheque.'

'I'm sorry,' I reply, 'I'm a stranger here myself, don't often play this course.'

Another long silence. 'You sure you're all right?'

'Perfectly,' I assure them.

With that they pull in their sails and draw away. I can't believe it. After eight weeks with no one to talk to, they're leaving without even an invitation to coffee. I wanted to say something really mean but the best parting shot I could think was, 'you haven't seen my bloody golf ball have you?' The I-hate-barnacles hour that night was extended by 30 minutes.

On Monday, May 3, 1976 the noon sight put us 47 miles from Hiva Oa. Looking back over my life I seemed to have done few things right so now I want desperately to recompense by making a good landfall. I had nothing to confirm my longitude calculations, apart from some days when I had taken two sights, morning and afternoon, which gave position lines crossing at about our latitude.

Slow progress, a flat sea and clear skies helped my navigation. Today I checked and rechecked a dozen times, for failure to sight land next morning would mean I had let down *Solitaire* yet again. In the afternoon I decided to test the engine which normally I ran every two or three weeks, just to circulate the oil and top up the battery. I turned the key but nothing happened so I went over all the connections. Those on the solenoid seemed loose and dirty. Cleaned and tightened we had a motor again!

The Marquesas Islands stretch for about 200 miles, half a dozen of them 3,000 ft high or more, and on a clear day they should be visible for 30 or 40 miles. Hiva Oa, at 3,520 ft, should not be difficult to spot, despite having no lighthouse or radio direction beacon. But, with one error of more than a thousand miles to look back on, anything was possible! As night fell the sky filled with stars, although a sea mist obscured the horizon. *Solitaire* should have been within a few miles of the island but I could see nothing, no lights, no black shape. The sea was empty. I dropped all sails and waited for dawn. As the sky grew lighter there was still no land. The sun had not appeared but it was daylight. Now I would settle for anything, a smudge in the distance, even land birds. All one could see was sea. I could not face another Brixham, another Brazil, another broken marriage. I went below, recorded another failure and made myself a cup of tea. All I could do now was to take fresh sights and try to discover my mistake. Defeated I climbed back into the cockpit.

I heard the Hallelujah chorus so loud it almost took off my head and tears of joy ran down my face. She had been there all the time, hiding beneath the early morning mist, the most beautiful island in the world. Her purple and blue mountains reached up for the sky, green palms swaying in the breeze, surf breaking on golden sands. After 68 days at sea *Solitaire* and I had made it and had got something right. I savoured every precious second.

Terrell had lent me one of his charts from which I had sketched the island. The anchorage was at the far end of a bay and we spent the morning motoring there, *Solitaire* still rolling drunkenly with her cargo of barnacles. This morning I hated nothing, not even the blasted barnacles.

The bay we wanted turned back on itself. There was a moment of doubt when I could not see it, then I spotted a beach, palm trees, a few homes up in the hills and two boats at anchor. *Solitaire* turned to meet new friends, a blue ketch flying a French flag, an American flag on a trimaran with people on its spacious decks.

I dropped anchor and started to put *Solitaire* in order, making a final entry in the ships log: '23.15 hours GMT. Anchored Hiva Oa, distance by trailing log 3,655 miles after 68 days at sea. Onboard one gallon of water, two pounds of rice, two tins of corned beef, six Oxo cubes'.

A dinghy left the ketch and started across. The men and women aboard could speak good English with a heavy French accent. Did I need anything?

Where could I buy bread? There was a store in the village, an hour's walk away. They left but the man was soon back with half a loaf, a jar of marmalade and a can of beer.

Later another dinghy came over from the trimaran with an Englishman in his early thirties and a beautiful doll-like creature whose golden skin and almond eyes showed traces of the Orient. Jeff and Judy would be the couple I would spend most time with in the Marquesas. There are few men I have grown to admire more than Jeff. Born in Britain, he became a veterinary surgeon and moved to the west coast of America where he built his trimaran, *Dinks Song,* to escape the more mercenary practices of his profession. Each day shared with him brought fresh surprises. It started with his playing the guitar, singing in a voice that would have earned him a living anywhere in the world; went through numerous instruments which finished one spell-binding night when he stood on his foredeck at anchor in the bay at Fatu Hiva, playing the hauntingly lonely music of Scotland on his bagpipe – unforgettable!

I learned more and more about this man, mostly from Judy. He held an aircraft pilot's licence. With his high-powered rubber dinghy he waterskied and taught the Polynesian locals to emulate him. But what I remember Jeff for most was the three-mile walk to the village, his face covered with dust, sweat and pain, never complaining. Jeff had only one leg. He had lost the other as a small boy in a coach crash in Scotland. People like Jeff make you humble – even after your first true landfall.

Now that *Solitaire* was about to be cured of her barnacle sickness, I found that I had contracted a terrible disease, the worse because you inflicted it on your friends. It is a disease of brain and mouth and is particularly prevalent among single-handers. It normally lasts for a few days after any long voyage and is called verbal diarrhoea. The brain keeps sending messages, 'for god's sake shut up, you are boring the pants of everyone,' which the mouth refuses to receive and continues to spew out garbage. On that first night in Hiva Oa Jeff and Judy made the mistake of inviting me back to *Dinks Song* for dinner. Judy, a first class cook, had spent most of that day baking. I completely demolished her work and was finally got rid of in the early hours, being bundled into their dinghy with a mouthful of cake, still trying to talk.

I awoke next morning from a deep sleep to a glorious day. A warm breeze rippled the still lagoon, palm trees barely asway while *Solitaire* slept on. I tried not to disturb her as I moved forward to check the anchor but managed to shake her slightly whereupon she yawned and stretched. Her chain lay limply on its sandy resting place three fathoms below, looking as if it could be touched from the boat. I walked softly back. 'Sleep on, love, you've earned a holiday.' With a contented sigh she snuggled back into her clean, warm bed.

There was no movement from the other boats; perhaps Jeff was watching from behind portholes, frightened lest I return for more cake and conversation. Then I heard a faint chugging and round the headland came the bow of a boat, standing on which was an attractive woman complete with movie camera. Her long, blonde hair streamed down her back, caught by the breeze but held partly in place by a fawn-coloured topee of Indian vintage. The bow belonged to a lifeboat with an ultra-short mast. At the tiller, like an old-time film producer complete with thick black glasses and also hiding under a fawn topee, was a man. Ye gods, I thought it's Bogie and the *African Queen*. They circled around the lagoon a couple of times still filming. I dashed to comb my hair and emerged in time to see them anchor whereupon I rowed across. Juli and Dontcho were Bulgarians permitted by their government to carry out an experiment in the *Kon Tiki* vein.

They had left the coast of South America intending to sail to Fiji proving that you could survive long periods at sea by dragging a fine mesh net behind and collecting plankton, the small organisms that

71

are found in the oceans. Soon after leaving they had lost their mast and were making do with a jury rig. Dontcho was a scientist with black hair to compliment horn-rimmed glasses. Shorter than myself he was a bit overweight so the plankton must be doing their stuff. He could speak little English and relied on his lovely wife Juli, a concert pianist, to translate. Slim and tall, she could well have been in films, her skin darkened by the sun to contrast strikingly with her blonde hair.

Their lifeboat was madness. The Bulgarian government had insisted that they carry a powerful transmitter and had supplied a 24 volt set, knowing the boat had only a 12 volt supply so that it could never be used. Heavy gauge stainless steel bottle screws and shackles that made my mouth water were used to put tension on thin ropes. The fibreglass water tank had been built with the wrong resin, souring their water. Their method of navigation included timing sunset to obtain longitude. They had been trying to correct their watches with BBC time checks ignorant of the constant time signals from the American station WWV. Although they had three portable receivers onboard only one worked, and that poorly.

After all my own blunders, and remembering the help I had so freely received, it was satisfying to contribute in return. We soon had all three sets blasting out WWV signals, and the water-tank cleaned. Doncho and Juli made a great deal of any kindness shown them, a truly brave and lovely couple of whom I became very fond.

Solitaire and I will always look back on the Marquesas as a Shangri-la, an earthly paradise. On the morning after our arrival I walked to the nearby ramshackle village situated on a hillside. Looking down on the lagoon I could see *Solitaire* still slumbering in clear waters. I cleared the French Customs and then tried the village store. Some of the things on display, eggs and tomatoes for instance, I was not allowed to buy. Items in short supply were kept for the villagers, but there was no shortage of mouth-watering delicacies.

Stalks of bananas, coconuts and bread fruit, which makes the world's best chips, were plentiful as was that goddess of fruits, pamplemousse, a grapefruit as large as a football, sweet and streaming with juice. Eaten for breakfast with a cup of coffee you were set for the day. I bought some of the cheaper food including flour, rice and baking powder.

Everyone was going back that night to dine and watch some native dancing. Tickets were three dollars each, so I decided to give it a miss. I had less than 60 dollars left and there seemed little chance

72

of my finding work until reaching New Zealand or Australia, more than 5,000 miles away.

On the way back to *Solitaire* I spotted the Canadian boat we had met in the Pacific and went over, minus golf clubs, to inquire if they had managed to cash their cheque. They apologised for not stopping with me longer and made up for it by inviting me to dinner the next day. At six that evening I sat on *Solitaire's* deck drinking a coffee and watching the other yachts and their crews preparing for the native dancing. As the dinghies moved ashore Jeff and Judy came over to *Solitaire*. The crowd had realised, by the food I had bought, that I was short of money and had clubbed together to buy me a ticket, deciding not to collect me until the last minute so that I could not refuse. I tried always to repay this sort of kindness, but it seemed that I always ended up at the wrong end of the stick. An American yacht with five young men onboard came into the lagoon, with alternator-charging problems. A broken holding bracket was the only trouble so I fitted one of my spares for them. During our conversation it was mentioned they had a taste for English gin and as I still had two bottles on board left over from my Brazilian beach party I wanted to make a present of them, but this they refused, insisting on paying the full local price. The battle went on for a week, with me holding the ace and the only two bottles on the island. I would go over with my gin and describe the pleasure of rolling this nectar around their mouths, of feeling it trickle down parched throats, watching them grow more desperate. It seemed like stalemate. On the morning they left, I waited until they had their anchor up, rowed over and placed the bottles on their deck as they slipped by with cries of 'up the British!'

An hour later they were back again with engine trouble so I went over to lend a hand. The battle of the gin bottles was not mentioned. Good, I thought, they've accepted their defeat with grace. At dawn the next day I was rudely awakened as they sailed past *Solitaire* to raucous Yankee battle cries. I waved them good luck, then breakfasted on pamplemousse and a 20 dollar bill they had stuck in my coffee jar. One of them must have swum over while we were messing with the motor. There was a note, 'no Englishman's going to get the better of a Yank!'

One of the people never to visit *Solitaire* was the filthiest old Chinaman I have ever met. The store had run out of bread one day and I was directed to an overgrown path on the village edge down which, they told me, was a bakery. I pushed through the creaking

73

door of a ramshackle shed into a black interior, adjusting from the tropical colours to dusty gloom within. I felt rather than saw the diminutive Chinese who shuffled forward smiling, saying the only words I ever heard him speak, 'me British'. He reached in a pocket and brought out a tattered British passport. Reluctantly I bought one of his hot rolls and, halfway down the path, hungrily broke off a piece. My taste buds turned my feet in their tracks to buy another.

Each day thenceforward I bought two of his rolls and each day he would show me his passport and say, 'me British'. I wished I had had an old medal to give him if not for his bread, then for being a true patriot.

Solitaire and I loved our easy life. A freshwater stream ran into the lagoon diluting its sea-salt concentration. The goose barnacles nodded their heads worriedly, turned black and died. I had relished much contentment, particularly during my second marriage, but if now you had asked me whom I disliked or envied I could have named none. It was a feeling destined to last until I returned home nearly two years later. Him I would normally have disliked I now only pitied, the wealthy in their homes or yachts I no longer envied, but once evening fell I uneasily needed to return to my boat. Money of course would have helped me to do more for *Solitaire*, buy the best anti-fouling, more sails, charts, pilot books, but I had chosen this life and regular wages would have meant regular commitments. I expected to pay my way, but I wanted to choose the method. My pleasures were cheap: I had never smoked and drinking was for special occasions. My clothes would consist of shorts and an open-neck shirt, my feet bare.

I felt affection for the people I was meeting; they did not consider the world owed them a living. I would visit their yachts and if the owner happened to be working would simply join in. I had boxes of spares left over which always came in useful. My rubber dinghy allowed me to ferry large loads ashore and my five-gallon containers proved useful for getting water to the other yachts.

Since there was only food to buy, money had little meaning for the natives. *Solitaire* inevitably had more fruit onboard than I could ever eat, picked by myself or traded for things I no longer required. Natives would place stands of bananas and the odd fish on deck. It was normal practice to row across to new arrivals and discover what help they required.

The cruising world is both large – meeting people from many countries – and small, particularly when greeting new arrivals and receiving news of old friends. People are like mirrors and reflect what they see: if you are genuinely pleased to meet someone and bubble inside, that feeling will be returned. But if you did not fit in and took advantage of friendships, you would be slowly ignored, wither and fade away.

When subsequently I looked back on the time I spent in the Marquesas Islands I remembered half a dozen eggs. Juli and Dontcho were among my first friends to leave and on their last morning in Hiva Oa I wanted them to breakfast with me, the first time *Solitaire* had guests for a meal. I spent a good deal of time deciding on the menu including pamplemousse for starters, of course. Tinned butter could be obtained in the village, a bit expensive, but a special treat which would go down well on the crusty rolls from my Chinese countryman. I would buy a couple of eggs each for the three of us, and finish with the marmalade given me by the French couple. All went well until I discovered there was a shortage of eggs on the island. After trying the village store, I chased every cock-crow in the hills. All the other yachts were reduced to powdered eggs and that night I went to sleep knowing that I would have to accept second best. It was quite late when two strangers in a dinghy woke me. they had just arrived in the lagoon and having been told by the people on the other yachts of my quest for eggs, they had taken the trouble to bring them over. I think that's what cruising is all about.

It was time to waken *Solitaire* from her slumber. Fatu Hiva, where many of our friends were, would be our next stop, with no navigation problems this time. Although the island was 50 miles away, on a clear day you could see her majestic peaks reaching into the clouds so I decided to sail through the night and arrive at dawn. There were a dozen yachts at anchor when we hove to but not a soul to be seen on the boats or beach. The anchorage is small compared with the size of the bay which must be one of the most impressive in the world. A shelf extends off the beach for a few hundred feet, then quickly drops away to 15 fathoms. Winds are invariably offshore and now and again blast down between the mountains at 60 miles an hour. For all that it is a safe and beautiful harbour, once berthed.

Solitaire circled the other craft feeling like a child that had not been invited to her best friend's birthday party. Meanwhile I'm blowing on a whistle and shouting. Jeff's trimaran is there; it crossed my mind that he had warned the others of my verbal diarrhoea and I imagined them hiding in their cabins, the natives concealing themselves behind trees, in case this new horror spread to their village.

Solitaire nudged her way between *Dinks Song* and another yacht as I peered through portholes, expecting beady little eyes to peep back.

When the echo sounder showed less than 20 feet, I let go the anchor. *Solitaire* moved slowly astern sulking, as much as to say 'I know when I'm not wanted'. Everything is as dead as a dodo. Should we drag our anchor, no harm would be done, as only open waters lie behind us. If *Solitaire* feels she has been cast aside and sneaks away in the night the worst that could happen would be bringing a reluctant child back against wind and tide.

After a cup of tea I put down my head and slept. Jeff woke me the following morning to tell me that one of the village lassies had been married. The yachtees had joined in happily, the ladies helping to prepare the bride. *Solitaire* and I fell easily into the life of receiving guests and visiting other craft although most of my time was spent with Jeff and Judy. As there seemed to be a shortage of girls on the island, Jeff arranged to take a dozen of the village boys to another island which had a similar problem – in reverse. The islanders spoke French which both Jeff and Judy could understand so there would always be a few Polynesian men on *Dinks Song* through whom I was introduced to two new forms of food. When approaching the island, I had seen palm trees perched on the sides of the hills sheltering sloping tables. These were used for drying bananas which retained their flavour but became quite chewy. I later found them in Tahiti where they were far more expensive. The second food was a piece of giant ray that came into the lagoon. Apart from a seat in the front row we had a running commentary from the boys. With a half dozen lads on the paddles the chief went out in one of the native canoes, by tradition the only person allowed to harpoon it. We watched him jump from the bow of the boat onto the ray's back, putting the full weight of his body behind a thrust. Then he virtually flew from the water as if dropped into a cauldron of boiling oil. I asked one of the young gentlemen how often the village acquired a new chief.

When the poor ray was dragged ashore it looked more like whale worked on by a persistent steamroller. The natives started to hack with meat cleavers and the shore line reddened with its blood, the sea taking on the appearance of a washing machine that had gone berserk as the sharks came in to feed. The yachtees who for days had swum over to *Solitaire* started using dinghies, but memories are short-lived and soon Jeff was giving his water ski-ing lessons again. When he and Judy left with their cargo of amorous young men it was to be for only a few days. In fact it was the last time I saw them.

4

IN A WAY JEFF'S DELAYED RETURN turned *Solitaire* into a harvester of yachts. At sunset I would spend my time looking out to sea on the off chance that Jeff's transmitter had broken down. If I saw navigation lights I would switch on *Solitaire*'s powerful 24 watt light at the top of the mast, a beacon in an otherwise dark bay. I caught two beauties this way, one a lovely 48ft Swan with two married couples aboard from the south coast of England, one husband a furniture manufacturer.

The owner of my second catch was also a furniture manufacturer – from France and was accompanied by his wife and two paid crew. In the dark they anchored near *Solitaire* and later started swinging into us. Although the bay was still crowded, there was no real reason why I should not shift my berth so I explained my intentions and, despite their protests, moved away. The following morning they came over to thank me and invite me back for a drink, another couple I grew to like. During the war the owner had been a submarine commander in the Free French Navy which occupation could be seen in the design of his boat. Virtually you could close yourself below and sail it. He made quite an occasion of introducing his wife. 'Leslie, I have the pleasure of introducing my charming wife to you . . .' I warmed to this old world courtesy which showed the affection he held for his wife and made me feel important to meet her. They owned a private island and I was invited to call there but alas never did. Instead I decided to sail to Papeete in Tahiti and made plans to lift anchor on June 10, 1976. Tahiti lay 750 miles to the south west and again there would be no navigation problems. In fact the island at 7,339ft was twice as high as anything I had seen up to then and also possessed a powerful RDF station and full navigational aids. The winds should be kindly at force three to four, mostly from the east to south east.

The quick and the brave sailed a direct course calling at the Tuamotu Islands which are well worth a visit as the natives are friendly, laying on feasts and dancing. However the low lying Tuamotus are surrounded by strong currents and at times a palm tree can be the tallest thing around. I have never taken star sights but, if I did, this would be the locality where I would use them constantly as it is vital to know your position to a tenth of a mile because over the years their reefs have claimed many fine boats. Climbing high in the rigging is advantageous passing through these reefs but as a single-hander I could not do that and steer *Solitaire* at the same time. I decided to take no risks and, in golfing terms, made a dog's leg of it, sailing above the islands on a course more like west-south-west. That way one arrived with a yacht and not on foot.

After leaving the Tuamotus *Solitaire* made 375 miles in the first three days then the winds fell light with the odd shower. There is a low lying island 20 miles north of Tahiti called Teriaroa, owned then by the film star Marlon Brando. Although I kept a good look out all day we must have passed it as I saw nothing and *Solitaire* arrived off Tahiti at nightfall. There is a reef to go through to enter Papeete Harbour, well marked and used by cruise liners, but as I was thinking of navigating it, the last of the sun's rays fell into the sea and went out like a candle. Suddenly Tahiti was a blaze of lights making jokes of channel markers. *Solitaire* groaned, 'please, please not again!' So we turned away and I distinctly heard her give a sign of relief. We entered harbour at dawn on June 19, 1976, our log showing 755 miles. As Bastille day was not far off the harbour was packed with some 90 boats waiting for the festivities to start. The Bastille was a French prison demolished in the times of the revolution but, so far as I am aware, the British were never blamed for this.

Solitaire circled the harbour a couple of times nodding to many of the craft she had met before, the boats anchored stern to shore. I saw a space next to a bright yellow Ericson 36 with an American in his early thirties sitting on the foredeck. 'Is there room for one more? I asked. 'Are you single-handed?' he replied and on my reply waved me in. In fact I had told a lie because at that stage I was anything but single-handed. We had about six dinghies tied to us. How and where *Solitaire* berthed had been taken out of my hands. I heard the anchor go down, two lines were taken to the shore and she was slowly eased back to lie 20 feet off. Remembering our arrival in Fatu

Hiva, I could almost hear her saying, 'now this is more like a welcome'.

Many of our visitors I had met in Panama and they had been concerned by my slow passage to Hiva Oa. After any voyage I enjoyed making physical contact with friends, shaking hands with both of mine, and hugging the ladies. You can say a great deal with the strength of a hand or hug.

As this was a Saturday morning Customs would not re-open until Monday. *Solitaire* spent the rest of the day receiving visitors which kept me busy making endless cups of tea for her guests. That evening I managed to sneak away to a party on another yacht, after which I found Dontcho's and Juli's lifeboat and left a message on its closed hatch.

The following morning my American neighbour came over and introduced himself as Webb Chiles. I have never met a more determined person. Twice he left his home port of San Diego for a single-handed voyage around the world via Cape Horn. On the first attempt he had been forced to turn back before reaching the Cape leaking badly and with broken rigging. He called in at Tahiti, made repairs and tried again, only to be turned back once more to San Diego. Finally he made the voyage on what was virtually a sinking yacht. He had visited New Zealand and had recently arrived in Papeete where, at the time of our meeting, he was writing his book *Storm Passage*.

I learned much from Webb, the first true single-hander I had ever met and remember talking to him on the sidewalk when a woman reporter asked if she could visit our boats and interview us. She wondered if we had a death wish, a daft question, particularly when put to someone who has just sailed around Cape Horn fighting for his life. I would have advised anyone with such an outlook not to step into a dinghy let alone a seagoing yacht and Webb said much the same thing only more trenchantly.

Although not yet half-way round on my first voyage, I had already committed myself to a second and these chats with Webb dictated the route for my next attempt – around Cape Horn. Always ready to joke about my early navigational mistakes and the Brazilian hospital, I was finding it increasingly difficult to live with my errors. My confidant would forget about it the next day; I would carry it in my mind for the rest of my life and wanted to square the account which made me believe a second voyage around Cape Horn might help. Later the woman reporter visited *Solitaire* by which time Webb had sailed for home which was just as well after reading the story she wrote. Under the headline, 'Yachtsman Lucky Les earns his nickname', and I've never been called Lucky Les in my life, it started, 'Les, while sailing here from England, was lost at sea, shipwrecked, hospitalized and suffered from hunger.' As I said at the time, 'I hope my luck never runs out or I'll be in real trouble'. In fact the story helped in two ways. The paper was given away to all the boats in harbour, and as a result I was invited aboard many of them. If I was not asked to any I thought looked interesting I would contemplate chipping a golf ball on to their decks to wake 'em up!

Through the same article I met Tim Beckett, fresh from England and who, for some reason, I always thought of as a college student with a delightfully dry sense of humour. With him was the co-owner of *Huzar* and they were waiting for Tim's father to join them before continuing to New Zealand. When visiting him he would send his ropey rubber inflatable across on a pulley arrangement. Once you were aboard it would wrap itself around you like a starving octopus. If you survived you were greeted with a chamberpot of tea. Tim later lost *Huzar* on Lady Elliot Island, 60 miles off the coast of Australia, saving only the engine and his address book.

The morning after my arrival in Tahiti, Dontcho and Juli made their appearance and I spent a week visiting places of interest and working on their boat, always with the movie camera churning away. Then they had to leave for Fiji because of the schedule laid down by their country. I made arrangements to sail for Australia the following day, a schedule dictated not by HM Government but by my pocket: I had less than 30 dollars left. It seemed an age since I had established two rules to govern my life at sea: the first that I would always sail alone, the second that I would never accept payment for working on a friend's boat.

Next to Dontcho's lifeboat was a 45ft steel boat belonging to a French aircraft pilot, Peter, who had a beautiful wife and two lovely blonde children. On the day Juli and Dontcho left, Peter and his wife invited me to a local restaurant and asked if I would stay on for a few weeks to fit out his boat. Since he was working and making good money he could well afford to pay me. After a long talk I agreed somewhat reluctantly to bend my second rule and except owners in employment. In Peter's case the pay would be low, the local Tahitian rate for unskilled workers being four dollars an hour and, since I had to get used to my new rule, I would take no more than a dollar an hour. During the next few weeks I worked a 60-hour week and by

80

saving two-thirds of my earnings pushed my 30 dollars up to nearly 200. Then Peter told me Kodak Laboratories wanted some fibreglassing done and would pay four dollars an hour, the outcome of which was that I started on one of the worst and most dangerous jobs in my life.

The Kodak building itself was a modern, single storey factory with a slightly sloping roof of corrugated aluminium. The maximum space between the roof and the ceiling was eight feet, diminishing to a few inches. To prevent the heat discomforting their employees, rolls of fibreglass had been laid in the loft. Particles of this were now falling through cracks in the ceiling onto the film processing machines so they wanted the fibreglass rolled up and replaced on sheets of plastic. Entering the loft was like stepping into a cauldron and it was impossible to wear a mask to prevent glassfibre being sucked into the lungs. Joists, four feet apart, were all I had to stand on up there. I would take a gallon of water with me and work through an eight-hour shift. Now and again they would call me down for a break, but I would explain that if I ever left their hell hole during the day I would never go back. Each night they promised me a native worker whom they reckoned would be more accustomed to the heat. Now and then a black face would pop through the trap door, the whites of the eyes would start to look like two fried eggs and the face would drop out of sight. Why I carried on with the job apart from wanting to finish something I had started, I shall never know. The only good thing to say about it was that it was great when you stopped.

The laboratory had some splendidly hot showers, the first I had used since leaving Panama. I would stand under them for ages to open up the pores and rid myself of the itchy dust and glass and then return to *Solitaire* knowing that I had more money to spend on her. For three weeks I worked a 45-hour week. Then they asked me to knock two rooms into one. After that would I build some storage racks. When they suggested building some car ports I decided I was getting too civilised and left to prepare *Solitaire* for our trip to Australia.

Just before leaving Tahiti a young French couple, who planned to start teaching on one of the nearby islands, came to see me. They had bought a 35ft wooden yacht to use as a home which they considered a good buy until they discovered Toredo worm in the stern-hung rudder and then could find no one to build them a replacement, so I stayed on two more weeks to do the job. My one regret about sailing was that I had not started when I was a young man, fitter, stronger and able to give *Solitaire* more care. Tahiti strengthened my regrets. I wished I could have seen these islands and met the Polynesian people before 'civilisation' had spoiled them.

Only in smoke-filled night clubs could you watch their beautiful native dancing. If you saw a Polynesian thrusting his canoe through the water with muscle power it simply meant that his outboard had broken down and he was on his way back to the garage to get it fixed. Large white cruise liners would dock and release a flood of even whiter chattering mice, all wearing the same brightly-coloured shirts, hats, sun glasses and cameras. False teeth flashing even falser smiles they would stream past the dancing girls swaying to Hawaiian guitars. The tide would flood the shops to devour everything in sight, prevented only by pavement vendeuses holding out armfuls of shell necklaces and beautiful woven straw hats. Cameras would click click, then their Pied Piper would toot toot on the ship's siren and the tide would reverse. The heavily-laden mice would be sucked back into a hole in the ship's side . . . a puff of smoke on the horizon and they were gone. The natives would count their profits and a street cleaner remove the last traces of their presence. Weeks later postcards would arrive in New York, Tokyo and Scunthorpe, 'having a wonderful time in Tahiti, wish you were here'.

When I recalled Hiva Oa in later years I remembered an English Chinaman. Tahiti, for me, meant a small American boy. The local paper printed my story on a Saturday and next day it was customary for children from the cruising yachts to attend Sunday school with the locals. I was walking past the church when an avalanche of these terrors descended. Within seconds I had them climbing over me, one even trying to pull off my shorts, so small I had to get on my knees to hear what he was saying. 'Mister, I'd sure be proud to shake your hand,' he said. It was like holding a butterfly. For days after I would smile when I remembered his serious face. He made me feel good inside, wishing that he could always stay young and innocent and not change with the years like Tahiti.

Sunday was always the best day of the week. Now that I was earning good money I could afford to buy the excellent French wines, the crusty rolls and make crisp, fresh salads. The harbour front was Papeete's main street and *Solitaire* was only a few yards from the sidewalk. Sunday was the day that the visits I had made in the week were returned; a day we all looked forward to.

My last hours on the island were spent scrubbing *Solitaire*'s anti-

82

fouling, not a particularly pleasant chore as the waste from 90 yachts was dumped in the harbour. The sensible thing would have been to go over to the unspoilt Moorea, but there had been too many delays and I had to push on.

Saturday, September 25, 1976 was set for my departure and I had chosen Gladstone, about halfway up the east coast of Australia, as my destination. It was just below the beginning of the Great Barrier Reef, the ideal place from which to start the following stage of the voyage. Another consideration was that I would have to remain in port for five months during the hurricane season and, as Gladstone had a large aluminium plant and was building a power station, it should be possible to find work there. I would have liked to have visited Auckland but New Zealand was further away and had few job prospects: I would make the final choice half way through the voyage when the current started to swing south towards Auckland.

The first leg would take us just below Rarotonga, 700 miles to the west-south-west, 200 miles south of Tahiti, which had a strong RDF station to confirm our position. After that our course would be virtually due west, dropping only another 200 miles in the next 3,000. Provided we did not go further south than Gladstone's latitude we should have a good passage. The pilot charts showed much the same pattern as our previous voyage: winds over our stern from the east to south-east, around force four with only three per cent calms and a few gales close to Australia, but no worse than an English summer, in all a voyage of 4,000 miles, no more than 40 days at sea if the pilot charts were correct.

The most upsetting thing about the trip was the places we would miss: magic islands whose names rolled off the tongue, Moorea, Huahine, Bora Bora, Tahaa, Fiji. Each year that would change as more and more hotels and flats destroyed them. It seemed foolish to be wishing I could have been in the South Pacific 50 years ago when they would change that much again in the next five. I was giving up seeing them just to sail round a piece of rock called Cape Horn.

As food in Australia would be cheaper than Tahiti's I kept my stores to a minimum although the cash situation was quite good; in fact I was richer than when I left England and now had 700 dollars in hand. The tucker I would not be running short of was onions as an Australian yachtsman had asked me if I had plenty onboard and was amazed when I told him I had never even considered carrying them. Onions last for months and were full of vitamins he lectured me, and to make sure I got the message he turned up with a sackful.

He must have told the story to all the other cruising people because *Solitaire* was soon packed with them!

The one thing I did not take was a cockroach, although Tahiti breeds some of the world's finest. After dark you could see whole families of them walking along the sidewalks, every now and then stopping to inspect a yacht before deciding whether or not to make it their new home. I believe every craft suffered from them, certainly all those I ate on. You would be eating dinner when they would walk across your plate splashing through the gravy without so much as a by-your-leave. Because they were a topic of conversation and, cockroachless, I could not join in, vicious rumours were spread. It was reported that they had been seen walking up *Solitaire*'s shore lines and that on reading her name on the stern there had been a panic to disembark again. It was also claimed that I spent half the night trying to entice the poor creatures onboard with bits of cheese which was a lie since I discovered they did not particularly like it! When *Solitaire* sailed through the reef to start her voyage she had not a single cockroach onboard and at the time I was concerned, remembering stories of rats deserting doomed ships. We had arrived in Tahiti on June 19 and left on September 25, 1976 after *Solitaire* had been rested for more than three months. The early stages of the voyage went well enough with a pleasant sail close to that island paradise, Moorea, but during the night things started to go wrong. We ran into fierce squalls and a batten pierced the mainsail which meant that the batten pocket could not be used again that trip and a five gallon water container burst, nothing to worry about at that stage since I still had another 25 gallons left.

I picked up Rarotonga's RDF signal on the third day out, 400 miles away! A week from Tahiti and Rarotonga hove in sight 20 miles to our north. The pilot charts had been correct up to that point. From then on had I reversed the information it would have been near enough correct. Instead of stern winds from the east at force four *Solitaire* was pushing into winds from the west dead on her nose, anything from force six to complete calm. Under these conditions we could not sail close to the wind as short, choppy waves kept pushing her bow to one side. *Solitaire*, facing a fighter with a long, left jab, would shake her head to recover and try to move forward, only to be hit again. At the halfway mark, passing under the Tonga Islands, I nearly decided to give up and head for New Zealand, 1,000 miles to the south.

Had I changed course then we would have had a current of 10 to

15 miles a day in our favour and, had the winds stayed constant, we would have been sailing with them abeam. *Solitaire* staggering like a punch-drunk fighter, refused to give up but carried on for Australia and Gladstone.

We had one particularly bad storm that led me to conclude that I should dispense with battened sails. Battens were forever fouling the shrouds, particularly when running, and if they broke they inevitably damaged the sail. Certainly they allowed a larger sail area with a roach but the increased speed was not worth the trouble as I was racing no-one. In future I would have battenless mainsails with a straight leech and would also change my reefing system. Although roller reefing was fitted to the boom, I had never used it, preferring to slab reef since all my halyards led back to the cockpit.

For the first time in this particular storm I decided to try the roller reefing. The job was nearly done when a squall strained the leech where it wrapped around the boom. The sail shredded in half, making its repair a lengthy project. For the rest of the trip to Australia I had to tie the main off at its last reefing point, cutting the sail area by more than half!

This was turning out to be another protracted voyage thanks to light winds and a small sail area. We were becalmed a few times and I went over the side in the dinghy to clean the waterline which was largely unencrusted. When 700 miles from Australia the split pin holding the self-steering rudder broke and I made the rest of the trip without its help. Normally I would have lost the rudder but since I had never liked this method of attachment, I had drilled it and connected a safety rope. Our landfall was Lady Elliot Island, 60 miles off the Australian mainland, which we passed on November 30. That night we had an electrical storm and I sat watching the lightning under bare poles as if in daylight.

Next day we drifted by the Bunker reefs, sighting land with the dawn. I motored all that windless day to arrive at six o'clock local time in the broad creek on which Gladstone lies after the longest time we had spent at sea so far, 69 days, beating our previous record by a day. We had logged 4,212 miles.

Australia is psychotic about the import of animals, plants, seeds or food. Normally when clearing customs I have been asked if I had drugs, guns or drink but the Australian customs man who boards *Solitaire* could not care less if I'm the head of the Mafia or carrying an atom bomb. 'Right, naaaaaa, do you have any pets onboard?' is the first question.

'No sir,' I reply, 'not even a cockroach!' We go through the plant and seed bit.

'Right, sport, I want all your food laid out on deck.'

So I go below and fetch my remaining bag of rice which I place in the middle of the deck and stand looking at him with my tail wagging and my tongue out, like a cocker spaniel that's just done its business in the dirt box.

'Maaaaaaate, maaaaaaaate, aaaaall of it!'

Much later I have turned out every locker and cubby hole trying to find something I can give the poor man. I keep inviting him to come below and search *Solitaire*. 'Maaaaaaaate, I don't want to search your flaming boat.' At last I find two slices of dried meat in a glass sealed-jar, which I think the Americans gave me in Panama. My maaaaaate smiles and locks it in his brief-case.

While this is going on a tramp has been sitting on the side of the dock taking it all in and swigging from a pint of milk through his matted beard. By the time he has heard my story there are tears in his eyes and he offers me his bottle without a word. I drain it in one gulp and hand back the empty.

Mr Customs asks the question I've been dreading. 'How long do you plan to stay in Australia?' During the past two weeks I have been picking up their radio broadcasts and apart from learning of a shortage of work, it seems that every disaster that occurs is due entirely to the English or, as he is better known, the Pom. Poms run the unions and are responsible for the strikes, Poms run the government and are responsible for the country going to the dogs, they control the weather, and that's the reason for all the bush fires. There is a disc jockey I've been listening to whose pet saying is, 'punch a Pommie every day!'

By this stage I'm thinking I might be allowed to take on water before being set adrift. With the hurricane season coming on I really need a visitor's permit for six months and when I explain this, I am told to call at the Customs Office next day to pick up one for a year!

The officer told me about Gladstone and the best places to eat, several times asking if I was all right for Australian currency. In fact I bought myself some fish and chips and ate them in *Solitaire*'s cockpit, during which time I was invited to dinner the following night by one couple and to a barbecue that weekend with another. My mooring problems were solved when an Australian offered to share his berth free of charge. Sometimes I think that certain types of radio broadcasters and newspaper reporters would be better employed collecting garbage rather than dishing it out.

Over the next few days I tried unsucessfully to find work. I could not be taken on as a skilled electrician because I had no Australian licence and unskilled work was carried out by apprentices, but my luck changed when I called on the local boatyard to buy a shackle. The manager, a Yorkshireman, asked if I needed work and then said I could cut the grass around the boats on hardstanding. After that it was making racks to store wood, fibreglassing, painting. In the end I spent all my time working for the boatyard. Sometimes I would help tie up ocean-going cargo ships; my last job was putting the yard's transport in shape and, as in Tahiti, I could have stayed on as the company wanted to build fibreglass dinghies and there were opportunities to work on charter boats. I liked the people who were always more than fair: even grass-cutting carried the same wage as everyone else's in the yard.

I managed to stay in Gladstone for more than five months without getting into serious trouble, although I nearly managed to kill myself when working on a large charter boat that could carry 300 passengers. One lunch time, having just returned from buying some fish and chips, I had reached across and put my meal through a ship's window and, stepping onto a cat walk to board, fell ten feet into the water twixt ship and dock. Luckily I managed to grab a rope and haul myself out before the gap closed. My first thought was to eat my fish and chips before they grew cold, but as fast as I ate all this funny red stuff was running down my front resoaking my shorts and shirt. When my workmates returned I was rushed to hospital.

On the operating table blood from a gash under my chin is flooding the place and half a dozen pretty nurses gather round me. 'I'm sorry for being a nuisance and making such a mess,' I apologise. 'We need the practice,' a chippy one replies. 'Lift me off the table and I'll go break a leg,' I offer. 'You do, sport, and we'll break the other one!' Which started me laughing and the blood gushing. Even when they were stitching me up I was still laughing.

There were few things I disliked about Australia. Food was reasonably priced and for a dollar I could fill my frying pan twice with chops or steak. Flies were a pest, particularly the little sandflies which looked like specks of dust but could bite like tigers.

Terrell Adkisson and I joined up in Gladstone for the first time since Panama. *Altair* was berthed 100 miles down the coast but he spent a week on *Solitaire* and we made arrangements to sail through the Barrier Reef together. While in Gladstone I met *Brolga of Kiama* with Rob and Lyn Brooks who were just about to start their voyage around the world. New arrivals in Gladstone creek were not normally greeted by fellow sailors but I had always liked the Pacific Islands' friendly custom so, although only a visitor myself, I would always row over to newcomers to see if I could help. Rob and Lyn have always made a point of the fact that in their own country it had been an Englishman who had first enquired.

While in Australia I managed to acquire some new sails from England. I had been well satisfied with my original Lucas sails so I had ordered from them again, including a battenless main with three sets of reefing points as I still had to round the Cape of Good Hope, where it can blow. The last reef would so contract the main that it would double as a trisail. At the same time I stepped up the weight of cloth from six to eight ounces, and ordered a new number two genoa, also eight ounce, and a new storm jib.

The boatyard let me haul out *Solitaire* free of charge and I had another go at the crack in the hull, although it had not leaked since Panama. The anti-fouling had vanished so I applied a heavy barrier coat followed by two coats of top quality finish. I also bolted the self-steering rudder to the drive shaft thus making it a more permanent fixture. I still had 1,400 dollars left (£700) or twice the amount I had left England with and *Solitaire* in many ways was in better condition than when I had set out, even though she had looked after me for more than 16,000 miles. Now she was taking me home, about the same distance again. I had not yet told *Solitaire* about Cape Horn!

The next leg of our trip would be from Gladstone to Thursday Island in the Terres Straits, 1,000 miles away. We had crossed 8,000 miles of the Pacific Ocean on just two charts and a few sketches, now I needed 30 charts for our next trip and a couple of Australian friends, John and Penny Pugh, lent them to me. Often I would go to their house for dinner and a bath and they did most of the chasing around for my supplies. Apart from the food parcel they gave me they also made a going-away present of a heavy fishing line (a lifesaver on my second voyage).

The Great Barrier Reef starts about 60 miles offshore at the bottom end, closing to a mile or two at the top. Most of the navigation would be by sight or, as the Americans call it, eye ball, and for much of the time we would have the mainland and a few islands in sight. I still enjoyed single-handed sailing but if there was ever a time when I would have liked a female crew member aboard this was it. The Great Barrier Reef must be one of the finest cruising areas in the world, anchoring behind your own private island after a day's sail with plenty of fish in the sea and oysters ashore. The sea, protected by the reef, is shallow and flat.

Terrell came into Gladstone Creek to collect me but as my sails had not arrived he went on ahead. Before I left, the boatyard threw a party for me where I tried to uphold the best British traditions by keeping up with some of the young bloods. After dinner the party continued at the Pugh's of which I remember nothing. Dawn woke me with a thick head, a foul mouth and to a weird sound. I had been sleeping on somebody's lawn and was covered by every dog in the neighbourhood, snoring their heads off.

Solitaire's mooring lines were cast off on Wednesday May 18, 1977 and as I had not let her touch bottom since Granada, anti-fouling apart, and my navigation had improved, we both felt more confident. A dozen cars followed us on the shore, blasting their horns as we set off, by far the best farewell we had had and one of the hardest to make. I caught up with Terrell on Friday, June 3, two weeks out from Gladstone. We met in Cairns, about halfway up the Reef where he had picked out a berth for me alongside the town quay. Cairns was another low-sprawling Australian town, so different from home where everything seems condensed. Here there were modern supermarkets, a cinema and a heavenly laundry. We spent a few pleasant days there, talking to a good many English who had settled in the area. Terrell's nephew Leo had gone back to the USA and had been replaced by an Australian crew member. Things improved once we joined up: with four eyes on the other yacht Terrell always took the path-finding position up front which allowed me to nip below for the occasional cup of tea without worrying about the constant changing picture of mainland and islands.

Cooktown was quite unlike Cairns. You could walk through it in a few minutes but it was well worth the visit if only to see the museum. The day we arrived they were to re-enact Captain Cook's first landing and on the jetty a goodly crowd had turned up for the spectacle. Three men came ashore in a rowing boat and the people promptly started to drift away. 'When's Captain Cook arriving?' I asked. 'He just did, spoooort,' came the reply.

Another advantage of being in company with a cruising yacht is that you can take it in turns to visit and cook dinner. We were having dinner on Terrell's boat where, since it was my turn to play host the following night, I asked, 'how do you fancy fish tomorrow night?' Both seemed enthusiastic, so I asked their preference and was

89

requested to catch a few mackerel.

Next day I took out the line John and Penny had given me. I put the nine-inch long spinner, about the size of any fish I had ever caught, over the side and seconds later it pulled tight with a blooming great mackerel nearly as long as my arm on its end, enough for three people. To make sure I thought I would catch its smaller sister which turned out to be twice as fat as the first.

I was concerned about possible waste and as I thought Terrell who was astern might also be slaughtering fish, I decided to wait for him. I halted *Solitaire* by luffing into wind and when Terrell came within hailing distance, I stuck two fingers in the air and pointed over the side. The effect on Terrell was instantaneous: he belted off in the other direction and I failed to catch him until much later. When I asked Terrell what his problem had been and why the panic an argument ensued. Two fingers in the air and pointing over the side, means I'm over a reef two fathoms down, Terrell insisted, while I claimed any fool knows it means I've caught two mackerel. Although we stuffed ourselves with fish much was wasted which, coupled with the fact that I had not enjoyed watching a living thing die, made me put the line away, believing they would be the first and last fish I would ever catch at sea.

Thursday Island lies between the most northern part of Australia and New Guinea where the current can reach six to seven knots. We anchored 20 miles away, timing our arrival to take advantage of the flow. When we reached our anchorage it was to find marker buoys being pushed under by the force of churning brown waters, the last place to drag or break an anchor chain. Thursday Island, which we reached on June 23, 1977 after a month's sail inside the Great Barrier, was a disappointment. In the days of sail it was known for its dusky beauties who, it was said, would outswim the fast-flowing current to ravish the poor unsuspecting seamen. After a quick walk through its shantytown of drinking houses we decided to push on for Darwin. Any dusky maiden would have been repulsed with a boat hook, after which I would have called a cop.

Darwin was 700 miles away but wind and current should be mostly with us. Gales were rare in the area but a bad sea could build up quickly in high winds. In company with *Altair* and two other yachts, we left on Monday, June 27. Although we had our sails up it would be wrong to say we sailed from the island, it was more like being fired from a cannon and we had to start and run engines flat out to keep control. We shot away like cars on a racetrack, trying to correct for drift which was great fun while it lasted, and circling the course with three other boats made it that much better. Darwin was approximately half way across the top of Australia so our course would be due west.

On Friday, July 1 we ran into a storm off Melville Island with some of the worst waves I had seen, not so much in size as in shape. There was little *Solitaire* could do against them so we dropped sail and lay a-hull until Saturday morning when the storm died. Until then we had been making good progress, covering 565 miles in just over four days with a best-ever day's run of 149 miles. When I tried the engine I found it had seized and impossible to turn even with levers direct onto the flywheel and this wasn't the best place to have it happen. Melville Island and the 15-mile wide Dundas Straits protect Darwin in much the same way that the Isle of Wight protects my home port of Lymington. I had in fact to sail between them which turned out to be terrifyingly difficult thanks to the speed of the tide.

Approaching from eastwards you pass through the Dundas Straits with its tidal current of two to three knots. The land then falls away to form a large bay which curves back to the island 60 miles on where 12 miles separate mainland from island, those few miles filled with smaller islands and reefs. There is a marked channel on the land side, about one mile across. Once through it Darwin lies only a few miles further on. As I had no tide tables and no engine I decided to sail up to the reefs and then anchor for the night.

We passed through Dundas Straits on Saturday night and had a fast sail next morning. By Sunday afternoon we were in sight of the islands and their surrounding reefs, Darwin's voice, 30 miles away, coming through clearly on the RDF. Having negotiated the reefs we seemed to pick up speed but the land was falling away. *Solitaire* was being driven astern – onto the reefs! The tide had turned.

I let go the 15lb CQR anchor on 50 feet of chain plus a good length of strong rope which thankfully held in coral. The seas, an Amazon in flood, raced past us, the anchor rope vibrating like a bow string forcing me to keep a watch all night, checking the depth from time to time. By Monday morning the tide had slackened then gathered strength in Darwin's direction. I had missed my chance. Instead of heaving in the anchor during slack water I had to struggle manfully to haul it in against the tide – and failed. So, deciding to wait for the next slack, I slung back what I had retrieved. When the tide eased again I found that the anchor had fouled and would not haul in. We had been there 40 hours and there was only one solution. It broke

91

my heart but I had to do it. I cut the rope and lost the anchor and 50 feet of chain.

From then on it was a doddle.

There are two bays in Darwin, the first, big and shallow, houses the yacht club. Next to it is an area for ocean-going ships. You can anchor in either and catch the bus into Darwin. On Tuesday, July 5, 1977 I anchored near the club after a journey of 753 miles. Our stay in Darwin was marred by engine repairs and the sickly smell of diesel. The final diagnosis was that a sump plate fitted to prevent oil splashing about had broken loose cracking the main bearing and jamming the reduction gear. Deciding to sail engineless and non-stop to Durban I cabled Sabb requesting them to send on a new bearing and timing instructions.

Terrell and the other yachts arrived a couple of days after *Solitaire*, having run for shelter during the storm which shows, perhaps, the different thinking between a single-hander and a crewed yacht. In bad weather I would always run from the land, an attitude I was never to change.

When we arrived in Darwin they were sinking piles in front of the club for members to tie-up and anti-foul. Terrell and I were among the first to use this facility which, at five dollars a time, was much cheaper than being hauled out by a boatyard.

From Darwin I planned to sail to Durban, approximately 5,600 miles away, my longest voyage so far, broad reaching again in the south-east trades. We left Darwin on August 2, 1977. *Solitaire* was surrounded by other yachts and as there was not a breath of wind Terrell shouted he would pull us clear. For the first time I accepted a tow. Up to then I had felt lonely only once when the Canadian yacht left us in the Pacific but as Terrell let go my lines I felt abandoned. I think it's watching the other yacht pull away that's the problem. During the first 24 hours light winds kept us out of trouble, but the next two days brought variable winds from the west and we found ourselves beating into choppy seas. That first week we covered 596 miles, thereafter we were into true trade wind sailing and logged 884 miles in the second week, followed by 912 in the third.

When a thousand miles from South Africa I started to pick up their radio broadcasts which is always good for morale. The pilot charts for once had proved accurate and we made good time. I preferred the blue, lively Pacific to the grey, overcast Indian Ocean for things to watch. The seas above Australia had a few surprises: black and brown snakes, giant rays that leapt out of the water only to slam back again, and then, towards the end of the voyage, nightly visits from dolphins which invariably cheer up life.

Thursday, September 22 was our 50th day at sea and, after sailing 5,555 miles, we had another 400 to go. I was trying to make our landfall well north of Durban to allow for the Agulhas current sweeping us south.

On Monday morning we were nearly run down by a tanker, not in fact one of the super type although I thought it then the largest ship ever built. Because I could not keep my lights on all the time I had been standing in the hatch keeping watch in poor visibility when, hearing nothing, I saw a ghost-like bow loom out of the dawn mist. At first I thought she was cutting across *Solitaire*'s bows but she was already turning. Looking up I could see her two anchors ready to drop on us as, a mass of rust and rivets, she swept down our side and back into fog. Never had I been so glad to see a ship disappear. There were many more after that but she was the closest. We arrived off Durban before first light on Thursday morning and sat watching the traffic signals and flashing neons. Durban has a long finger of land that points north, called The Bluff with a breakwater beside it, the entrance into the outer harbour. It would have been possible to sail through but I could hardly keep my eyes open and the wind was fickle so, when I spotted a charter fishing boat preparing to enter, I beckoned them over and requested a tow. The people onboard had a flight to catch but promised they would radio for a police launch to bring me in. After clearing Customs in only a few minutes a power boat arrived from the club to take me in tow.

Solitaire arrived at the Point Yacht Club on Thursday, September 29, 1977, nine years after her conception there on a Sunday morning in 1968, on the very jetty she was now moored to. Her log showed 5,952 miles, the longest journey so far. One day I would ask her to carry me non-stop nearly five times that distance!

The international jetty lies directly below the club house with its showers, restaurant, lounges and bars. The cruising season had barely started when we arrived; only four other boats were moored to the jetty, one an old junk owned by a German couple, another an American Choy Lee ketch, and two self-built ferro-cement yachts, one made and sailed by Susan and Graeme from Yarmouth in England, the other owned by a lovely Rhodesian couple with their three young children on board together with a crew who knew as much about sailing as I had when *Solitaire* first left Lymington.

After a shower in the club I was taken to meet the secretary and given a visitor's membership card. Durban must have had a dull week for news because when I returned to *Solitaire* reporters were waiting to question me about my Brazilian adventures and the voyage from Australia. I was also asked to broadcast by a chap who ran a navigation school to which I agreed provided my talk was based on mistakes so that others could learn from them.

That first night I was too tired to sleep and walked the streets seeing how the other half lived, wandering around in sloppy flip flops, tattered shorts and open shirt, comforted by the knowledge that *Solitaire* was waiting to take me anywhere in the universe I wished to go. Our stay in Durban was a happy one. *Solitaire* had a safe berth, the lights from the surrounding flats sparkling at her as I went to the occasional party. On Sundays the yacht club and several large hotels would put on a self-service meal with a double-feature film show all for £1. Food was as cheap as we had found anywhere and the local wines were first class and equally inexpensive, so much so that I threw a birthday party on *Solitaire* on October 24, 1977 without considering the cost. We set a new record of 16 guests in the cabin with lord knows how many on deck.

These fine wines led me to a brief affair with an Australian lady. I had been invited by a couple of English lads to a party given to celebrate the launch of their 40ft yacht. When I arrived I found their boat had been rafted onto the end of nine others. With a bottle of grog in each hand it was hard going clambering from one craft to the next. I had nearly reached my goal when I came across a boat turned the opposite way from the rest. Hitherto I had walked over the foredecks in approved social manner, now a cockpit faced me. I should have walked up the deck and crossed in the middle but instead I tripped on the life lines and fell into the cockpit which is where I made a terrible mistake. It seems that a crowd of hob-nailed boots had already passed that way en route to the orgy. The woman who attacked me came out of the main hatchway like a bull terrier, a fat one. From Australia. Suddenly I was a flaming Pommy trying to kick holes in the side of her flaming boat. Where the flaming hell did I flaming think I was? Flaming Piccadilly Circus? I secured my retreat only by promising never to darken her cockpit again.

The wine flowed freely and things were slightly blurred when I left the party but I managed to remove my flip flops and cross the decks barefooted. When I came to the Australian boat, I remembered my promise and, going forward, fell through a hatchway onto spongy flesh. The sound was reminiscent of the air raid sirens in the last war, low pitched at first but reaching a teeth-shattering screech. Since the lady appeared not to appreciate my company I decided to leave. 'We have lift off,' I'm sure I heard as I came back out of the hatch like a missile leaving a Polaris submarine.

Terrell turned up in Durban two weeks later. After letting go my lines at Darwin, he had sailed to the Cocos Islands where he had picked up the crew of a wrecked American boat which was lucky for him. Halfway across the Indian Ocean *Altair* was thrown on her side by a rogue wave and Terrell finished up in the sea. He could think of no reason why this wave had formed. The sea was flat and wind moderate and there seemed no reason to wear a life harness. As he lurched overboard he grabbed a yellow seat cushion which was all the crew could see when later they came on deck. They homed in on it to rescue him.

I wanted to be in Cape Town for Christmas and the jetty, where *Solitaire* had lain snug for two months, was becoming crowded with visiting boats. It was time to move on and I planned to set out for Cape Town on Wednesday, November 23.

My biggest regret in Durban was that I had been unable to see Rome, although we kept in contact by mail. He had called his Norwest 34 *Adhara* and had been given leave from the RAF to compete in the OSTAR, single-handed transatlantic race. Having put up a good performance in that he had been selected to navigate the service entry, *Adventure,* in the Whitbread round-the-world race. On completing the first leg to Cape Town, he had been asked to navigate to New Zealand and was now in Cape Town between stops. We tried to arrange a meeting but had to make do with a few phone calls.

Whether a voyage is easy or difficult depends on the yacht's crew and weather; strong winds from the south combat the Agulhas current which rushes south at anything up to five knots. Gales from the east send waves sweeping across 4,000 miles of Indian Ocean to pile up on the ledge that runs close to the South African coast. With so many supertankers in the area a single-hander can never find the voyage hazardless, even in ideal conditions. The 1,000 miles voyage from Durban to Cape Town can be made in stages; East London after 240 miles, and Port Elizabeth a further 140 miles, both readily accessible. Thereafter the harbours are more difficult to enter in bad weather. The best plan seemed to be to wait for a settled weather forecast, then sail close to the 100 fathom line taking advantage of the current, closing ashore at the first signs of bad weather.

Solitaire's motor was still very tight. The new main bearing sent on by Sabb had been fitted and the instructions for re-timing carried out. Despite changing the oil a couple of times, small particles from the smashed sump plate were still finding their way into the gears and I could not rely on it to start in an emergency. Fortunately the engine started for our departure. Outside the harbour we found light south-westerlies but after two days we were within sight of East London, having logged 151 miles when our true run was 240 miles: the Agulhas current had pushed us 45 miles a day. Although we had sailed in strong tidal currents before, this was the fiercest in a constant direction. The afternoon was spent becalmed outside East London. With the setting sun I decided to enter harbour, but it brought up a steady northerly so I ran south intending to go into Port Elizabeth. On reaching there the winds swung to the south and increased to gale force so that for the first time we were beating into fast seas with three reefs in the mainsail and flying our brand new storm jib.

A week out of Durban and we still had 300 miles to fetch Cape Town but the constant presence of tankers prohibited sleep, even making relaxation difficult. Then the wind rose to storm force, the working jib blew out and I let *Solitaire* lie under bare poles close to shore in shallow water but well away from the steep ledge. I went below for a few minutes for a cup of tea and closed my eyes to rest them. I opened them again after a few minutes and discovered that six hours, with no control over whether I lived or died, had passed. I had been lucky.

My confidence in the ability of tankers to avoid yachts was shattered when I saw two of them wrecked on the beach east of Cape Town, one of which had broken its tow line. I'm not sure why the other was there, maybe because he thought the first was lonely, certainly not from trying to miss a yacht. Our last night at sea was spent becalmed so we motored the last 35 miles into Cape Town, passing through a mass of lights on what I think were native fishing boats. Somehow I managed to lose the log's trailing spinner, possibly taken by one of the fish the natives were trying to catch. It must have had sharp teeth for the line was cleanly cut. I had seen hundreds of seals in the water who liked to play around *Solitaire* but I'm sure they didn't take it, unless they carried razor blades!

Cape Town, with Table Mountain in the background, often wearing her cap of white cloud, is one of the most beautiful and impressive harbours to enter. *Solitaire* passed through the breakwater on December 5, 12 days after leaving Durban and all I wanted to do was sleep for the next 12. A pilot launch led us to the yacht club where the manager, Peter, took our lines. The Royal Cape Yacht Club I will ever remember for its kindness and hospitality. On my arrival I was taken as I was – barefooted, in shorts and tattered shirt – to meet the Commodore and a lady I had heard a good deal about, Joan Fry, the club secretary. My apologies were brushed aside and they asked what the weather had been like on the trip down. I said I had run into gusting conditions which they seemed to find amusing. Gales apparently had been sweeping the coast, the Town Harbour had been closed and one ocean-going ship had been forced to enter with a damaged bridge. Was there anything I needed, they asked. 'Sleep,' I said. Other interests besides sailing? 'Golf!' I said. I went back to tend to *Solitaire*'s needs and when tidying up I heard my name being called over the loud speaker to say I was wanted on the phone. Puzzled, because no one knew of my arrival, I picked it up. 'My name's Frank Minnitt, I understand you play golf, Les,' came a strange voice. 'Are you free tomorrow? I'll pick you up at nine o'clock in the morning.'

No yacht club should be without a Joan Fry. Not only did she know all her members and their interests, she took the trouble to make a complete stranger a welcome guest and after arranging my golf game I felt far less tired. Rome had given me the name of a family friend whom I phoned. Betty was a keen ballroom dancer so I promised to escort her to a Christmas dance: after that I had my first decent sleep in nearly a fortnight.

Frank Minnitt arrived next morning in a white Jaguar. Maybe a little older than I, very pro-British, he had fought with us in the second world war and was the owner of a Contessa 32 which he had shipped from England. Apart from sailing he would take on anything that had been cast aside as useless and make it work again, his favourites being old British cars and motor bikes. His dog was an English cocker spaniel which was blind in one eye and inevitably named Nelson. On one occasion when invited to his house for dinner and having had my one suit cleaned I found myself in his garage helping him to take a car to bits. He had a son in the Navy and a charming wife called Solfrid.

I have often heard yachtsmen talking about the effects of long voyages, some claiming that the land appears to move. I can't say that I had this experience although my golf seemed to suffer! I would play more for the pleasure of watching other people swing a club correctly and to see beautiful greens set in rolling hills, feeling the lush grass under my feet. On the course I met Neil Nisbet who became my partner in a four. Later I went back to have dinner with him meeting his wife Beverly and their two teenaged daughters, and ended up spending most of Christmas with them.

Frank Minnitt gave a dinner at his club on New Year's eve and I found myself sitting beside another lovely lady, Caryll Holbrow, who had three grown up sons, one of whom, Andrew, was forever turning up with picnics to help work on *Solitaire*. Caryll's home was in sight of Table Mountain and was as beautiful as its name, Moon-rakers. It was not only the hospitality of these people that made Cape Town such a memorable stop. The yacht club was always active. Following the departure of the Whitbread round-the-world race they were running the Rothmans week.

Terrell turned up just after Christmas with a new crew member. Again he had made all the stops from Durban. *Rolling Stone* rolled in with Graeme and Sue. Another ferro-cementer was in Cape Town when I arrived. Her owners, Glen and Norma Harvey, farmers turned sailors whom I had met in Durban, had completed their 45ft craft in nine months. Knowing nothing about sailing they had paid a skipper to bring them down to Cape Town. Their two children accompanied them along with two cats, one of which was blind and was led around by the other. The family were adventurous, hard working and with a pioneering spirit, characteristics that were missing in some of the older established countries. Eilco Kasimier was a well-known and well-liked Dutch single-hander whose wishbone ketch, *Bylgya*, was alongside *Solitaire*. Eilco had sailed in the single-handed transatlantic race and from America had continued around the world the wrong way via Cape Horn. A Dutch hotelier and an experienced seaman, he taught me much.

I had to tear myself away from Cape Town where there was always a reason to stay longer: to play another round of golf, go to a party, a concert. . . . *Solitaire* was given her last coat of anti-fouling before setting off for home. Although the slipway had been heavily booked by the Rothmans racing boats, the club manager had fixed it for me to slip her for eight hours thus ensuring our departure would be eased by the knowledge that the hull was clean, and so speed our trip to St Helena, the next port of call 1,660 miles away. Our course north-west, the charts suggested lightish winds over *Solitaire*'s stern from the south-east but as we had a high pressure area to pass through there could be a few calm patches. For the first two or three days I could expect little sleep until we cleared the shipping lanes and the area of gales. Navigation would present no problems as St Helena is small but mountainous and there could be no mistake in recognising it, the nearest neighbour being Ascension Island, 700 miles further on.

After clearing the harbour *Solitaire* found a gentle southerly as we headed north, a broad reach under main and genoa. Table Mountain dropped sadly below the horizon. On the second day out a disturbed sea brought problems in holding a course, with the odd bad broach as the winds did not match wave size. Two slewed us and a third knocked *Solitaire* flat, breaking three of her stanchions.

I dropped all sails, a mistake. I could have continued to run with them but perhaps my judgement was impaired by finding myself with no secure lifelines to starboard. Later, when the winds increased to match the seas, I hauled up the working jib and sailed comfortably. I made an entry in the ship's log next morning and spotted the date, Friday January 13. 'No wonder!' I wrote.

On Monday, January 30 the entry in the log read, '0300 GMT, St Helena sighted'. It always warmed me to see land loom out of the dark particularly when, as with St Helena, there is no lighthouse! I waited until morning before entering harbour, after logging 1,607 miles which meant we must have had a strong helping current.

St Helena was where Napoleon found himself interned in 1815 after his defeat at Waterloo by the British since when the island has changed little. Many of the battlements built to prevent any attempted rescue, can be seen from the harbour. There is little industry for the 5,000 inhabitants so many of the young men emigrate to find employment elsewhere, leaving a surplus of attractive ladies with time on their hands. As there is no airfield the only outsiders who call regularly are yachtsmen.

When the customs boat came over I asked them what the main entertainment was or, at least, what the second was. I was told there was a cinema show three times a week. What they neglected to say was that they were the same three films, one of which consisted of coming attractions that never came.

As soon as practical I rowed ashore, walked through the old town gates and up a sloping cobbled street where the islanders, a friendly lot, crossed the street to greet you. At the local tavern I asked the innkeeper to bring me a tankard of his finest ale and as I got stuck into this became aware of a toothless wench weighing close to 18 stone sizing me up. She told me that the town was holding a beach barbecue that night for which I thanked her kindly and promised to attend but, tired from the voyage, I slept and failed to make it. Next day I was talking to some of the local girls and expressed sorrow at missing the big event whereupon they started to laugh. It seems the only people on the beach that night would have been me and toothless. She already had 12 children and was trying for a record 13. After that my stay on St Helena was like having both my mother-in-laws with me. She would swim around *Solitaire*, a cross between a shark and whale, and I had to keep explaining she could not come aboard because we would sink.

Local dances started at seven-thirty but I was warned to stay away because of the danger of being attacked by man-hungry dark-skinned ladies. At seven o'clock I would be at the door trying to start a queue, only to find, once inside, the blight of my life. The night would be spent with her not so much sitting on my lap as flowing over it, every now and then uttering a war cry reminiscent of a Gordon Highlander. On one occasion, when I saw a crowd of yachtees and girls leaving early, I asked the reason. They explained that although the beach was of pebble, there were cardboard boxes to lie on and did I want to reserve one? Not bloody likely!

Many of the South African boats came into St Helena while I was there including Eilco Kasimier on *Bylgya*, later to continue to Holland for a hero's welcome, and Glen and Norma Harvey on *Chummy* which was to hit a wreck off Brazil and sink. Fortunately all were saved although I'm not sure what happened to the cats. Six boats were lost at sea between leaving Tahiti and reaching England but luckily all my friends survived. Another boat from South Africa, *Sundance Kid*, came in just before dark one night when I was able to help, an attention which they repaid later in spades. Aboard were Doug and Mary Solomon, with two teenage boys and John, a crew member. They had run out of diesel and were coming in under sail. Although Doug was a first class seaman, the light was poor and as St Helena sometimes has a 30ft swell at that time of year, anchoring alone is not particularly healthy. It is far safer to have at least one rope onto a mooring buoy so I rowed out with a torch and directed them to lie alongside *Solitaire*.

Life on this island must be a paradise for any able-bodied seaman but after 10 days I felt as pure and as disappointed as a snowflake falling in summer. Next stop was Ascension Island, 700 miles away for which we sailed on Saturday, February 11, 1978 in company with *Sundance Kid* only to watch them pull away under poled-out headsails. The conditions were much the same as before, with following winds from the south-east. The trip passed without incident, apart from the sextant falling to bits which I soon cured with a few elastic bands. After logging 671 miles we arrived on Saturday, February 18, quite blasé about our navigation, despite a sick sextant. The island, emerging from the ocean like a dirty-grey volcano, I spotted 30 miles away. I was thrown a curving ball in that the powerful RDF transmitter was off air. One would think that when you approach an island that is packed with satellite-tracking equipment, a BBC relaying station and a modern airfield, not to mention their own Russian spy ship, there would be little problem in keeping a simple transmitter serviceable. One would think. I had the confidence not to worry, although I did pray for the sun to come up every morning so that I could take sights. My prayers increased in tempo when I looked into the anchorage.

It is always difficult to judge a breaking wave from the back, even taking a picture of a really terrifying one from this angle will show only a comparatively flat sea. I could see things were quite interesting by the bashing the sea wall was taking and the puzzling way everything kept disappearing, now you see it, now you don't. One minute there would be landing barges and yachts, the next the anchorage would be empty. Obviously a monster swell was responsible for this illusion so I considered giving it a miss and pushing on to the Azores but, as there were two yachts at anchor and I wanted to post some letters, I decided to take a closer look. In England I used to watch an American TV show called *Hawaii Five-O* which always started with some nut on a surfboard inside a wave. During the next few minutes I was to become that nut. I began to enter the harbour under power with sails stowed and conditions looking not too bad. Then, as everything went dark, I looked up expected to see a black cloud across the sun; instead I saw water reaching for the top of the mast. We were inside a breaking wave, with no way out. If I tried to turn we would broach, capsize and finish as a wreck on the rock-strewn beach. To do nothing meant surfing in at lord knows what speed to smash into the harbour wall. The wave took the decision out of my hands as it fell on us. Even as the cockpit started to empty I was turning *Solitaire*, bringing her around to face the threatening seas, clawing back out to sea. I could now see where the breakers started and finished so I made for a marker buoy and rounded it to make another attempt but, as we closed, the other craft still kept vanishing, clinging to their mooring buoys. The wind was off shore so that whenever the swell came in the boats would rear mightily, surge forward, and then be driven back by the wind as the wave passed through. There were no free buoys but I would be unable to leave the tiller long enough to secure a line anyway. The nearest yacht was *Sundance Kid*. I decided my only chance was to get a line onto one of the landing barges and hang off its stern. I went round the nearest a few times but there was no-one to take a rope.

I closed Doug's boat intending to shout goodbye before continuing on to the Azores when John, the crew member, dived over the side and started swimming towards me, risking his life. I just could not see how anyone could survive in that sea. Had Lana Turner been alone on the other craft, begging me to step off *Solitaire*, I would not have gone, even after my disappointment in St Helena. In that situation I think I would have gone below and quietly cut my throat. No way would I have left *Solitaire*.

After getting a line to John he managed to clamber onboard. When we had chewed a piece out of the bow and twisted a pulpit he succeeded in getting a line onto a bollard on the stern of a barge, whereupon I played out as much rope as I could without endangering the craft astern of us. Each time the swell bore in the rear barge would lift like a bird of prey, come screeching down for the kill and then stop a few yards short of *Solitaire*. Next moment we would be shooting up in the lift, looking down on the craft ahead, before plunging for its decks. My stomach muscles relaxed when I became confident that this vessel would move forward before we struck. It is terrifying to realise you have so little control over the life of your craft and, for that matter, your own.

John told me *Sundance* had arrived the day before. The people on the adjoining boat had gone ashore with Doug's wife and the boys whereafter the swell had started. Those ashore had been forced to spend the night there with no chance of returning until things eased. In fact it was 48 hours before we could land and the island newspaper reported it was the worst swell, rollers and resultant undertow for years. Concern was felt for the Giant Turtle eggs that were destroyed, Ascension Island being one of their few breeding places. *Sundance Kid* had been watching when I made my first approach and as the first wave hit *Solitaire* it seemed she had gone down like a stone. Later some of the Americans and British, who had been standing on the surrounding hills keeping an eye on us, confirmed that even the mast vanished. Having decided that we were lost and that they should start looking for survivors on the beach, *Solitaire*'s bow shot back from her grave to live again. Tongue in cheek they offered to take a collection for a repeat performance!

I told them bluntly what to do with their cameras.

Ascension, in many ways, is the opposite of St Helena which is green and reasonably fertile with a surplus of girls and little to do, a tired island living in the past and totally isolated from the twentieth century. Landing on Ascension, in comparison, is like landing on the moon. Barren of greenery, the island is grey and dusty, growing only tracking and transmitting aerials charged with static electricity, a man's island with few spare ladies. Although it is under British control Ascension depends on the gigantic American air base for its life blood. I have played golf in some unlikely places, in the deserts of South Yemen and Saudi Arabia, on a beach in Brazil but Ascension has a golf course which its members describe as the worst this side of hell, and after playing on it I was forced to agree. It is more like playing on a pinball machine. Having hit your ball you can relax awhile watching it leap from rock to rock. When it settles the game turns into hide-and-seek. At this stage you realise that this is also a very expensive course to play since every time you hit a ball you are virtually kissing it goodbye.

Everything possible is done for the serviceman and contracted civilians working there. If you weary of the black and grey landscape or looking out to sea, there are always the latest films to be seen nightly at a variety of clubs. The airforce base has a fine restaurant that looks as if it has been freshly shipped from Hollywood, the meals cheap, the food fresh. Spending most of my time in the clubs talking to BBC and service personnel, I never did get to see a film.

I cast off from the stern of the landing barge on Friday, February 24, 1978 with England 5,000 miles away and Cape Horn a further 20,000. We left in a mood of uncertainty. If I sailed direct to England spring would hardly have sprung. Should the weather prove too cold as we pushed north it might be advisable to stop off in the Azores and wait for a warmer welcome home. There was enough food and water onboard for a non-stop voyage. I would play it by ear. *Solitaire* had now sailed close to 30,000 miles since we took our first stumbling steps with Rome in the Solent. Considering the punishment and adventures we had shared, she was still in good health, although her motor gave concern. On top of that the working jib that had seen us round the world was on its last legs, broken stanchions needed welding, and the sextant was held together by faith and elastic bands. The self-steering needed new nylon bushes but at least it still worked well.

On Tuesday, March 21, *Solitaire* crossed her outward bound track, tying the knot and completing her first voyage around the world. In the past I had run the motor every week or two, now I was exercising it every few days, but each time it became more difficult to start. I ran it for long periods to circulate the oil and charge the battery but every mile north the problem increased. As the Atlantic grew colder the seas sucked through the engine froze and thickened the oil, adding more problems to those with which we left Cape Town.

Wednesday, April 5, 1978 found us close to Horta in the Azores after logging 3,330 miles from Ascension. Land's End, England, was approximately only 1,200 miles away. I had heard many heartwarming incidents about the Azores and its people so the temptation to call in was great but, above all, now I wanted to see my family so we sailed on. The waves that broke over *Solitaire*'s decks were touched with ice and her cabin grew cold, damp and dreary. Slowly I increased my clothing, first long trousers and sweater, then heavy socks and sea boots which I left on for longer periods until finally I slept in them.

The motor grew even harder to start and 900 miles from England it groaned for a few minutes, slowed down and coughed as though it had consumption, exhaled its last breath and died. I performed every operation I could think of to bring it back to life, bleeding its system, stripping it down, taking off its head. Its dismembered body was strewn over a heaving cabin floor and I did everything possible bar give it the kiss of life. I accepted the fact that we would have to sail up the English Channel without its backing, conserving the battery for navigation lights.

The last days of our voyage were insistently cold as we beat up channel into wind, rain and fog, tacking back and forth through heavy shipping. At last I heard a faint RDF signal from St Catherine's Point on the Isle of Wight which grew louder and louder as I turned towards, the gloom and mist pushed aside. Here at last were England's white cliffs and green fields to welcome home two weary travellers.

Then fate played its last dirty trick. Tacking past the Needles in company with other yachts we looked into the peaceful Solent anchorage at which point the wind dropped and the tide turned. The rest of the boats took down their sails and started their engines, leaving *Solitaire* to be swept back to sea. Enviously I watched them leave us for hot meals and baths, soft beds and warm arms. Rejected, we turned away and heading for Christchurch bay there to

104

spend another watchful night at anchor.

Although lacking tide tables I had noted the time the current had turned the night before and I knew that an early start would see us safely home so we swept past the Needles that Sunday morning, April 30, 1978 on a fast tide. Then the wind dropped again although the current bore us past Hurst Castle. Lymington river came up to port and I tried to edge over into its mouth but still the tide carried us. After a frantic dash to drop an anchor, a long wait ensued until a zephyr came up in the afternoon allowing us to start for home. Again it died to leave us helpless, drifting towards the mud banks as a motor cruiser closed us.

'Could you give us a tow into the marina? The motor's packed up'.

'Sure,' they say, 'we'll put down fenders and tie you alongside.' Then, 'you're flying a yellow flag. Where have you come from? France?'

'Ascension Island in the South Atlantic,' I reply proudly. 'I've just sailed around the world.'

The cameras came out. Wine, chicken, chocolates and cups of coffee showered on *Solitaire*. It was the Easter holiday and the marine was full, but we were allowed to tie alongside the wall, *Solitaire* still secured to the cruiser. The customs launch that had followed us down river soon cleared us. Standing on top of the wall was John the rigger, the first person to steer *Solitaire* three years ago.

'Nice to see you back, Les,' he shouted. 'What kept you?'

SUNDAY 1 FEBRUARY 1981

20·10 NO NOON SIGHT. NO VIS, RAIN, FOG DRIZZLE.
LOG READING 25 MILES (TOTAL 18,425 MILES) 83 MILES 24 HOURS
VERY LITTLE WIND DURING NIGHT AT TIMES BECALMED, WINDS
STARTED FROM NORTH THIS MORNING WITH RAIN AND DRIZZLE
INCREASED TO PRESENT GALE FORCE. WORKING JIB ONLY
MANAGED TO KEEP REEFED MAIN UP BY STAYING ON TILLER
AND CAUGHT ABOUT 4 GLNS OF WATER OFF BOOM. VERY PLEASED
AT LEAST EASED ONE PROBLEM A LITTLE. MID DAY BUT QUITE DARK
BELOW, BEING ONCE MORE CLOSED IN. TEMP DOWN A BIT AT 58°F.

MONDAY 2 FEBRUARY 1981

17·00 SIGHT TAKEN FOR LONGITUDE. LOG READING 06 MILES.
19·55. NOON POSITION LATITUDE 50°36 LONGITUDE 115°34 WEST
LOG READING 20 MILES (TOTAL 18,520 MILES) 95 MILES 24 HOURS
THE LONGITUDE SIGHT ONCE MORE PUTS US AHEAD OF OUR D/R POSITION
THIS TIME BY 20 MILES, I WILL TRY FOR FURTHER SIGHT THIS
AFTERNOON, HIGH SWELL MAKES ANY SIGHT A BIT TRICKY.
DISPITE DRIZZLE MANAGED TO PUT MAIN UP LAST NIGHT
WITH 2 REEF, WEATHER CLEARED THIS MORNING. NOW HAVE
WINDS 5 TO 6 FROM NORTH WEST, FEW GUSTS BUT NOT TOO
BAD. BLUE SKY, FAIRLY FLATE BLUE SEA.
FIBRE GLASSED IN REAR HATCH THIS MORNING, LAST JOB
BEFORE TRYING TO ROUND CAPE HORN. IF I WISH TO START
ENGINE NOW HAVE TO CRAWL THROUGH. SOLITAIRE TO REACH
EXHURST SEA COCK.

TUESDAY 3 FEBRUARY 1981

19·45 NO SIGHTS, GALE FORCE WINDS
LOG READING 35 MILES (TOTAL 18,635 MILES) 115 24 HOURS
GALE STARTED LAST NIGHT FROM THE WEST HAVE JUST
REDUCED FROM W/J TO STORM JIB, HOLDING GOOD COURSE.
SEA VERY COLD, ME VERY COLD. WE HAVE SOME HOT NOSH
WEARING THE TROUSERS MARGARET GAVE ME, JUST THE JOB.
DISTANCE COVERED WEEK 30- 679. MILES.
CAPE HORN NOW APPROX. MATLY 1,700 MILES⊙

WEDNESDAY 4 FEB 1981

19·35· NO SIGHTS- GALE
LOG READING 32 MILES (TOTAL 18,732 MILES) 97 MILES 24 HOUR
VERY FIERCE GALE, SOLITAIRE BEING THROWN ON HER SIDE.
SQUALLS ARE UNBELEAVEABLE. DIDN'T NOT WINDS COULD
BLOW SO HARD, SKY KEEPS CHANGING, BLUE, BLACK PINK,
FANTASTIC. PHOTO'S WITH ROME AND PETERS CAMERA'T
STORM JIB ONLY.

• A page from the ship's log

PART TWO   Second time round

1

THE FIRST CIRCUMNAVIGATION, leaving Lymington on Monday August 18, 1975 and arriving back on Sunday, April 30, 1978, had taken 12 days under two years and eight months. The east to west voyage had been made far too quickly and I had missed out many of the countries I would have liked to visit. Such an exploration, of self as well as the world, should take a minimum of ten years and anything up to a lifetime. Now my main driving force was to make a fresh start and to round Cape Horn.

The distance *Solitaire* covered on that first voyage was roughly 34,000 miles with a best day's run of around 149 miles and the longest time spent alone at sea was 69 days with a best non-stop distance of about 6,000 miles; not that any of this was important. *Solitaire* and I were neither equipped for nor desired to set records. It's what is in your head and heart that's important, not what Joe Soap, who has never stepped on a boat, thinks. Was it a good sail, a warm day, did the sun set in a blaze of colour, did the dolphins visit, were we contented? Those are the questions whose answers matter.

I shall never forget or forgive my first navigation blunders. After the Brazilian disaster I made yet more mistakes but thenceforward I kept a mental note of *Solitaire*'s position, the weather conditions she was in and the dangers she might face. When laying out a course, I would draw lines from point to point, trying to skirt around areas of calms, storms and shelving sea beds, using such charts as I possessed. Sometimes things go wrong and three or four problems are thrown at you together. Then there is no time to think and you must react instinctively, preferably having the cure ready before you catch the disease.

For me the time taken on a voyage was important only as far as food, water and the boat's condition were concerned. If I could make 100 miles a day I would be content. Had I had the funds I would have worked out the stores required then doubled them, but I was in no position to do this until towards the end of the voyage. The second circumnavigation, this time west to east, broadly speaking, depended on three things. First, my family's reaction. Both parents were now in their 70s; my mother had been in poor health for some time and brother Royston had spent much of his time caring for her and father while I was gallivanting. If Roy wanted to alter his way of life or the voyage distressed my parents then it would have to be delayed. Second, my friends had an influence. Hitherto they had only encouraged me but if they tried to dissuade me I would sail for Cape Horn no matter although I would be apprehensive, really alone for the first time on any voyage. Third, finance. I had to find work quickly. I left England in 1975 with £300 and returned with the same sum which I had saved in Australia. But to carry out modifications, equip *Solitaire* with new gear and stores would cost at least £2,000. My best way to make this money quickly would be to try for an overseas contract in electronics.

I spent my first night in England with Group Captain Rex Wardman and his wife, Edith, who welcomed me warmly with a hot bath, sizzling steak and a bed, full of sleep. Later that week Rex

DEPARTURE 9-7-
ARRIVAL 3-6-81

FISH CAUGHT
11-4-81

LESLIE POWLES' SECOND CIRCUMNAVIGATION, EAST-TO-WEST

1 = End of first week, 2 = End of second week, etc

KNOCK DOWN
8-2-81

CAPE HORN
24-2-81

drove me home to Birmingham where the news was good.

If my family, who had moved into a small, semi-detached house, did not exactly encourage they certainly made no attempt to discourage me, their attitude being that the sea was my life and I would be off again. On my arrival I found a couple of reporters. In writing to my family I had omitted or glossed over the bad times, but when talking to the press I forgot this and mentioned some of the sailing's gorier aspects which caused the newspapermen and my family to blanch. My photograph duly appeared in the papers, not that that means anything, but parents like this sort of thing, provided it's not just before they hang you!

Three days later Rex drove me back to Lymington whereafter I spent a week with Rome and his mother, catching up on my writing. I contacted Sabb who told me to take my engine to Savage Engineering in Southampton where the motor was stripped, cleaned and serviced and the fuel pump attended to for an all-in charge of £20! After that I had no further trouble, making up for all the problems I had experienced after leaving Australia. Most of the remainder of my time was spent talking to Rome about the modifications I wanted. The major task was to change *Solitaire* from sloop to cutter rig and perhaps add a bowsprit which would put her headsails further forward and thus help prevent her broaching when on a run. Cutter rig would also give me a bigger choice of sails. When beating into storms I could get a better slot effect with the main by using a small staysail which would also serve as a back-up for self-steering. The one objection against the mod was that I might have to fit running backstays which did not appeal. When Rome sailed his transatlantic race he fitted an unsupported inner forestay on his boat but agreed it was not worth the risk in the Southern Ocean. Having experienced the roaring forties on *Adventure* in the Whitbread Race he told me about the conditions, explaining the problems in his quiet, precise manner, never discouragingly. Later Brian Gibbons came to see me and designed a new mast support, then Rex Wardman joined in. I was no longer alone.

My stay in Lymington had been a good one. I had overcome the initial problems on my list and *Solitaire's* engine was in perfect condition. All that was left was finance, and that was tricky as the work situation boded ill. I had no luck with my old firms, most of whom were cutting back on staff, and the Job Centre could offer nothing. The public moorings cost £10 a week and the £300 with which I'd arrived home was shrinking so I decided to take *Solitaire* to Dartmouth and anchor in the river. Although an overnight stay was prohibitively expensive it was possible to pay by the season which was comparatively cheap and the plus point was that I had friends there I wanted to see, and could spend the rest of my time writing.

Rome said he would sail as far as Poole with me whereupon I suggested we tack there. 'What do you mean by a tack, Les?' 'How about Cherbourg and back?' The tack to France was 120 miles and so, for the first time in her life, *Solitaire* made a voyage with a crew of more than one. Since a boat can have only one skipper aboard, Rome got the job and I dropped a rank to first mate.

After anchoring at Dartmouth I contacted Ann and her daughter Susan who had moved there soon after I had set off on my first trip. I stayed with them and Richard Hayworth, a quietly spoken man, forever throwing bones at me to growl over while he sat back with a twinkle in his eye. A fighter of lost causes with the tenacity of a bulldog and as gentle as a lamb, he was English to the core.

John and Diana Lock invited me to dinner at their beautiful home. John was a retired RN commander whose name had been given me by Caryll Holbrow in Cape Town. Later I helped crew his boat in a race but I'm afraid the round-the-world sailor impressed no one. When asked how to make the boat go faster, I said, 'start the engine'. One night when I was dining with the Locks I had opposite me a

110

very young man whom I imagined was probably still at university. He produced some cheese which he said he had bought in France that morning. I could not work out what form of transport he had used: the time he gave for the journey was too slow for an aircraft, too fast for a yacht. Allen turned out to be the captain of the warship that had escorted Naomi James home the previous week. As a result of this fortuitous meeting I was invited to a cocktail party aboard his ship, then the petty officers had me back next day for dinner.

In turn this led to an experience which, at the time, disturbed me. After my visits to Allen's ship one of his officers invited me to spend the day at the Naval College with his sister, her husband and their three children, one a baby. Despite being embarrassed by their praise of *Solitaire*'s voyages I enjoyed my time with them and played a good deal with the baby whose tiny hands clung to my fingers. I started laughing. 'She's a beautiful baby but if she doesn't let go of me you'll have to take me home with you.' The mother's face glowed. 'Do you really think she's beautiful?'
'She's lovely,' I replied.
'Oh I'm so glad, you see she's mongol.'
For a moment I could not take in what had been said by this young woman with a child she would care for all its life, a woman with far more guts than those who get their names splashed in the papers.

Because I had no work my financial situation was worsening daily. I was now pushing 53 which age, in the electronics field, made me ancient. Many of the government contracts I tried for were of a secret nature and for a successful response you had to be British and able to prove your movements over the past three years. No employer could be expected to undertake that on my behalf.

I heard there were some mud berths at Cobbs Quay in Poole where, reputedly, the mooring fees were low but my move there in August, 1978 with £100 in my pocket was to prove my biggest mistake since hitting the reef off Brazil. Not only were there no vacant berths but those boats already there were being asked to leave because it was an 'unscheduled development'.

Solitaire could be lifted out, her mast dropped and put in a cradle for £60 and I could live onboard for two weeks. The fortnight passed without my finding work, apart from a couple of private jobs in the yard. One paid £50 and the second should have been £200, but the owner found it convenient to flit by moonlight without paying me.

In October I saw an advertisement in the local paper asking for electronic wiremen and rang the firm for an appointment. 'I have to tell you I'm 53 years old,' I said, having been turned down so often that I believed I had no chance. I turned up with my last £10 note in my pocket – and got the job. If the basic wage was unexceptional there was plenty of overtime and by saving hard I reckoned I could still leave for Cape Horn the following June. I walked and ran the four miles to and from the factory which helped build up my legs and get me fit for my voyage. *Solitaire* was the one I really felt sorry for, sitting forlornly in her cradle with her mast down, dreaming of her warm bed in Hiva Oa sunshine. As winter progressed the marina became more like a graveyard, the snow-covered boats so many tombstones.

To save money I spent Christmas in the marina trying to hide from the manager but he caught me on Christmas day before I could dodge behind the tombstones. His weekly enquiry as to when I was going to remove *Solitaire* changed to, 'are you still here?' I remembered vividly my last Christmas which had been spent in Cape Town when it had been, 'can't you stay longer?' Rome collected me on New Year's day to spend it with his family and Annegret, a girl he had met in Cape Town, an air hostess with a German airline who was to play a major role in my second voyage.

Work fell off after the holiday so I moved to Plessey Electronics on a six-month contract with good money and more overtime. For £25 I was offered an old banger which had six months left on its MOT and was taxed for a month. I bandaged the broken silencer but never managed to cure the carburettor which drank petrol like an alcoholic so I threw the bum in the dustbin and got another from the scrapyard. I needed a car for work and, more important, to start fetching equipment and stores for the voyage.

I drove to Derek Daniels' home to order a second Hydrovane self-steering gear. He would service my old unit free of charge for the feedback information it would provide and I could then use it as a back-up. He guaranteed the delivery date on the new one with ten per cent discount. From Kemp Masts I ordered a new Jiffy reefing boom. With this system of slab-reefing I could feed all the down-hauls back to winches in the cockpit and use the old roller boom as a stand-by. Meanwhile I had been buying ship's stores from the supermarket and the boat's lockers, unlike Mother Hubbard's, were starting to fill.

As the weather warmed I hired an industrial sander and spent my spare time on *Solitaire*'s topsides, finally giving her four coats of International 709 paint and bought some anti-fouling to be applied just before the boat went back into the water. This time I would not risk strangling *Solitaire* as I had in the South Pacific. I splashed out, too, on wet weather gear, having it heavily lined to combat the freezing conditions in the Southern Ocean. There were changes to make on the rigging for safety's sake. The lower shrouds of six millimetre stainless steel wire had to be stepped up to eight millimetre to match the rest of the rigging. Sails were the major item. It might be possible to pick up some strong secondhand headsails, but I needed two new working jibs and a new mainsail on which I held very definite views. The mainsail would be similar to the one Lucas had sent me in Australia with a straight leech, no battens and three reef points, the last reef point to provide a virtual trisail. And I needed a heavy luff rope, not only to give strength but to grip on in icy conditions. The seams had to be wide with three rows of stitching and, had I been able to afford it, all panelling seams would have been taped with further stitching. The sail was to be at least eight-ounce material and heavily reinforced. All eyes, clews, tacks were to be stitched rather than pressed in position, for in the past such eyes had inevitably pulled out. My old Lucas mainsail was still good enough to serve as a back-up. The working jib was to be made to the same specification apart from stainless steel, not rope, in the luffs and the piston hanks had to be heavy duty because on my last journey I had worn out two sets.

I consulted a number of sailmakers, all of whom said they could supply to specification and deliver within ten weeks at prices ranging from £400 to £500. A local sailmaking firm had several advantages: they were only five minutes' walk from where I worked, they claimed to specialise in heavy cruising sails, their price was competitive and there were no transport costs. I called at their office on March 14, 1979 and we had a long talk about the specifications and my reasons for them. If I paid cash with order the price would be £400 with delivery on May 14.

I handed over a cheque for the £400 within a week along with my Lucas sails to act as a pattern. 'Do make them strong enough to take me round Cape Horn,' was my last request. 'We will make them strong enough to lift the boat out of the water,' they promised. Later I received a confirmation of order and delivery date.

Calling in to pick up the sails on May 14 I was told they would be completed five days later. On May 19 an employee tipped me off that they had not even been started and it was the same story on May 26. After more phone calls and visits I was finally told they would be ready on Saturday, June 2, 1979. Handed three plastic-coated sailbags I asked to see the mainsail. At first they refused, claiming that they did not allow sails to be removed from their bags and inspected on the premises! Finally they let me pull about four feet of the sail from its bag. The first thing that came to light was what I thought was a large tack or eyelet which had been pressed in and not stitched as agreed. Then I realised it could not be either since the material was too narrow, but could only be the head of a sail with the headboard missing! The reinforcing was limited, there was no rope in the luff, the cloth merely turned back on itself, small diamond-shaped pieces had been sewn on into which eyelets had been pressed to take the plastic slides, and the seams were too narrow. My first reaction was that I'd been given someone's poorly-made dinghy sail by mistake. 'You've given me the wrong sail,' I complained, whereupon they asked if I had paid for the sails in full. On affirming this I was told, 'in that case the sails are now your property and you have no case'.

I contacted a solicitor who was also a yachtsman. He made an appointment to inspect the sails but the sailmaker failed to keep it. I contacted the Association of Sailmakers but since my sailmaker was a member of theirs they refused to act as arbitrators. On June 27 my solicitor advised me to contact the Office of Fair Trading at which stage I knew I had little chance of leaving for Cape Horn that year as *Solitaire* was not fast and we would be unable to reach the Horn before winter set in. I considered all the actions I could take, starting with taking the sails to the nearest rubbish dump and burning them.

To set off on a voyage without first class sails would give concern to my family and would be unfair both to them and *Solitaire*; to walk away from the legal problem could mean that other yachtsmen would be taken advantage of, so I visited the Office of Fair Trading and stepped onto a merry-go-round until 1982 when I staggered off as sick as any long ride on the legal circuit can make you.

Once more I was to feel as if I were in hospital, this time one for the insane. Three teams of surgeons came to operate. First were the solicitors, talking softly and incomprehensibly; second were the judges, entering your stomach not with scalpels but with bare hands, twisting your guts into knots; and third were the get-on-your-bike-and-look-for-work brigade whose speciality is the heart. They remove you from the operating table and sit you in a small cubicle where a girl, young enough to be your grandchild, asks, 'have you looked for work? How much money do you have? Prove it!' You are then allowed to leave their hospital, reporting weekly for your dole prescription, wishing you were a thousand miles away and had never heard of British justice.

The Consumer Protection Department advised collecting the sails and having an expert's written report whether or not they were of merchantable quality and fit for their purpose. I was further advised to apply to Poole county court for a hearing before the registrar which was arranged for August 4, 1978. The sailmaker failed to turn up. The case would now go before a judge after I had engaged an expert witness. Then my contract with Plesseys ran out and I could not afford the repairs to get my car through its MOT so I sold it for £18. Meanwhile I had promised to leave the marina by the end of June for Cape Horn and when this fell through I was put under more pressure. *Solitaire* was put back in the water and I sailed for Lymington in mid-August, entering Lymington Yacht Haven for a winter berth on September 25. From now on this friendly marina would always be looked on as *Solitaire*'s home.

The court case dragged. First there were problems in finding an expert witness and a sailmaker made it all clear when he said, 'dog doesn't eat dog'. In other words doctors don't appear against doctors which outlook is shared by solicitors and sailmakers. Since Vectis cloth had been used for the sails, I tried its makers, Ratseys, who used this as a reason for not inspecting the sails! However they recommended I should contact the chairman of the Association of British Sailmakers who turned out to be with Bruce Banks Sails and he could not help. He recommended a surveyor who, after examining the sails, said, 'your troubles are over. I'll appear for you in court'. Whereupon he jumped on an aircraft and was never heard from again.

The court case was set for May 5, 1980. I found another naval architect who inspected the sails and said he would appear for me. The trial went so well that at times I thought the defendant's solicitor was working for me. When I was in the witness box he asked, 'did you ever write an article for a yachting magazine called "Barbados or Bust"?' I had expected my own solicitor to bring up my past sailing experience, not the opposition.

'Are you the Leslie Powles who sailed from England with only eight hours sailing experience?'

'Yes, sir.'

'Are you the Leslie Powles who was over 1,000 miles off course?'

'Yes, sir.'

'Are you the Leslie Powles who then came back to England with his tail between his legs to tell my client how to build sails?'

'No, sir,' I replied, 'I'm the Leslie Powles who then sailed 30,000 miles around the world and even managed to find Australia.'

The Australia came out in that country's accent, Austraaaaaalia. There was laughter in court, the judge's face reddened and that line of questioning came to an abrupt halt. It was one of the few enjoyable things about the trial.

The next insinuation infuriated me. They claimed that I had become frightened to make the non-stop attempt and had used the sails as a reason not to go. Finally the judge accepted that the sails were unfit for their purpose and that the sailmaker was in breach of contract. My £400 would be returned and my costs paid, but the expense of bringing *Solitaire* back into a seaworthy condition was refused, the judge taking the view that these costs were in the nature of living expenses and would have been incurred at the end of the voyage. A second blow came in one of my solicitor's letters, 'the court costs are limited to the appropriate county scale. We will obviously temper the wind to the shorn lamb, but in reality by the time the costs position with the Law Society is resolved you will not get the whole of your £400.'

Shorn lamb! I felt more like a sacrificial goat. By living off *Solitaire*'s round-the-world stores during the winter months I had managed to keep £850 of my savings, but by now we were in a sorry state. The last of the food had gone and *Solitaire*'s hull was covered with weed and had to be taken out of the water for anti-fouling. Her battery needed replacing, the rigging needed changing, and the fuel tank leaked. Time was running out.

At the age of 55, and for the first time in my life, I wanted to abandon the country of my birth. I had left England a dozen times before but never because I wanted to. Now I wanted to storm out, a spoilt child, the angry husband on the way to the pub to cool down, a feeling, true, which would pass. I was still a free man able to come and go as I pleased but this time go I would, even if it meant rowing my boat down the channel without her mast.

Once more I started to ready *Solitaire*. Once more I ordered a mainsail and two working jibs, this time from Peter Lucas of Lucas Sails who, after hearing my tale, agreed to help all he could. There would be no problems over the specification, I could even have my stainless steel wire in the luffs of the working jibs. The price was the same as the duff sails, £400, with a couple of bonuses thrown in: my old

116

sails would be checked and reconditioned free of cost and his wife would do all the running about. In fact I received a third bonus. His wife was a lovely Canadian girl, bubbling with encouragement and I even found myself whistling *Land of Hope and Glory* again!

I gave up the idea of changing *Solitaire* from bermudan to cutter rig as the cost was too high. The best I could afford was to step up the lower shrouds from six to eight millimetre wire, matching them with the rest of the standing rigging. I had used a local Birmingham firm when I first rigged *Solitaire* in 1975, so I wrote them asking for a quotation for the stainless steel wire fitted with swaged ends. They answered by return with a price out of my reach. I had just finished reading their letter when there was a knock on *Solitaire's* hull. The company's representative had called to explain that the price was high because the firm did not do their own swaging. The rep said that since he dealt with local companies doing this kind of work he could put it through at trade cost, and he spent three days chasing back and forth. The modification still cost £85 but what really warmed my heart was that a home town firm had gone to so much trouble. I still had to change the rigging connections at the top of the mast but that was only a day's work.

A ship's battery, something I could not take chances with, cost £80. *Solitaire's* motor can be started by hand but only with difficulty and after months at sea I might be too weak even to try swinging it. New halyards and sheets took another £75. Rome managed to buy charts, almanac, radio and navigation books through the RAF at a discount, but it was still a drain. Some of my original charts could be used again. At one stage Rome pointed out that I had no chart of Australia which led to our having words. 'Since I've no intention of going within 200 miles of that coast I don't need a chart,' I told him. Rome finally walked away shaking his head after my last remark, 'that it was six months away and I'd worry about it when I got there'.

Lack of money was forever raising its head not simply because I could not afford to buy the things I needed but that I had tried to prevent friends realising just how broke I was. Peter and Fanny Tolputt, who owned a local guest house, took me along to the wholesalers for stores, where I spent £120 buying the cheapest food I could find. They were convinced that I just did not like tinned steak, duck or salmon! At the very least I needed to buy double the amount of food already on *Solitaire*; the eight connections on the mast's top rigging had to be changed, say £60 for that, and I had to buy at least one used headsail for running before the winds in the Southern Ocean.

Each day I rang my solicitor's secretary (her boss had long since stopped talking to me). On June 10 with less than £100 in my pocket and two weeks to *Solitaire's* departure he wrote me from his office in outer space and I stopped whistling *Land of Hope and Glory*. 'Dear Mr Powles,' he wrote. 'I refer to my secretary's recent call from which I gather that you are not minded to return the sails until the question of costs is resolved.' Then came the body blow. 'Unhappily I have to report that the other side have not been prepared to agree costs which will therefore have to be taxed by the court. This process will take at least three months and there is not the slightest prospect of resolving this matter before your intended departure this month.'

I was no longer the angry husband slamming out of the house. Since I had been rejected I would look around for other attractive company with whom to have an affair. I remembered all my American friends and the kindnesses they had shown me on my first voyage. July 4 was their Day of Independence so it would be mine, too, mine and *Solitaire's*, the day we would sail.

Perhaps at this stage a normal individual would have considered finding a sponsor, but I was dead against, my feelings stemming, perhaps, from my working class background. With a sponsor's money I could have a yacht built with electric self-reefing sails, sensors that would record any strain and reef the sails while I stayed below watching the latest video, relaxed in the knowledge that our satellite navigation aid was keeping us on course for Cape Horn. Without a commercial sponsor I would be cold, hungry and afraid, but I would be using the gifts given to me by the only sponsor I was responsible to.

The closest I came to being caught in this rat race was when I met Dr Herbert Ochs who came to see me about using a new anti-fouling he had invented. A chubby, jolly man, he must have been a bit older than me. I liked him on sight, a down-to-earth character I could have spent days talking to, a man I could trust to keep his word. When I told him my feelings about sponsors he said, 'there's no question of your considering me a backer. I simply want you to put a gallon of my concoction on *Solitaire's* hull, take it round the world non-stop and let me inspect the results. Er, should you hit a reef, run aground or sink I'd be grateful for any last minute photos you manage to take.' While we talked in the cabin I worked on my old plastic sextant which still had the handbag mirrors I had stuck on in Panama. The adjuster had been held together by elastic bands, now perished, and I was replacing them with the finest money could buy. Dr Ochs, or Herbert as he had become, grew more and more agitated. Unable to contain his curiosity any longer he asked what I was doing. 'Getting my sextant ready for this trip,' I replied, whereupon he turned a lovely shade of green.

'Not with my .... anti-fouling you're not,' he exclaimed. He promised to replace the sextant and a week later turned up with a beautiful Zeiss product. After much discussion I agreed to accept it on the understanding that when I returned *Solitaire* would be taken out of the water to have her hull inspected but that I would not be required to express an opinion. I felt thoroughly ungrateful, but I did not want to be obligated.

Lymington Yacht Marina allowed me to haul *Solitaire* out of the water early on Saturday morning and leave her in slings until Monday. This kept down the costs and was far more efficient than rushing the anti-fouling on a six-hour tide at the Town Quay.

Rex drove me to Birmingham to farewell my family and leave the duff sails with Tony and Irene Marshall. If they had heard nothing from me after a year the sails were to be sent to my solicitor, otherwise I'd deliver them myself when I returned and carry on with the court case. Driving back to *Solitaire* all I could remember was my father's big, rough hands, my mother's frightened eyes and her last words, 'keep warm and be sure to have plenty to eat'. I would remember those words later! On my return to *Solitaire* I entered the half world that I knew well from past voyages. Normally the transition was made one or two days before sailing; this time I had been slipping in and out of it for two years. I badly wanted to hold on to what people said to me, record them on tapes in my mind to be taken out in the months ahead to be used, gone over slowly and to enjoy when I had more time to think. But life became more and more difficult as there seemed so much to do in so little time and questions merely served to trigger more problems.

The July 4 departure date had to be postponed. Keith Parris became my unpaid uncomplaining press agent. He and Ann were two people who sneaked up on me and I can't now remember when I first met them. Both were school-teachers who owned a boat in the marina, Keith with time on his hands. Without really being aware of it I began to rely on them more and more as my sailing date neared.

A couple of nights before I sailed Rome and Annegret threw a party for me at which were his mother Grace as was his sister Terry and husband Martin. All had presents for me which, since it was late, Rome would bring to *Solitaire* the next morning. Sure enough

119

Rome and Annegret turned up and loaded an unending stream of parcels. I could not really appreciate it all, staggering over water containers and trying to store the presents on top of the bunks. Annegret excitedly tried to explain that for weeks Rome and she had been making ten of the parcels which were to be opened at different stages of the voyage. One was marked 'Crossing the equator', another 'My birthday', besides 'Rounding the Five Southern Capes', 'Christmas' and so on. Over the coming months I tried to log just what these parcels meant to me. At one stage tears of frustration streamed down my cheeks, unable to transcribe my feelings into words. In the end all that would be written was, 'God bless them'.

On my last day there was another rush of gifts, mostly paperbacks and food. A parcel from Peter and Fanny included a tin of salmon and a bottle of champagne for rounding Cape Horn and two fruit cakes, ideal for the early days at sea. A Dutch friend somehow had obtained ten boxes of NATO army rations, each box supposed to last 24 hours. From the local bakery I had bought 70lbs of flour housed in two five-gallon sealed containers. Another container held five gallons of sugar! A last minute purchase of 30lbs of onions, another of

● **Leslie Powles ready for his second round-the-world voyage**

potatoes. Fanny gave me three dozen fresh farm house eggs. I had food enough for a six-month voyage.

With help from my guardian angel I would be at sea for nine months . . . I was saying ten when I would surely end looking like Twiggy. The morning of July 9, 1980 brought light northerlies and a few scattered clouds in an otherwise clear blue sky. I had been up since dawn, *Solitaire* becoming the stage for a farce I played every time we sailed. Before learning this game I would get into all kinds of trouble trying to do three things at once while carrying on as many conversations. The engine had been run and was still hot, but this did not prevent my remarking, 'I hope the motor starts, otherwise you've come for nothing'. Rigging, halyards, sheets and sails had been checked a dozen times but I still walked the decks pulling and kicking things as though seeing them for the first time, allowing me to concentrate on the things that really mattered. Will the wind push *Solitaire* onto the berth or away, how will the current affect her until she attains speed and can be steered? I wanted to say nothing that would leave behind a bad impression because tomorrow I would not be there to say I was sorry.

In Tahiti I became close to an American family whose daughter would row over each day while I was at work and put a letter on the chart table for me to find when I arrived home. On the morning I sailed she was there with a garland of island flowers. As I put out to sea I turned for a last wave, the flowers still around my neck, and remembered that today was her seventh birthday. I had planned it for ages but at the last moment had forgotten. I could not turn back, too many people had come to see me off. The voyage to Australia lasted 69 days and that's a long time to be sorry.

After preparing *Solitaire* for her departure it was the crew's turn, another ritual carried out before each voyage. My thinning ginger hair had given up the ghost the night before when Annegret had butchered it in, what else, but a crew cut. The pasty white body scaled a grossly overweight 14 stone, for the first time something to be pleased about since it could live off its own blubber during the early stages of the voyage, and it had delighted in its last soaking in fresh hot water where pores had opened and been cleaned. From now on there would be showers direct from the sky but the pores would always contain salt. I dressed it in clean clothes. Yesterday my laundry had been done since then I was to wear my oldest gear, keeping the best for the long months ahead.

At 0830 on July 9, 1980 I walked down the pontoon to *Solitaire*. All

121

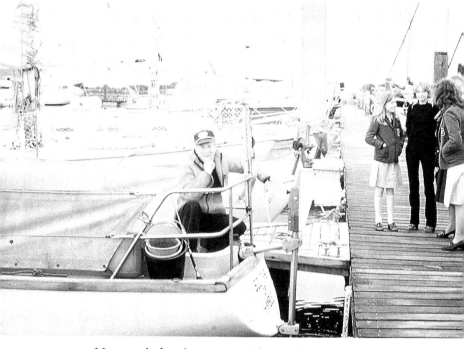

● **Moments before departure on July 9, 1980. Margaret's trousered figure in centre of the group on the pontoon**

I had in my pocket, in fact all I had in the world, was £60 of which £40 had been given by a TV company a few days before. They had promised £20 at first but after the recording had doubled the amount. With a few violins it might have been further increased. On my return I learned that they had interviewed another single-hander at the same time and put us both on the same show. The difference was that the other chappy was sponsored. His yacht had cost £350,000 and a further £40,000 a year to run but the funny thing was that after all the money and shouting he never even sailed!

Solitaire waited for me to step aboard, her old red ensign now a faded orange, her spray dodgers dirty and rust-streaked, her new golden boom with an unused mainsail, her old number two genoa hanked on to one forestay, the new working jib on the other.

These I could see as the visitors saw them, perhaps shaking their heads, believing me foolish to set out on such a voyage so ill-equipped. It was what they could not see that would have convinced them I was mad, the equipment I lacked that most sane yachtsmen would require for a voyage across the channel let alone around the world: liferaft, radio transmitter, barometer, flares, charts, wind speed indicator. The list was endless. A sane person would work out stores he needed, then double them. I had worked it out and halved

122

it, not from choice, but because I had stopped being rational after depending on others for justice and fair play.

Aboard *Solitaire* things speeded up. A quick interview with a TV crew, Keith Parris saying they would follow me down river in the marina launch for last pictures; asking if I would put full sails up to leave the mooring, and I explaining that I would have a following wind and could not. Once clear of the berth I would put up the genoa, leaving down the mainsail until we reached the Solent. I looked for people I could trust to let go and spotted Peter Tolputt and Margaret Brown. A shout to Peter, 'will you take in my fenders,' then to Margaret, 'please take in our springs'. A dash to start the motor. Back on deck, collect the fenders and drop them below. 'Peter, the motor's on slow ahead. Will you let go our bow line then come back for the stern?'

At 9.15 *Solitaire* severed her links with land for 329 days. A quick wave to Rex and Grace. 'Tell Rome I'll see him in ten months' time.' (He had a flying detail that morning and could not be present.) Hard over with the rudder to pass between the other row of berths, then heave up the genoa which, with my excess weight, went up easily without need a winch handle. A quick chase up deck when its sheet snagged. Waving to friends on other yachts then into the river, pursued by the Yarmouth Ferry and the TV crowd, trying to take instructions from one while not being sucked into the other. Then my own request to Keith, the last for 329 days, 'phone Mom and Dad and say I'm on TV tonight'. Their shouts of 'good luck', before they turned back to their safe homes.

Solitaire cleared Lymington river into a surprisingly empty Solent and headed for the Needles. Her new self-steering gear had its bright red wind vane set for the first time, already proving it was more sensitive than its predecessor. The trailing log's spinner was put over the side, registering more miles to add to the 34,000 already recorded. Our new mainsail was hauled up, the reefing ropes passing through eyes on the leech of the sail then back through the boom to a block on the foot of the mast, thence to a winch in the cockpit, all designed to make reefing easy. It snagged but needed only a small adjustment; nevertheless I was glad I hadn't tried to be too clever while friends were around. With the main up more contrasts: pure white against patched grey.

The lines that had tied *Solitaire* to shore now secured me to her, as a priority on leaving harbour was to run them from cleats in the stern along the deck to a bollard in the bow. In the old days I would

123

step into the cockpit and secure my lifeline, but for this trip I had taken another precaution: a large U-bolt had been put within reach of the main hatch so that I could fasten on to this in rough weather before leaving the cabin.

Approaching Hurst Castle there was time to nip below to check for leaks, grab my wet weather gear and get back to the cockpit with a few minutes to relax in and catch my breath. Broad reaching up the Needles channel to the Fairway buoy I eased *Solitaire* onto 254° by adjusting the self-steering vane and hauling in the sails as we came onto a spanking reach, day and wind both perfect. I should have stopped the motor and used the large genoa but decided to leave well alone; maybe I was lazy, but the number one genoa would have restricted my forward vision, and anyway it was best kept for future use. There was a good reason for running the engine: I needed a fully-charged battery to power my navigation lights and give me a better chance of dodging shipping. But the main reason was to reach the open sea. Already I was feeling the old freedom and no longer responsible to the laws of the land. There were no courts of law out here, and if I made mistakes they would be mine with no one else to sit in judgement. Just God, *Solitaire*, and me.

Every voyage consists of steps. A year ago, when I believed we would be making the voyage fairly well equipped, there had been only two: England to Cape Horn, then an easy step home; now the steps had become more of a drunken stagger to provide for possible trouble. First clear the English Channel then cross the equator to Ascension Island where, if the rigging broke, the Americans would help. On to Cape Town and the Royal Cape Yacht Club where I could carry out repairs. In Australia, if I had to, I could buy more food and still round Cape Horn. The Falkland Islands, even if I arrived under jury rig, would allow me to fix up something to get us home. All vague thoughts. Privately I intended sailing around Cape Horn non-stop even if I finished up eating stewed boots and barnacles. *Solitaire* might have to give up if the rigging broke, but as long as she kept going I would not be the first to throw in the towel. Not that she had any thoughts of giving up; romping along, throwing spray in all directions, alive for the first time in months her joy was infectious. I started to straighten up the cabin. The two bunks looked like a double bed, singles joined by the water containers so I completed the picture by spreading my sleeping bags across them. At the back of the containers was about a yard-and-a-half of floor space, enough for a bit of disco dancing but a tango was surely out.

124

For a moment I was taken back to South Africa and my first thoughts about sailing when I had told people I wanted a boat to carry me, my suitcase and a set of golf clubs around the world although then I had not meant non-stop. Here I was setting up another record: the first round-the-world non-stop yachtsman to carry golf clubs.

Back in the cockpit with tea and cake I watched a coastal steamer change direction to head towards us, the crew lining the decks and cheering. After waving back with the tattered remains of my red ensign I decided to stow it away and bring it out only for important occasions. The day stayed warm and pleasant, the land standing out clearly but in my wet weather gear I became tired, hot and happy, and to the slow beat of *Solitaire's* motor drifted in and out of sleep. By early afternoon we were six miles south of Portland Bill, 34 miles in five hours, not bad going considering the weighty stores onboard. Start Point light came in view at 0010 Thursday morning, July 10, our last sight of England for nearly 11 months. In the first 24 hours we knocked off 125 miles en route to Ushant; it was 75 miles away and took another 12 hours. At first I thought our navigation had been spot on. I had intended passing no closer than five miles then to bring *Solitaire* hard on the wind to cut through the shipping lanes out into the Atlantic before coming onto our southerly course, but the land drew closer and buildings, including the lighthouse, came into sight. Blast, I thought, annoyed with myself. This was downright lazy sailing, dozing when one should have been taking RDF bearings. Ushant was sighted at 2115 that Thursday, 36 hours out of Lymington, the last land I would see for 326 days. As darkness fell coded flashing lights from the lighthouse slowly worked their way to *Solitaire's* stern, then became just a loom on the clouds as man-made lights disappeared to be replaced by nature's.

Heavy shipping cut off our retreat from the possible storms in Biscay to the open Atlantic, their steady stream of lights making our sail more like a quick dash across a motorway rather than a safe withdrawal from danger. A ledge runs around the Bay of Biscay and when seas hit it terrifying waves can build up. The quickest way to get off this ledge was to cut straight across. With constant winds from the present westerly direction we would have them just forward of the mast, making for a fast passage but it meant staying inside the shipping lanes. Even so I could still snatch a few hours' sleep in reasonable safety. I set *Solitaire's* self-steering to head us 50 miles west of Cape Finisterre, 360 miles across the Bay, and slowly the lights of the ocean-going ships dropped below the horizon.

After seeing nothing for an hour I went below to eat; and then to lie on my bunk to think of family and friends. It has always amused me that on my return from a long voyage I am an immediate expert on loneliness which bears no relationship at all to being alone. Loneliness is caused by people and places and the real experts are the old age pensioners who wonder why the children call only once a fortnight and then can't wait to leave; the people with families who wake up one morning to find they have nothing, not even each other. Loneliness is staring into other people's windows at Christmastime, and thrives in railway stations, in airports and divorce courts; but you are never lonely because you are alone. How little people know about themselves surprises me; few have been alone for more than a few hours, and yet they claim they could never survive so many weeks by themselves at sea because they confuse missing someone with being alone and lonely. I did not miss my family and friends because I simply took them with me and had time to remember them and what they had said which is no different from re-reading a good book. Indeed in some strange way I became even closer to them at sea.

I had known the other side of the coin: leaving my family to join the RAF, for instance, and a railway station in Toronto when my first wife returned to England. Perhaps the loneliest experience of all is being with someone who no longer wants to be with you.

Friday morning found us 250 miles from our home port ploughing into a choppy sea in a light drizzle with poor visibility. I was still using local time in the log, navigating with RDF bearings on Cape Finisterre and dead reckoning. Once the weather cleared I would change to Greenwich Mean Time, take my sun sights and log our position every noon. The day was spent sorting out food which even now seemed to be shrinking as I stored it away. Even the number of paperbacks diminished as I sorted them into boxes. When they had been given to me I had said, 'I hope you won't mind if once I've read your book I dump it overboard'. As I normally read a book a day the idea of dumping was already forgotten. I planned to read the best first and keep them for an encore towards the end of the voyage.

The food situation was far worse than I had imagined, even though before leaving Lymington I had estimated that the stores would have to be doubled to ensure a non-stop voyage. When I started to receive presents of food things began to look up and by sailing time I reckoned I had enough to provide a meal a day for nine months. Only when everything was listed and stored did I realise

126

how serious the food problem would become after reaching Australian waters.

Stews 15·3 oz tins		Greens 10 oz tins	
Chicken	12	String beans	12
Beef	12	Peas	12
Steak and kidney	12	Mixed vegetables	12
Savoury mince	12	Total	36
Minced beef	12		
Total	60	**Fruit, small tins**	
		Fruit salad	12
Baked beans 8 oz	48	Grapefruit	12
Spam	24	Total	24
Sardines	12		
Marmite 1 lb	2		
Bovril 1 lb	2		
Jam, small jars	12		

Flour 70 lb in two five-gallon plastic containers
Sugar 60 lb in one five-gallon plastic container
Rice 60 lb in sealed buckets
Eggs 36, Onions 36 lb, Potatoes 20 lb.

Coffee and tea posed no problems, because at worst tea bags could be used twice. I had ten food parcels from Rome and Annegret, ten NATO 24-hour rations from my Dutch friend, two fruit cakes and other bits and pieces for special treats.

My diet would be easy to work out proscribed as it was by the provisions themselves and the time they would last. In the past I had baked six bread rolls every three days. Until we were halfway round, say five months, I could carry on doing that, but after five months at sea the yeast would be useless. So bread would be a basic food until Australia when any remaining flour could be used for pancakes. On the other hand rice would last for ever so it must be kept for the second half of the voyage. The voyage's first turning point would be when we passed under the Cape of Good Hope, 65 days away if we averaged 100 miles each 24 hours. Meanwhile I could have an egg every other day! Onions last well and make spicy sandwiches with Marmite or Bovril. I intended using the NATO rations early on, since they were a bonus, and the first of Rome's parcels on crossing the equator. Rivers of rain water, running down the mainsail to cascade off the boom end like a broken house guttering, would ensure a water supply. As we carried nearly 80 gallons there was no need to replenish until we were homeward-bound.

The winds were from the west just forward of the beam across a flat sea as we approached the middle of Biscay Bay with 2,000 fathoms of water beneath us. Saturday, July 12, our third day at sea, I spent adjusting the rigging and making up a new kicking strap; and I had Peter and Fanny's salmon for dinner that night accompanied by onions and boiled potatoes. On Sunday the weather brightened and I brought *Solitaire* hard onto a light force three. I should have hoisted the number one genoa but there are times when things are so perfect that you hardly breathe lest you spoil the balance and speed seems of no importance. For the first time I removed my wet weather gear and shoes and socks. Freedom! I changed the ship's clock to GMT and at 0700 took my first sun sight for a position line and made a cross on it after my noon sight for latitude. Thanks to my new sextant I had no more worries about loose handbag mirrors or whether the elastic bands would hold long enough for me to take a sight. More freedom! Catching the sun in its flight and controlling it in a slow descent onto the horizon I turned the delicate micro adjuster with reverence, like a jewel thief about to break into a safe. A perfect day with a perfect end: stew with extra potatoes for dinner.

I'm wary of saying in the log how well things are going because when you are on top of the world, and start shouting about it, someone inevitably comes along to knock you off, but my extended stay ashore had made me forget that lesson. My feet started to slip early on Monday morning after I had wakened to find strengthening wind, breaking seas and poor visibility. By noon we had two reefs in the main with the wind backing south-west, and were being pushed towards the land 30 miles away, *Solitaire* taking punishment as she tried to smash through fast-breaking waves. If we continued on our present course we would soon be in the shallower seas around Cape Finisterre. When night fell phosphorescent seas continuously buried the boat, allowing her only seconds to clear herself and gasp for breath.

Her surrender, when it came, was not because of any lack of determination on her part. On a brief visit below I found seawater streaming down the mast support and believed that the deck had cracked; it was my first panic of the voyage. I had to take the pressure off her but as I dropped her reefed sails she came beam-on to the seas

128

which slammed into her side. She rode the blows, giving ground and heeling to protect decks. With *Solitaire* looking after herself I made a closer inspection of the damage by torchlight. The mast is deck-stepped into a shoe secured by six bolts through the deck onto a steel plate and the top of the keel. After wasting time trying to find the source of the trouble I pumped out the bilges and lay down to sort out my thoughts. Had I put sealant on the securing bolts?

With dawn on Tuesday, July 15 came light and lovely north-westerlies. I discovered that the mast shoe itself had cracked but by making a plate to fit over it I felt confident we would see the last of the leaks from that direction. I was unable to get a morning sight due to overcast skies, but by noon they had cleared and the latitude taken put us approximately 60 miles west of Cape Finisterre. My log for the first six days showed 632 miles, despite making only 35 in the last 24 hours thanks to the storm; but we were still ahead of our 100 miles a day target to the Cape of Good Hope.

That night I wore pyjamas for the first time on the trip. When a few gusts of wind threw *Solitaire* off course, I removed them to go on deck wearing just a safety harness. Having dropped the mainsail, I replaced the pyjamas and snuggled back into my sleeping bag listening to the contented murmurs of my faithful companion no longer fighting the sea but living with it in peace.

Our first week at sea ended on Wednesday, July 16. By noon we had logged 750 miles. I should have reset the main; but on a broad reach, with just the number two genoa up, it would have blanketed the jenny as I had no whisker pole to hold the headsail in position and it would have slammed every time a wave passed under us. Normally this is acceptable but as the genoa was already weakened I did not want it to take too much punishment. I started to realise how different things would have been with a new number two jenny. Ah, well!

For all that, I was happier than I had been since completing my first voyage. *Solitaire* bubbled along, sharing a contentment that came from doing what you wanted to do in ideal surroundings. At the day's end a simple meal. Margaret had given me bread rolls that could be popped in the oven and baked, and as each NATO pack contained a small tin of cheese, hot baked bread, cheese and onion followed by delicious coffee, it provided all I needed. As I watched the sun set my cup and belly were full. Deep satisfying sleep! In our second week we covered 780 miles and the log is full of contented entries. It was not simply finding one's sea legs, the pleasure went deeper than that: it was a feeling of belonging, of walking into a strange room and knowing that you had been there before, of meeting a stranger and recognising a mutual bond without a word being spoken. To have taken me from the sea and placed me in a square box miles inland would have brought as much confusion as if you'd done the same thing to *Solitaire* herself. That week's log read,

'Thursday July 17, 1980. Eighth day at sea, good night's sleep. Not a cloud in the sky. Winds light from north-east three to four. Number two genoa only as, with main up, it is blanketed causing it to slam and wear. I'm not complaining, guardian angel working well. Distance last 24 hours 124 miles.

Friday July 18. Ninth day at sea. Wind about 25 degrees off the stern, should do more sail-adjusting but content to read, eat and sleep. Logged 986 miles, 112 miles in last 24 hours. Position for the amateur yachtsman, 170 miles due west of Lisbon. Big head!

Saturday July 19. Tenth day at sea. First five gallons of water used. Winds becoming lighter. Have hoisted main and tried to use the heavy aluminium pole to hold out the genoa but too much strain on the sail. Lovely warm conditions. Winds from the east, force three. Few scattered clouds. On book five. Very happy. Logged 104 miles in past 24 hours.

Tuesday July 22. Thirteenth day at sea. 0915 Madeira approximately 35 miles to port side. Starting to warm up, could be changing to shorts tomorrow. On my sixth book.

Wednesday July 23. Fourteenth day at sea, 1,530 miles travelled, 109 miles a day average, better than expected. Celebrated by using two cups of water to shave and trim my beard and wash all over. Basked in the sun in shorts with a cup of delicious coffee.

The following week brought sunburn, progress and setbacks; the first because I spent too much time in the cockpit wearing only shorts; the second when we passed 110 miles west of the Canaries; and the third started on Saturday, July 26. First the skies turned grey, giving the impression an atomic war had just finished. For a while we had a milkily faint sun, then the wind started to increase, gusting from force six to eight with *Solitaire* surfing on a broad reach, the odd wave breaking over her. I should have changed down to the working jib, but I thought I'd try for a fast sail to make up for two days' lack of wind; and make up for it *Solitaire* surely did with a run of 141 miles. Sunday night was a bit hairy with *Solitaire* still going like a dingbat, the old genoa straining out its heart to keep ahead of breaking seas. I had been checking the sails during the night with a torch, but when dawn broke on Sunday I saw that the two-inch seam along the bottom of the genoa had ripped and was trailing over the side; so I replaced it with the working jib and hoisted the main when the wind abated. The rest of the morning was spent repairing the genoa by folding the seam twice and wrapping it in the first panel of the sail. The log however showed that our mad ride through the night had given us a run of 121 miles, a ride I was to spend two days paying for, sewing sails until Monday night. From now I would treat the number two genoa as though it were spun from pure gold for use in ultra-light winds only. On Tuesday, July 20 I started to record the sails I should have had, with a feeling of having let down *Solitaire*, asking too much of her without giving her a fair chance. By noon that day the log read 2,175 miles, 86 miles in the past 24 hours. 'Conditions a little better. Hazy sky. Pretty good sights. Will continue heading westerly to clear Cape Verde Islands. Number two genoa in use with main. I'm afraid we have little chance of establishing any records thanks to our lack of sails, poles, etc., but happy to potter along in my own sweet way. Still not eating much, but thirst back with vengeance. So far have eaten four tins of fruit and have been swilling down Margaret's fresh fruit drinks. Anti-fouling coming off self-steering blade. No undercoat applied could be the reason.

Wednesday, July 30, 1980. Despite the ripped sail we have still managed 760 miles this week. Have cleared Cape Verde Islands, and now on course 220°, blue skies, lovely weather. *Solitaire* broad-reaching well. Genoa seems OK after repair. Will not mess about with poles any more but keep them for jury rigging (I hope not!) Still not eating well, another tin of stew yesterday followed by tinned grapefruit. I should be baking bread but the thought turns me off. I can't understand my lack of appetite. It could be the 25,000 miles still to travel, missing friends, concern for *Solitaire* and her lack of equipment. Perhaps it's reaction to delay in starting the voyage, or just my oversize waistline bouncing about. I'm even worried it might mean the start of appendicitis. I'm not lonely, I'm enjoying the voyage. Maybe with a few more miles under our belt I'll start eating. We have RDF signals from Cape Verde Islands so no navigation problems. New sextant works like a dream. 1340 GMT noon position 31° north, 24°50 west, log reading 2,291 miles, 116 miles in 24 hours, which could have been much better with decent off-wind sails. Will bake bread for the first time, lovely with sandwich spread and fresh onion. We are 250 miles due north of Santa Antao, Cape Verde Islands. Should clear on this tack with luck. Going well. Good old *Solitaire*.'

This was one of the longest entries I have ever made in the log. I was confused by my feelings and thoughts but by putting them into words they would perhaps sort themselves out. When I lived in Canada I had a similar experience and went off my food for no reason at all. On my return to England I found that my mother had been seriously ill then; I had not been told to save distressing me.

The damage to our only reasonable running sail was a setback. If we had nothing bigger than a working jib in the Southern Ocean we would be cutting speed by a third but none of this accounted for my unease. Before setting out I had estimated my chances on a voyage of some 28,000 miles. I believed that with the strong winds in the Southern Ocean pushing us along we should make our 100 miles a day, say 270 to 290 days at sea. The difference between a broad reach in force five to six using a genoa (140 miles on a good day) and a smaller working jib (95 miles a day) was 45 miles. But the longer we spent at sea the more chances there were of the rigging going and I was uncertain how long the masthead connections would last. From the records of other Cape Horners I knew I could expect at least one roll over which *Solitaire* might survive, but not two or three. I had known this before leaving and accepted the risk, so I could not understand my new apprehensions, or why I had become so finicky over food, eating tinned stews and fruit which should have been kept for the later stages of the voyage.

July 31, 1980 saw the start of the fourth week at sea with flying fish rising from under our bow. I have no idea why they were ever so called as they don't flap wings but simply leap along the tops of waves to get up speed, then launch themselves into the air to glide on delicately transparent wings. There's intense pleasure in watching them, particularly when a setting sun showers them with colour and I feel like apologising as *Solitaire*'s eager surge displaces them in a shower of noise and panic. By night they fly into the sails. In our early days I would crawl about in the dark trying to reunite them with their families but they damage their wings too badly to return them to the jungle that is the sea. I remember holding one, its eyes popping, gasping for breath, or should that be water? I heard a voice say quite clearly, 'don't just lie there, say something,' and was even more surprised to realise the voice was mine. I believe they lock away people who talk to fish. This Thursday there were six on deck, a record. I have read of seamen breakfasting off them, the fish fried in butter with browned potatoes and onions to accompany them. Had they been served that way I would have eaten them with relish, but having heard their death struggles my entry in the log simply read, 'six large flying fish came onboard during the night. Very sorry, I hate to see anything die.' By now I was on my eighth book, the *Master Mariner*, one of the finest books I have ever read. Its pages would become worn as I read and re-read it.

'*Friday, August 1.* Grey skies, sun about to pass directly over my head,' was all I noted. It would be two or three days before we could get a decent sight for latitude. We would then be facing north when we took our noon sight instead of south, which I would have to watch out for when applying declination, remembering my last boob and my subsequent appearance in a Brazilian maternity hospital. I made a large note of the change in the ship's log.

Next day *Solitaire* was approximately 100 miles west of Santo Antao in the Cape Verde Islands. Because the noon sun was still above us I did not try to pinpoint our latitude; what interested me was *Solitaire*'s longitude, 27°45'W. After leaving England *Solitaire* had headed south in a gentle westerly curve to sweep around the tip of Africa and the Cape Verde Islands. Now that we were well clear, we could start to swing back for our first major turning point, the Cape of Good Hope.

On Sunday, August 3, the sailing was marvellous with force three easterlies, the waves small compared with the past weeks perhaps due to their coming from the coast of Africa and feeling its protection. Blue skies with a few scattered clouds to make it interesting, but no dolphins. I remembered reading that Japanese fishermen were killing them off by driving them ashore. Bloody Japanese, I muttered. I started drinking tea again after two weeks of not being able to stand the stuff. And a further note, 'remember, clown, that the sun is now north of us'.

Next day calm conditions gave me a chance to lean over the side and check the anti-fouling. There was no slime or growth, although the paint had changed in colour from a reddy brown to light fawn, the seas having stripped the top coats. I checked the motor, sprayed it with oil and turned it by hand for the first time in three weeks. I was saving it for the doldrums we would soon be entering. As I was taking my noon sight my old pals, the dolphins, showed up for the first time, so the bloody Japanese had not killed them off after all. To prove the point they came back again that night to put on a special performance. The last two days of our fourth week brought lighter winds and slamming sails in a high swell, a final day's run of only 44 miles. Nevertheless we still managed to make good 692 miles for the week, 2,983 miles in 28 days. Not bad going.

On the last day of our fourth week something terrifying happened. We sighted our first ship for two weeks, not that that scared me. I started the engine and the fan belt broke. That did not worry me either as I soon fitted a spare. By afternoon the wind had dropped completely and I was forced to lower all sails when I found that I had read 19 of my supply of books. None of these things caused much concern. But what did petrify me was that I nearly committed hara-kiri by ripping open my belly. It was one of those stupid things you do when not concentrating on your job. I had been trying to cut a piece of canvas with a particularly sharp knife and, like a fool, was cutting towards me. The knife slipped and next second I was looking at a six-inch pocket I had made in my shorts. When I removed them I found I had blood running down my stomach. Fortunately it was only a scratch, but half-an-inch deeper and I could have been in real trouble. Three inches lower and I would have been the laughing stock of Birmingham.

'Why did you give up sailing round the world, Les?'

'Well I cut my Thing off!'

Perhaps one should not curse the Japanese even if they are slaughtering your friends.

We had now reached the stage in the voyage when life begins to speed up. I'm often asked how it is possible to spend week after week living in boredom. Most people on holiday find that, although the first week goes fairly slowly, the longer they are away the faster the time flies, particularly if they are enjoying themselves. It's the same with sailing. You wake and perhaps bake bread, take the morning sight, have a coffee, read a book. After noon sights, the main meal. More reading in the afternoon followed maybe by a bit of a snooze. Watch the dolphins play with a last coffee. Another day has passed. Work and storms interfere with this fast-moving clock. In moments of danger it stops to freeze you in a lifetime's terror.

Wednesday, August 6, 1980, the start of our fifth week at sea, our latitude 12° north of the equator and longitude 27°W. Another 720 miles to Rome's first parcel for crossing the line. We start edging to the east to sail down the middle of the South Atlantic, reducing the longitude to around 20°W. No point in heading for the Cape of Good Hope because a large, high pressure area lies off the coast of South Africa. Better to stay clear of its calms, not that there would be much chance of a direct passage anyway. Since leaving England the winds had started from the west and slowly veered, moving clockwise to

134

north then north-east giving lazy days of sailing with stern winds. Now they were blowing from the east. The doldrums would bring confusion to the winds. It would be possible to have days, even weeks, of calms to be broken by squalls, short sharp gales from every point of the compass. Flat seas, angry seas. You paid your money and took your chances. Once through the doldrums the wind should settle, blowing constantly from the south-east, and the Cape of Good Hope, our next turning point.

Whenever I think or write about the weather my thoughts seem always to affect it. After writing in the log that we would soon be in the doldrums we lay in a sea of grey steel; every now and then someone would shake its corner making it swell and ripple. We spent the night with just the reefed mainsail up, even so there was much slamming and banging, and for all the noise we covered only four miles, and lost two of our three buckets. How I could be so stupid as to lose two buckets one after another I have little idea. The handle came off one as I was trying to bring seawater on deck and fell like a leaf through the transparent blue water; without more ado I tied a second bucket to a rope and dropped it over the side with the same effect. Neptune must have thought it was raining buckets but at least he had a matching pair. The last bucket now took on a new importance. Although I have a flush toilet onboard, once in the Southern Ocean, with its high seas, it would be more sensible to close it down at its seacocks and use a bucket. Fortunately the remaining bucket was stronger than its companions so should render valiant service. Thursday night brought a vicious electrical storm with black, racing clouds, breaking waves, skin-smarting driven rain; and our first visitor, an unwelcome one, a butterfly, in the middle of an ocean, bringing only sadness with it for its certain death. As with land birds they last only a day or two as you try to feed them, but they always die. Sometimes you wake in the morning and they are lying stiff on the cabin floor. At other times they disappear and you feel thankful. Days later you move a book or a chart and you find their lonely grave. It's difficult for people living ashore to understand the effect of such a loss. Unlike the human race a single small bird becomes your responsibility, you share in its suffering, it's the only living thing with you.

We had been in the storm for some time. Angry seas tore furiously towards us breaking over *Solitaire*'s bow and flooding her decks. The night sky, lit by a full moon and hundreds of bright stars, was brilliant. It is only when you watch awhile and notice how quickly the moon and stars are being switched on and off by racing clouds, fronts rushing through like stampeding herds, do you understand. I reduced to two reefs in the main with working jib and decided that before enjoying a hot drink below I would first clear up the tangled mess of halyards and sheets in the cockpit.

I bent to pick up the ropes and came up with a screaming monster in my hands. Jesus Christ! I flung it as hard as I could. Only when it hit the boom and its wings splayed out did I realise it had been a storm petrel. I watched it fall into the sea with horror. I had committed murder and the loss of this bird was to stay with me for the rest of the voyage. I would be reminded of it every time I saw other birds gliding past *Solitaire*'s white hull or landing in her sheltered wake.

Saturday, August 9. One calendar month out of Lymington. Still making progress in squalls and confused sea with runs of 60 to 100 miles a day. Hard on the wind most of the time with plenty of tacking back and forth. One night when we were hard-pressed I heard two loud bangs like a gun going off. I dashed on deck thinking the rigging had parted. By the time I had reached the cockpit, the thing I used for a brain had already accepted the fact and was calculating how to reach Ascension Island under jury rig. The rigging still stood and I could find no reason for the double bangs. I had heard aircraft flying through the sound barrier and this had sounded much like that, a cannon exploding followed by its echo. Possibly it was a high-flying jet or even a satellite passing overhead at 100 miles a minute, making unflattering comments as we crawled across the planet trying to make the same distance in a full day.

At this point in my log I made a remark about Francis Chichester. To be honest I've never been a lover of your conventional hero. My type are like Rome's sister, Terry, who had a cancerous breast removed just before I sailed. That did not stop her walking down to *Solitaire* or laughing at the party. During the second world war I wanted to be a pilot and envied those I saw walking the streets, wings on their breasts, popsies on their arms: the few who saved the country. But the real heroes for me were the poor devils who spent year after year in mud, covered in lice, until one day some idiot told them to stick their heads up and get them blown off. They received no medals, were never called 'heroes' but only because they were not of the few, but the many. Bloody millions of them.

Chichester, Robin Knox-Johnston, Alec Rose were people I admired for living full lives. Apart from Slocum I had read only one of their books but because I found Chichester's *Gypsy Moth circles the*

136

world among my paperbacks I read it to check my positions and times for different stages of the voyage against his. In the ship's log that day I noted that it had taken Chichester only 22 days to reach that day's position against *Solitaire*'s 32. No way could *Solitaire* equal *Gypsy Moth*'s times. We would set no records; our satisfaction would come from finishing something we had started.

Solitaire continued south through confused seas and grey, overcast skies, tacking back and forth, dropping off the top of waves, decks awash. Concerned half the time because we carried so little sail; worried the next because of sea falling from under us, an anxious eye on the weakened, straining rigging.

For a few days the sun sulked behind heavy layers of mist and clouds, the odd smile it managed so fleeting that it could have been imagined. Dead reckoning put us 300 miles above the equator. Since leaving England I had used one chart only to cover the 3,500 miles we had logged, one of the luxuries I had indulged in! It would have been safer to have had charts of the islands we passed, but a chart of even a harbour will cost as much as one covering several thousand miles. Chart two would have brought looks of disbelief from any self-respecting yachtsman. While in Darwin, Australia I had photocopied one of Terrell's charts covering the Atlantic from 10°N to 37°S, say 2,820 miles. It was in two pieces as it was too large for the machine in one go and made of thin, coffee-stained, pencil-marked paper. Alas, it did not even cover the 200 miles below the Cape of Good Hope which I needed to help avoid the fast-flowing Agulhas current that sweeps from east to west under South Africa. The lack of food, equipment, sails and charts I had accepted before starting out. My log complained constantly about this, but it was only my way of letting off steam. In the heavy seas *Solitaire* had started taking on water from the forward compartment and I needed to pump out her bilges twice a day. Once through the doldrums, with their squalls and confused seas, things would improve; but I felt useless as I watched the boat try so hard for so little progress, one working her heart out while the other sat around long-faced and complaining. That apart, my health was good. I still worried about small things like appendicitis, breaking a leg or simply needing a heart transplant. That's another thing I find amusing, being asked if it would not be safer to have two aboard for such emergencies. In fact all you do is double the chances of trouble.

The end of our fifth week found us 296 miles above the equator, 18°24'W. We had just finished one long tack to the east. Our next

137

would take us back to around 20°W. That week we logged 632 miles which sounds pretty fair until you look at the chart and find that all you have made good in the last 24 hours is 90 miles due east when you want to be sailing south! After 35 days we had travelled 3,615 miles, still holding onto our 100 miles a day, but only just.

In week six more living things, sea birds, started to join us, this time brown in colour. They needed constant winds for survival; perhaps, soon, we would be out of the doldrums: I was fitter than I had been for two years and my spare tyre had been worn away by *Solitaire's* constant movement. My skin had toughened so that I no longer worried about sunburn, and I had settled to my planned diet, baking bread every third day to accompany the eggs and onions. I was conscientiously leaving the food that would last until the end of the voyage.

The biggest lift to my spirits was that soon we would cross the equator and have Ascension Island within easy reach, and Rome and Annegret's first parcel to open. I started to look forward to that day with an enthusiasm I had not experienced since I was a small boy. My log became full of the event. On Monday, August 18, 1980 our noon sight showed us to be just 24 miles north of the equator. I could have cheated and opened my present then, arguing that with

● **The contents of that precious first parcel for crossing the equator outward bound**

138

● **The first whale to be spotted this trip making a friendly advance in the South Atlantic**

luck we would cross over the line before midnight. However I had promised myself that no present would be opened until the specified time. Nevertheless it slept with me at the bottom of my bunk. We crossed the line at 2200 GMT that night. Inside the parcel was a lovely tin of ham, enough for two meals, a tin of fruit, another of coleslaw, a can of beer, chocolates, sweets and a letter from Annegret. My log read, 'just opened my parcel. Over the moon with contents. I've been cutting down on eating my tinned food but tonight a special treat of cooked ham and coleslaw. I'll be drinking to Rome's and Annegret's health with the beer they supplied. Makes me remember the many times they've had me round to dinner. God bless them! Have taken pictures of parcel with Rome's camera.' Rome had lent me his, together with three rolls of 35mm film. Then Peter Tolputt had turned up with another easy-to-use camera and more film. It was one of the things I just had not even considered because of the cost; later I was to be pleased that my friends had.

At the end of our sixth week we were 4,155 miles out from Lymington, (the direct route by chart was more like 3,800). That week we had logged 540 miles, but by direct line, Wednesday to

Wednesday, noon to noon, only 440 miles. Despite the lost 100 miles there was much to be grateful for: the winds had settled from the south-east and were allowing *Solitaire* to sail close to them on a southerly heading. During the day I saw my first whales of the voyage, brown monsters that broke the surface half-a-mile away, blowing water vapour, disappearing, reappearing, bothering no one. That day's log finished on a cheerful note, 'now for fresh bread, the last of yesterday's ham, fresh onion and soup. Blue sky, scattered white clouds, winds south-east. A good book. It can't be bad.'

August 22. For the first time in nine days we have covered 100 miles in the right direction. Looking at the chart and reading the daily logged distance you would have thought the rest of the seventh week was sailed in the same blissful conditions: our pencilled course flew arrow-straight for 602 miles, never wavering from our intended longitude of 22°W. The noon positions were equally spaced, 86 miles, 81, 87, 87, 85, 77 miles. Only on reading the log do you realise how bad the conditions were. *Solitaire* has sailed in far worse seas, in fact the winds barely blew over force eight (34mph). Maybe it was just worry over the gear and the distance still to go, but I have never known my nerves so raw. For the first time I began to wonder what the devil I was doing out here.

It started that Thursday night with the entry, 'could be past Ascension Island in a few days if sails, gear and guardian angel don't let us down. Winds gusting, *Solitaire* dropping off the odd wave.'

'*Friday.* Changed down to working jib during the night, winds gusting force six. Lots of square waves give impression of climbing upstairs. Can't increase sail area because of slamming. All to be expected in this area with its high swells. Still managing to head south (slowly), blue sky, scattered clouds, 86 miles in 24 hours.

Saturday. No sights possible, very rough sea. 81 miles in 24 hours. Still working jib and one reef in mainsail. Charts show force four winds from south-east. Holding approximate course south, but sea throwing *Solitaire* all over the ocean. One minute becalmed, next screaming winds. Bilges constantly filling. Very little sleep with all the bouncing. Nerves get on edge when *Solitaire* is knocked about. Nothing I can do; if I reduce sail further we won't make any headway.

Sunday. *Solitaire* still being thrown about in high angry seas. Very high winds during night with impressive waves. Double-reefed main. Little sleep, moments of fear. Worrying to have *Solitaire* drop from the top of high waves. What will the Southern Ocean bring?'

Monday. Pram cover over main hatchway broken (can be fixed

140

later). Only making 80 to 90 miles a day. I can't push *Solitaire* harder in these conditions. Panic this morning, one clock was five minutes adrift, the other had stopped. This shaking can't be doing them any good. Changed batteries just to be on the safe side and wrapped them in foam. Thank goodness for the portable radio; at least I can get time checks and reset the clocks. Bilges full of water again. Have not been eating well. Impossible to go in cockpit with these breaking seas. No room to move about below with water containers covering the cabin floor. I spend hours grasping the chart table and looking astern. *Solitaire* feels as if she is smashing through doors without a chance to run at them, a steeplechaser with obstacles too close together. Not being given time to recover from one jump before finding the next racing towards her. It's just bash, bash, bash with no chance to build up speed. Suddenly to find herself plunging down into pits being brought up short with shattering jerks. The sea is shaking with mirth at our confusion. Mast and rigging alternately slacken and stiffen.

Tuesday.   High wind squalls started at 0300. Seas high and angry, double-reefed and working jib. Not my idea of sailing; one of the times I'd rather be watching TV. It's three weeks since we had a good day's sail. Anyone who thinks this is pleasant is mad, mad, mad.

Wednesday, August 27.   Noon and the end of the worst week at sea for a long time. During the week we passed 500 miles west of Ascension Island. It was while moored to a landing barge in 1978 that I'd been scared by some of the biggest swells in the world. The pilot book puts them at more than 30 feet. I'm confident the seas are due to similar abnormal conditions. To find such conditions in an area that the chart suggested were reasonable does not augur well for the areas shown as bad! It's difficult to work on deck and gazing over the stern from the cabin for hours hardly helps. Reading makes the time fly and helps shut out unpalatable thoughts, and it's warm.

When I was not frightening myself looking down at breaking seas I would sit on my bunk with a book or sort out the mysteries of the NATO food parcels. I found some plain chocolate that went down well and suddenly became aware that I was the proud owner of ten tin openers!

The eighth week at sea was a week of contrasts. The south-east winds from the Cape of Good Hope would soon start in a clockwise direction, veering first to south, then south-west, finally becoming the roaring forties 1,500 miles to the south. While they made up their minds what to do they swung back and forth, giving beautiful tropical days with time to sort out leaks and damage. I repaired the pram cover and the forward escape hatch, putting a beam underneath it and securing that to its hinges to ensure it would not fly open in a capsize. Anchor and chain were stored in the stern locker which also contained the exhaust outlet. Were the anchors to smash the exhaust seacock the sea would flood in faster than I could pump it out so I brought the anchor below and secured it under a bunk. Sorted and repacked our supplies, doing everything I could to prepare us for the storms ahead. The end of the week came with one of the trip's biggest surprises.

I was on my bunk with nose stuck in a book, enjoying one of the better days and thinking I might wander on deck for a noonsight, when I heard the most horrible sound as if we were in the middle of a herd of groaning, pregnant elephants. Ye gods I thought, the nearest elephant should be 2,000 miles away. I threw the book to one side and dashed on deck to find a few 20-ton whales making improper advances. We were in the middle of a school of these magnificent creatures, some so close that I could have jumped on their backs for a free ride. I rushed below for a camera and managed a couple of shots as they departed.

In the eighth week we logged 627 miles, 5,384 miles in 56 days. We had fallen behind our 100 miles a day. The Cape of Good Hope lay east-south-east, 2,220 miles away. The ninth week started well when the winds went round to the north-east. For the first time in weeks we had a free wind blowing at three to four and came onto a broad reach with the poor old number two genoa and a full main. We glided along without the old smashing and banging; then the sheet broke and the genoa flew free. However I soon had it repaired and we continued on lazily. Further south, a shirt joined the shorts I had been wearing during the day. At night I no longer lay on top of my sleeping bag but climbed inside for warmth.

September 9 celebrated two full calendar months at sea. Back home they would be making ready for an English winter while we sailed into a South African spring. I became more of a crew than skipper, following quietly whispered commands as I soothed Solitaire's occasional displeasures, taking the strain from her weak body. 'I'm hard pressed,' she would complain and I would reduce sail. 'You're driving me too hard.' I would ease the self-steering so she could take the waves on her quarter.

The ship's log grew repetitive, grey sky – grey sea – grey skipper. Beating into choppy seas, I really am sick, sick, sick of it. But repeti-

142

tion breeds over-confidence and stupidity. Returning from changing a headsail one stormy night I put on the kettle for tea and reached down to remove my safety harness – it wasn't there!

At the end of our ninth week at sea we recorded a distance of 776 miles, but the tenth was far worse with only 646 miles to show for it. I'm sure the slow progress was mainly my own fault although the pilot charts did not help too much. Tristan da Cunha now lay 550 miles south of us. The South African high pressure area with the light winds and calms was still to port. *Solitaire* had started to sweep in a gentle curve to the south-east to pass well under the Cape of Good Hope. It's a mistake that many people make in life: you see your target and head straight for it. I should have used my golfing experience and made a dog's leg of it, heading further south towards Tristan, perhaps entering the roaring forties before turning south and making for Australia. If it was a mistake to take the direct route it was one I could live with. Many better qualified yachtsmen had made the same mistake in this area. The pilot charts proved unreliable; instead of skirting the high pressure area we must have sailed into its outer fringes of calms. Well, as Gracie Fields used to sing, every cloud has its silver lining. The silver in our present cloud was that the calms allowed us to do more work sorting things out.

During my tenth week at sea I started to use words in the ship's log that would have been unusual on our first round-the-world voyage: 'nerves' and 'depression'.

Engine Run for one hour, diesel and water containers stowed.

Food and water Should have enough food to reach New Zealand, a quarter of water used.

Temperature Now 70°F, (90° on the equator), so am wearing sweater in early mornings, and really need sleeping bag at night.

Anti-fouling A few goose barnacles, seems to be working well.

Solitaire In better shape than when she left England apart from number two genoa.

Crew Has moments of deep depression, worrying about *Solitaire*'s gear and sailing under jury rig. Although Cape Town is 1,500 miles away and it was hoped to make it in 70 days, so far we have been lucky and I have no reason to complain of our progress. So why do I feel so depressed?

The end of her tenth week brought new records for *Solitaire*: on her first voyage her longest time at sea had been 69 days, the greatest distance travelled around 6,000 miles. These had now increased to 70 days and 6,614 miles, not an earth-shattering achievement but for the speck moving across the oceans it was important. We were sailing into the unknown with new problems that would have to be overcome. Somehow *Solitaire* had to survive the gales of the Southern Ocean, somehow round Cape Horn. If at that stage I had been asked my main concern I would have answered that it was my own part in the voyage not *Solitaire*'s. The urge to round Cape Horn was as strong as ever and nothing would stop me, but I could not understand my mental condition. Unless I could sort myself out I was likely to end the voyage in some form of mental strait-jacket.

A long-distance sailor on his own must be many things, captain, cook, navigator and doctor but, most important of all, he must be able to understand himself and recognise his own limitations, mental and physical. It sounds easy, but people living ashore pay psychiatrists thousands of pounds a year to understand themselves, despite having family and friends with whom to discuss their problems. *Solitaire* and I were cut off from the outside; we had no transmitter with which to make the odd call, 'I say, old boy, I wonder if you could help me? I'm in the middle of the Pacific Ocean and I've gone off my rocker'.

When I left England everything seemed so straightforward. I

- **'We ran with screaming winds'**

would sail around the world for my own satisfaction and would survive for my own love of life, the desire to see family, friends, and England again. To make the voyage I would be prepared for tiredness, cold, hunger and long periods of fear. On my first voyage I had been frightened only for short periods, mostly during the Brazilian episode. I believed I could stand this type of fear for five weeks or so which I felt would not attack me until I reached the Southern Ocean. But after crossing the equator and beating into seas that normally would have given little concern I had become frightened, my nerves rubbed raw for no apparent reason. At one stage I thought I knew why: some of Chichester's descriptions of the conditions I could expect were so vivid that I put down the book vowing not to read it again until we were safely home.

Solitaire's rigging might not survive a capsize, but all who had made this voyage had suffered at least one. What then?

I bitterly resented my lost year thanks to the sail manufacturer and the unjust outcome of the court case. That I felt so apprehensive so early in the voyage proved that, at heart, I was not brave. At sea I would turn anything I could to my own advantage, not an unusual trait. It's surprising how after spending their lives without a God, many become aware of him when in need. I used friends, 'what would Rome or Rex do in this situation?' Others had survived, why shouldn't I? Ah, well, time would tell.

Each day brought danger nearer. In the 11th week we logged 470 miles, six more than the previous week, in the same old mixture of calms and gales. The worst started on Friday, September 19, 1980 when we ran with screaming winds, under working jib only, while rogue breaking waves slammed into *Solitaire* ripping one of the heavy canvas spray dodgers in half. What worried me was that I was over-reacting to conditions we had been through a dozen times before. On my first voyage I had been unconcerned, indeed would have listened to the wave's onrush with interest, putting aside my book for a few moments to hold onto the bunk, awaited the impact, then continue reading. If I was reacting in comparatively safe conditions how would I cope with real danger when it came?

I spent two days repairing the torn dodger. On September 22 I recorded our longitude as 00°15′E, in other words we were 15 miles east of Greenwich. Once past that date line the working of our navigation would alter. And September 23 was the anniversary of my Brazilian adventure when I had started to think about a second voyage around the world. This time I would make the correct adjustments when using navigation figures. As yet I had no desire to contemplate a third voyage!

By the end of our eleventh week we had sailed 7,084 miles and, as the log reported, 'had rode one gale during the week and were becalmed for its last 12 hours. New Zealand will take forever at this rate. Plenty of sea birds about from small petrels to aircraft-sized albatrosses. Visits from my dolphins after staying away for two weeks. Nice to have my friends back. I have been photographing my fellow travellers with Rome's camera. Still managing to read a good deal. Thank goodness I enjoy books so much. Long days in these conditions would seem endless if you could not lose yourself in other times and places. I'm reading one of Annegret's books called *Hawaii* by James A Michener. Have hardly put it down for three days. Anti-fouling still working well apart from barnacles on the rudder, propeller and a few on the topsides. More than satisfied.'

The twelfth week started with Cape Town 720 miles to the east, a good week's sail to safety, steaks, hot baths and warm beds. We could be tempted only under jury rig. Once past Cape Agulhas I could open Rome's second parcel. I planned to round the Cape 300 miles south of Africa for two reasons: to keep well below the west-flowing five-knot Agulhas current, and to avoid the 90 fathom continental shelf. The seas, 12,000 feet deep beyond the shelf, would be kinder. The problem in sailing so low was that my charts ran out at 37°S. I covered the extra 180 miles by sticking an odd piece of paper to the chart and pencilling the lines of longitude and latitude onto that. *Solitaire* was about to round her first objective on a scrap of writing paper.

The week was wet and miserable, navigation made difficult by heavy rain clouds. The winds played tricks or were the pilot charts chuckling quietly having suggested winds from the north to southwest force five to six? Any of these would have been acceptable but *Solitaire* had to battle against winds on her nose – from the south. The odd day we had stern winds brought our first thick fog. At least we knew that no other ship would be within a couple of hundred miles of us, ghosts of lost square riggers excepted, for only a pigheaded fool would venture so far south. It was fitting that the thirteenth week should be the worst I had ever spent at sea, the week I thought I had lost *Solitaire*, the week that I lost my affection for England. Since leaving home I had been bitter, frightened and depressed. The bitterness I could understand but not the time I was taking to get over it. The court case had upset me deeply. Weren't the upper classes, the lords of the manor, supposed to look after the peasants? I could picture *Solitaire* beating up the English Channel, her red ensign streaming in the wind, with a certain pride in completing the long haul. But after 90 days at sea the picture had started to fade. And this was the day the storm started. The questions I had asked myself for nearly three months started to be answered.

Thursday, September 30. Our noon sight showed we were about to enter the roaring forties, 250 miles below South Africa on latitude 39°S. The morning winds, around force four, came from the north and were cold despite my heavy sweater, foulweather gear and sea boots. It was not just the cold that had made me put on the full gear; the day before one of the water containers had burst and soaked both my sleeping bags so that the only way I could sleep on them now was by wearing oilskins. I had been forced to stop using the old number two genoa a week before as we had been getting the odd gust that would have ripped it in half. We were reaching under working jib and main with one reef which had gone in when I had started to feel uneasy; although, cold apart, it seemed a perfect sailing day with a few scattered clouds in an otherwise clear winter sky. A swell started to build up and the hairs at the base of my neck began to stand on end. During the afternoon wind strength remained constant but the sky turned from blue to black in less than two hours as though coats of film, one atop the other, had finally turned sea and sky to jet. There were no breaking waves but the swell increased until the sea roller-coastered.

Normally I would have taken down the main but for weeks I had been over-reacting. Was I at it again? The only headsail strong enough for these waters was the working jib which meant I would have to keep the main up for as long as possible or the voyage would last for ever. Apart from running out of food we would be too late this year to round Cape Horn safely.

If we were to have any chance of maintaining schedule the old rules of the game would have to go by the board, starting with the first and oldest: reef or reduce sails as soon as you think about it. That afternoon I was trying to read *Hawaii*, so uneasily that I found I was scanning the same line again and again. Although *Solitaire* carried no wind speed indicator I know that during our first voyage outside Cape Town we survived winds in excess of 100 miles an hour (as later reported by ships damaged in the area). I know what they sound like in the rigging, what effect flying spray has on bare flesh. This storm did not frighten me as it lasted only a few hours and the

147

waves had little time to build up. My main fear was being run down by a tanker.

When the storm struck – without warning – it was with the force of one of these tankers. This was an assassin's bullet hitting before the victim heard the sound of the rifle. You're alive, you're dead, you're upright, you're on your side. There's a whisper in the rigging, then it screams. A panic-stricken dash to the deck to find the mast nearly in the water. Both spray dodgers have gone; the self-steering wind vane is pushed fully over and is vibrating against its stop. Sails are filling with the sea, their seams about to split. Both sheets are released; for a moment part of the boom and main disappear over the side and God knows what's happening to the headsail for I'm blinded by wind and spray. I claw my way to the mast and tug on the main's luff but the bloody thing will not come down as the pressure on the sail is jamming the slides. Finally I succeed in lowering it. I should return to the cockpit and pull back the boom inside *Solitaire*'s guard rails but if I don't do something about the headsail I'll lose it. Quickly I lash part of the main to the boom, nothing below me but white broken water. Once the jib was safely down I could return to the cockpit and retrieve the boom dangling in the sea. I tied a rope onto the wind vane and around my waist. When I released it from the self-steering unit it tried to take off like a rocket bearing me with it. I promptly had second thoughts and in the end managed to take it below where I wrapped it in a protective blanket.

Now I could think about my own needs. Luckily I had been wearing my wet weather gear on deck, the first time I had ever sat around with sea boots on. As I like to feel *Solitaire* moving under my bare feet, wearing sea boots is like going to bed with a woman wearing boxing gloves. I had had no time to put a towel around my neck so my shirt and sweater were saturated and as I realised this my teeth started to chatter. Then the risks I had taken without a safety harness dawned on me and the chattering increased in tempo. Tea would have tasted like ambrosia, but first I had to fit a shock-cord onto the self-steering rudder to prevent it banging back and forth, and I needed to retrieve the 30 feet of line on the log. One spray dodger was again ripped in half, the other hung over the side, held by a few odd ties: both had to be removed and stowed. At that stage I was merely thinking of just another stormy night at sea. I would put extra lashings on the sails and rubber dinghy, pump out the bilges, then settle down for a night's sleep lying ahull.

When the storm started I was confident that *Solitaire* and I had all the answers for hadn't we faced every situation, every type of wind, every type of sea? All sails were down. It would be hours before the seas built up and became dangerous. Lord, what poor misguided fools we are!

Without knowing it everything I had done so far had been wrong. I was working to rules from the first voyage, rules that said that provided everything was secured and there was a good depth of water, storms were nothing to worry about. There had been exceptions of course, when the storm brought fierce lightning, which I hated, or we lay off a lee shore or in a shipping lane. Then I would prefer to be sitting in front of a roaring fire, a dog at my feet, contemplating a stroll to the local for a pint with the lads. The rules from our first voyage were as outdated as trying to fight an atomic war with conkers.

I was starting to suspect even the preparation for the voyage. Money, or its shortage, decided what we could or could not take with us, apart from my wet weather gear which was the best I could find, being the type used by Rome on his Whitbread round-the-world voyage. It seemed to have everything I wanted, the jacket heavily quilted for warmth, the double-lined trousers had substantial plastic zips which in turn were protected by flaps. The trouser tops fitted snugly under armpits and the jacket had a built-in harness on to which the safety line clipped. The outfit cost around £150; it was money well spent. The first problem showed up when I tried to wear sea boots which I normally don only when close to English waters. Even at night, although my feet would be cold, I felt no pain and certainly had no frost-bite worries. In the old days in emergencies I would dash on deck naked apart from the safety harness. Now when I was needed there in a hurry, I first had to tuck my long trousers into my socks, pull on the outer trousers, put on sea boots then work the trousers back over the boots, tightening the tapes. The linings slowed down the drill.

I hit another snag trying to get back on deck – I could not get through the hatch! In storms I would lock myself below and wait for a lull, then slide back the hatch cover, remove the top board, step out and replace them. It was fairly easy provided you were not wearing padded jackets. After leaving England I had fitted two bolts to the top board to prevent its loss during a capsize. To clip on my safety line I had to lean over the boards to reach the U-bolt; it made feel sick. *Solitaire's* movements were so violent and the winds so strong that I had to keep my back to them and so powerful was the spray that I feared for my sight.

149

It had become very dark and I was becoming painfully aware that my feet were turning to ice. There was more than a foot of water in the cockpit. With the spray-dodgers lost, seawater broke over us more quickly than we could jettison. It forced its way up my wet suit and over the top of my boots, freezing my legs and feet.

Somehow the trailing log line with its weight and spinners had wrapped itself around the self-steering gear, and as it was nearest I decided to make a start with this. Waves continued to break over us and an aching body joined my frozen feet: for the first time my body temperature worried me. In winter's seas you might be lucky to last half-an-hour if you fell overboard off the English coast but if I went over in these latitudes I would have only minutes. For the first time I realised that many of *Solitaire*'s features that had worked perfectly on the shake-down cruise were a disadvantage in these seas. The skirt that ran around the top of the cockpit, three to nine inches above the deck, had prevented seas streaming into the cockpit. Now it also trapped and held them until *Solitaire* was thrown on her side and the seawater partly spilled out. The cockpit that had been perfect in Tahiti, Australia, and South Africa was far too large. Instead of holding parties of ten or twelve happy guests it was now holding tons of freezing sea water. The cockpit was made from a single moulding with a 14inch seat halfway down its side dropping to the cockpit floor. The seats lifted to provide locker space. I had modified the two lockers so that the channels around their covers were self-draining. On the first voyage the covers were held in place only by shock cords since I could not afford anything more expensive. I had attached half-inch ropes onto the hull, fed them through holes in the locker tops and secured them in this Mickey Mouse fashion. When leaving the cabin you stepped onto a centre shelf which held the mainsheet traveller. An adjustable pulley and block ran from the traveller to the end of the boom, holding the latter in place.

The main trouble with leaving the cabin was my heavy clothing coupled with *Solitaire*'s violent pitching and tossing. What I really needed was something to hold on to and use as a lever. The pram cover frame was far too weak to suffice.

I centred the mainsheet traveller which meant that the ropes to the foot of the boom passed in front of the hatch, giving me room to squeeze by and be used as a hand hold. All I wanted now was to strip off my wet clothes and brew tea, but once I had struggled below I remembered I still had to pump out the bilges. So back I went into the cold, the breaking seas and the howling winds. Then

150

came the bliss of holding the kettle on top of a dancing stove to produce a life-giving, hot, sweet cuppa. When I started to think about changing my wet clothes I realised I had insufficient replacements and those I had were the wrong type for these conditions.

The suitcase I had carried around the world in 1968 now contained one suit, a dozen assorted nylon dress shirts and sports shirts and five sweaters. Rex Wardman had also given me a lovely thermal jacket for Christmas, and Margaret a pair of quilted trousers. She had driven me to the Surplus Army and Navy stores in Southampton where they were selling off old ex-navy diving suits for £10. Unfortunately when we arrived they had sold out apart from one moth-eaten suit that was falling to bits. It was a green fur-lined one-piece affair that I tried on and spent an enjoyable half-hour running around like the Incredible Hulk frightening customers.

On the way back to Lymington I had asked Margaret if I could put it on again and lean out of the car window. At the time we were driving through the Southampton Red Light district. 'You do and I'll throw you out,' was Margaret's reply. The thought of a green man knocking on doors in that area had me chuckling for days. Funny how the mind wanders when you are cold and tired!

In a storm like this we could be badly damaged at any time so I had to keep on my wet weather gear. Even if I changed my sweater it would be dry only for a few minutes before soaking up the water from my jacket. The best I could do was take off my boots, empty them, and wring out my socks. After that I wedged myself on the floor behind the water containers and pulled a sleeping bag over my head to retain some body heat. At first it was too cold to sleep but, as my clothes reached body temperature, I started to drop off only to be brought back with a shock to find myself sitting in two inches of water covering the cabin floor. The bilges were full again despite my pumping them dry within the last two hours. We must have taken in well over 100 gallons in that time.

I waited for *Solitaire* to steady herself, slid back the hatch cover and put my head out into a shrieking, screaming world of horror. Massive seas were crashing on my poor boat, trying to bury her alive, giving her no chance to recover, to fight back. The cockpit was full of water. The lockers that I had made self-draining for the odd breaker were under boiling seas that would be gushing under their covers and running forward under the engine mounts to fill the bilges and then, more slowly, the cabin itself.

Given any other choice I would have gladly taken it. Instead I

151

picked up the bilge pump handle and pushed through the hatchway. Timing it wrongly I dropped up to my waist in freezing water. My boots filled and the seas worked up inside my legs. *Solitaire* rolled and half the water left the cockpit. I banged my face on a winch and started pumping. Mom and Dad would be warm in bed now. God, I'd love to see them! I kept on pumping. Sometimes I thought I had nearly finished only to have another wave break over us. For all I knew the cabin could now be completely filled with water, the dryest place in the boat precisely where I stood. If we were sinking, how long would it take to reach the sea bed, two miles down? The water grew denser the deeper you went. There were aquatic creatures down there without eyes, would they turn as we slipped past? *Solitaire*'s white shimmering shape . . . a lonely figure dressed in red still attached by life-line. How long would it take? Hours? Weeks? Would *Solitaire* blame me for letting her down? Was being tied to your mistakes for eternity a definition of hell?

Once the bilges are dry the pump passes air only and the handle needs little pressure to move it. When I believed I could be no colder, that I could no longer keep my eyes open for another second, the pump started sucking air. I staggered below, took off my boots, wrapped a towel round my feet and boiled a cup of tea, warming my hands over the flame. After squeezing the water out of my socks I put on my boots again longing for sleep and sank onto the floor behind the water containers where I found myself in deep water. Two minutes later I was back in the cockpit, pumping. The night lasted a millenium. Each time I thought I could close my eyes more freezing water streamed through the cabin floor. The seas were replacing the blood that ran in my veins, the heart pumping ice water to the brain faster than I could jettison it over *Solitaire*'s side. It was numbing, stupefying. At times I was unaware whether I was the bent body in the cockpit or the huddled shape on the cabin floor. At last the sky lightened with dawn. After so long in a black, screaming hell, eyes blinded by stinging salt water, I would see again.

I slid back the hatch cover and for a moment wished I had remained blind. This could be no storm; for storms had waves, the stronger the winds the faster the waves, the higher they reached. Waves marched majestically across oceans like regiments of soldiers. But this was no ocean, just a shrieking horror of unmoving mountains reaching up to a black sky. Suddenly a flock of small grey birds with outstretched wings in the distance tried to scramble up the lower slopes like so many little old ladies with raised skirts splashing through puddles. As we dropped deeper into the valley the howling wind seemed to slacken and *Solitaire* settled onto the sea's green floor. Over there was the perfect setting for a thatched cottage.

The real nightmare was that despite the deafening sound nothing moved. Then the top of a mountain turned white as though covered with snow and an avalanche descended, slowly at first, very slowly then, gathering speed, roaring down on us trying to kill its trespassers. I slammed the hatch shut, expecting *Solitaire* to be rolled over and over like a puppy at play. When the avalanche reached us there was not the crash I had expected. Instead the sea flowed over us, carrying us sideways for a few hundred yards before it released its grip and promptly ignored us, a matchstick in its path. For a moment *Solitaire* staggered upright in its wake and again I opened the hatch. The air was filled with stinging sleet. *Solitaire* lay buried in the snow, her outline marked only by the stanchions that stood up like sticks on a cold winter's day. *Solitaire* rolled, spilling half the water over her side.

Surely nothing could live in this mad world. Waves would kill us

● **The beginning of the storm**

without noticing. Somehow I had to get the boat moving to give her a fighting chance. The first thing was to replace the self-steering wind vane consisting of nylon stretched over an aluminium frame, no more than three feet long. But the screaming wind tried to tear it from me and it was a fight just to hold it. There was no way I could get it working.

I considered putting up a small headsail to try steering myself. But if I was at the helm I would be unable to pump. Even if I managed both the winds were still from the north so I would have to run south. And land to the north was more than 300 miles away. If I lost the mast it could take weeks to reach land under jury rig and any attempt to round Cape Horn would have to be put off for a further year. Suddenly I was aware of something I had been putting off all night. I had to use the lavatory or rather the bucket, for the lavatory was out of the question since I'd have been thrown around like a pea in a tin whistle. But the bucket and chucket method was far too risky. Then I thought of an idea that was to serve me well for the rest of the voyage. Plastic bin liners was the answer. In order not to foul the bucket I used one of these, putting a couple of sheets of newspaper in the bottom for added strength. After sealing the bag I waited my chance and threw it into outer space assisted by a wind blowing at more than 100 miles an hour. I believe it was the first time this type of payload had been put into orbit.

It was time to look after *Solitaire* again. I went back into the pumping routine, removing boots and socks, a cup of tea, then more pumping. During one of these periods in the flooded cockpit something happened that I would have given anything to reverse. Time seemed to slow. Whether it was the contrast between the howling winds and the stationary mountains I don't know. At times the illusion was so complete that I felt I could step off *Solitaire*, leaving her freezing cockpit and run down the green valleys, exploring their secrets. The only thing that stopped me was the knowledge that she would not be there awaiting me when I returned.

Another sequence of thoughts started after another wave hit us without the following swell that would have rolled *Solitaire*, partly emptying her. I found myself repeating, 'there was no need for this, no bloody need at all'. A week before leaving England a friend had given me a new bilge pump which sat in one of the lockers because I had been unable to afford the piping with which to fit it in the cabin. Had it been installed I need never have stepped outside; my clothes would have remained reasonably warm and I need not now

154

be standing in misery, tormented by sodden clothes, cold, tired, battered and bruised.

I started to understand the bitterness I'd felt since leaving England, a country I had loved as long as I could remember when to hear a choir singing *Land of Hope and Glory* would cause tears to spring to my eyes. I'm not sure when I started to lose this feeling for my native land. Perhaps it was the court case. Perhaps it was after watching an Englishman run for his country and collect a contract to sell a product on TV he had never used. Perhaps it was just that I'd grown old, seen too many lands, met so many friendly people. Whatever the reason the loss was mine and *Solitaire*'s. I regretted it, but the rest of the voyage would be made without the help of patriotic choirs.

At three o'clock on this day we had been storm-wracked for 24 hours. I had been unable to sleep during that time, I was soaking wet, had swallowed a gallon of tea but had eaten nothing. In the past I had survived much longer without food or sleep, but my main worry was the cold as I had no previous experience to fall back on. There was no point in putting on warm clothing when once in the cockpit I would be as wet as ever. I thought about leaving the stove turned on. We had three 32lb-bottles of gas onboard, and as on the last voyage I had used only one bottle every six months there was some to spare but essentially I wanted to keep the extra gas for rounding Cape Horn. In any case nearly all my time was spent outside the cabin.

After discovering that I could not replace the self-steering vane I started to consider how to live in the Southern Ocean by correcting my mistakes. I should not have tried lying abeam to these seas or removing the self-steering wind vane. I must always keep up enough sail to control our position to the waves. I could have done little with the self-steering gear at the time as the vane was much too big for the wind strength which demanded smaller, stronger, vanes. I had three plywood vanes from the first voyage which were unusable in their present state. The blade-holder supported only about four inches at the bottom of the vane and pressure had to be distributed; so I cannibalised one to supply feathering pieces for the other two vanes and finished just before dark.

Meanwhile the winds were still coming from the north at hurricane strength so that I could only sail south, deeper into the roaring forties. All I could think of was getting into the Indian Ocean past the Cape of Good Hope. Once there we would be less restricted and could ease our way out of these howling, desolate seas. With luck we would find warmer weather and give ourselves a chance to dry out and renew our strength for future battles.

I spent another miserable night praying for the winds to abate. If my guardian angel could not arrange that could he please swing them to the west, giving *Solitaire* wings to leave these watery mountains. No craft could continue to take such punishment and I felt like the condemned man waiting for the trap to spring. As I watched the sea break on us I could see the hangman reaching for the lever. Again we were lifted and carried effortlessly on a boiling cloud; and then, after a few hundred yards, released as a cat plays with a mouse. Sometimes I was permitted to pump *Solitaire* dry before it sprang again, sometimes I was halfway through the hatch dreaming of wrapping my hands around a hot cup and rubbing back the circulation into cold feet when there would be a roar and once again we would be buried.

I was reminded of the Germans outside Stalingrad during the second world war. Ill-clad in their normal dress uniforms they died in a Russian winter. I remember one upright corpse standing frozen, staring through dead eyes. Someone had stretched out his arm and pointed a finger, turning him into a road sign. At least it seemed a useful way to end your life. When I stood in freezing water up to my waist, unable to move my arms or open my eyes, I wondered if my last effort should be to point to Cape Horn as a service to following seamen. Instead I kept on pumping.

Dawn came and somehow we struggled through another day. In fact it went better than the first. Although the storm had not abated I felt it could get no worse and as we had survived one day, why not this one? The cat and mouse game the sea played with us was wearing a bit thin. It was not the dying I feared or even the method. I would rather drown than lie for years, suffering without hope, watching my family and friends walk past a shell for which I had no further use, hearing a priest quote from a book as unreliable as yesterday's newspapers. Yet there is some supernatural force, for without it *Solitaire* would have started on her journey to the bottom long ago. I had no wish to die. There were many things I wanted to do, horizons still to be scanned. And I wanted to see my family once more, just once more, so I kept on pumping.

During our third night of storm I realised that with the dawn *Solitaire* would have to take over the responsibility of keeping us alive. In the beginning I had worried that I was not eating, now nothing

156

mattered but the pumping. Sleep no longer bothered me; sleep was something that happened between life and death. If I closed my eyes now I would die. Dying bothered me but not sleep. All that mattered was the pumping.

With the dawn I would fit a new wind vane and hoist a headsail. It would make no difference if the winds failed to drop or if they still blew from the north. It was all I could do, my last card. All that mattered was the pumping, but tomorrow I would be able to pump no more. Most of that night I spent in the cockpit no longer crouching to avoid the breaking seas. *Solitaire* and I became one, moving in a numb stupor, beaten to our knees. *Solitaire* staggered defiantly while I worked the pump readying her for more punishment. My *Solitaire* had started as an idea in South Africa, something I would use as a common prostitute for my own pleasures after which I would pass her on to the highest bidder. My love affair with her had started on a reef off the Brazilian coast and our courtship had been long and happy. For two days we had celebrated our marriage, a ceremony far more binding than the others I had been party to. In sickness and in health, that was true, but till death us do part, never. We would survive or die together. I would never leave her.

Dawn arrived with no drop in the wind's strength, the sky still black although I could see over the mountain peaks to the limited horizon. Without their protection the wind screamed in the rigging, a loose halyard vibrating against the mast like a runaway machine gun. In the valleys I fooled myself into thinking the storm was tiring then *Solitaire* would rise to the sound of the stuttering gun.

When I had pumped her dry again I started to fit the small plywood vane drilled with an extra hole to take a rope which I tied round my wrist. I waited my chance and fell into the cockpit with it pressed to my chest. I gripped the pushpit and started to straighten up and for a moment thought I was in a January sale with a mass of bargain-mad housewives tearing at me as though I held the crown jewels. After nearly being swept over the side I managed to rope myself close enough to the self-steering to use both hands to slot in the vane. The blade was adjusted so that its edge faced into wind. The shock cords were taken off its rudder and I freed the locking device. After more than 50 defenceless hours at last we had a means of fighting back. By this time *Solitaire* badly needed pumping out again, but bloated by our small victory I decided to haul up a headsail. Both working and storm jibs were already hanked on to the twin forestay. The problem was which was the better to use.

157

When *Solitaire* left her home port she had been very much like a five-year-old family car entered for a round-the-world rally. Since sails take the place of a gear box in a car we could claim she had a five gear box. First and second gears were new but the third and fourth gears had been used already in one 34,000 mile rally and both were damaged. As *Solitaire* had no large running sails perhaps you could claim she had no fifth gear. The bolts that held the gear box in place – the rigging holding the mast – were the wrong type and had been used already on one world trip. And we were about to try to drive out of a land that existed only in a madman's nightmares. The trouble was the mountains were ice-covered and the screaming winds would try to push the car sideways. Our tyres were bald and we had no brakes. Any car driver would say the answer was simple: at the top of the mountain change into bottom gear to control the descent; at the bottom change into second and drive yourself back into position ready for the next mountain. But even in perfect conditions, with both sails in position, it would take me around ten minutes to make the change. With waves continuously breaking over the decks I would be lucky to hoist a sail in half an hour.

If I used the bigger working jib there was a chance it would rip to pieces on the exposed summits, or the rigging and then the mast go over the side. If I used the small storm jib there would be no power to control *Solitaire* in the calmer valleys. I had heard of yachtsmen running under bare poles in storm conditions but had been unable to understand how it was possible in a rough sea. I had heard of running with twinhead storm jibs poled out, but in these conditions it would have been highly dangerous to dive down one of these mountains. At the bottom the yacht's bow would dig in and the stern would come over like a pole thrown at the Highland Games. If you came off the dead run and the wind moved from over the stern one of the running sails would back. Heaven alone knew how long it would take to get sailing again, not to mention possible damage. I decided to use the bigger working headsail. True it might blow out but far better that that happen than be rolled out of control in the troughs.

The 30 minutes I reckoned it would take to hoist the working jib turned into an hour and was completed in an air of misery and bad language. At one interesting stage three waves buried *Solitaire* one after the other. The position I took up while this was happening was flat across the deck, my hand grasping a safety rope on the side over which the seas were breaking. Both legs had gone through the lines

158

on the other side and were hanging in space. Over the past three days I thought I had experienced every possible way sea water could enter my sea boots. The new method was more complicated and took a little longer, but its route was ingenious. It entered by a hose pipe forced up my sleeve, went over the top of my trousers and down my leg.

After scrambling back to the cockpit I slackened the sheet and hauled up the sail. At first I thought it would tear itself to shreds, but after adjusting the sheets the sail, its seams straining, started to pull *Solitaire* stern to wind. Then I adjusted the self-steering and main rudder to hold us on a broad reach, the only possible way I can sail *Solitaire* in such conditions. The main idea is to go down the waves much like a surfboarder, at an angle. The self-steering rudder is not always strong enough to control this type of sailing as the waves take over, trying to push the stern around until the boat lies beam on to the waves. I use the main rudder to control this, its power holding the skid.. At the bottom of a run the main rudder helps bring the yacht back onto course ready for the next breaking sea but every manœuvre has to be just right. Too much correction with the main rudder puts you on the other tack. Usually then the backed sail will tack you again, but the strain on the sails and the forestay sets teeth on edge. Getting it right took frightening minutes whereas normally the time taken is minimal but never before had *Solitaire* tried to sail down the side of a mountain.

Things looked up. Seas that had broken over us now pushed us forward in wild breath-taking surges. For minutes we would race in spray and a tumbling mass of white water. Advancing cliffs lifted us like a soaring eagle and we balanced above their snow-capped peaks before plunging down into emerald green fields, often out of control. *Solitaire* rushed forward, anxious to find peace and lick her wounds.

I fitted the trailing log line which curved in a half circle, the weight and spinner like so many flying fish skipping over the ocean's surface. The plastic compass was returned to its cockpit holder, our course south-east. The northern winds drove us deeper into the roaring forties, but we were clawing our way east, working our way around South Africa and its Cape of Storms. Dead on my feet I went back to pumping the bilges. Over the past three days I had often thought that I was finished, that I could pump no more, that I could no longer survive without sleep. The seconds had turned into minutes, to hours, to days. Now if something went wrong I felt I

159

could still carry on. I just hoped to God I didn't have to prove it.

When I started this voyage I thought that I could stand being afraid for five weeks and that at the end of that time I would still be sane and able to carry out normal everyday functions; it was a thought based on my past experience. I had not anticipated a situation when for three days I would believe every moment, every breath, could be my last. Oh well, three days gone!

After a while *Solitaire* settled down to look after us both. A few rogue waves still hit our beam; now and again we would have six or nine inches of water on the cockpit floor, but no longer were the seas flooding the lockers. Below I stripped off every stitch and felt the glory of rubbing myself down with a dry towel, putting on a clean shirt, trousers and sweater and for a special treat donned Rex's thermal jacket. My wet weather gear I turned inside-out to drip dry, had a cup of sweet tea and found some chocolate which I ate at the chart table with my head in my arms . . . my mother was shaking me. I was 14 years old and it was time to get up, go downstairs and eat my morning porridge, time to put on my overalls and join the bus with half-asleep men, nodding, coughing, grey-faced men moving through their lives like zombies. I did not want to leave my bed to live this nightmare, tried to pull my legs into my chest to squeeze so small I would never be found, but my mother was banging my head. My mother never bangs my head. I shocked awake, moving through 40 years in a second, exchanging one nightmare for another *Solitaire* was in the teeth of a wild beast viciously shaking her from side to side, and she was leaning the wrong way. On this new tack I had slipped sideways. My legs had jammed under the chart table and my head was beating itself to death on the engine cover. When I had freed myself I stood on weak legs trying to take in through blurred eyes what was happening. I slid back the hatch cover and looked into the face of a breaking wave, slammed the hatch shut and staggered back, only to fall on top of the water containers. From there I heard the wave hit and saw jets of water penetrating the hatch boards.

I threw off my jacket and sweater, for there was no point in getting them wet. It was then that I felt *Solitaire* start to swing onto her correct heading. Her backed headsail and the self-steering were striving to bring the wind on the right side of her stern while the main rudder that had been set to prevent her skidding and broaching would be working to keep the wind on the wrong side.

For a lifetime she seemed to balance on a knife-edge, rolling from side to side. I watched the breaking seas through her windows first on one side then on the other, feeling like a gambler who had bet his last dollar on the turn of a card. If she fell one way I would not have to go on deck but could have a hot meal. If she fell the wrong way I would have to put on wet storm clothes and return to hell.

If *Solitaire* could correct a backed headsail on her own it would mean I could sleep knowing she would take care of us. I tried to hedge my bet by throwing my weight behind it, bouncing off the starboard side as if I was trying to drive a hole through it. The bet paid off and *Solitaire* came back on course. The working jib swung across the deck with a shuddering whack whose vibrations ran through us for a full 60 seconds.

It was nearly noon so I must have been asleep for some four hours. Quickly I inspected the deck and headsail by holding onto the mainsheet and popping my head around the pram cover. All seemed in order, although the sail looked as if it might rip at any second. The storm jib was still tied securely to the pulpit. The ropes securing the mainsail to the boom were holding.

But the conditions remained terrifying. Any man who claimed that he was unafraid I would have dismissed as a liar. *Solitaire* still slid down the sides of mountains and at any moment might broach. Once she had rolled on her side at speed she would simply keep rolling. Even if we survived it would be difficult to reach land without a mast. After we had passed South Africa our chances would improve as the motor could then be used to stagger us into port under jury rig. At the moment if we tried to reach land, the Agulhas current would sweep us into the South Atlantic.

I was afraid, but that was something I could live with. My fears were less constant than they had been in the past three days, coming and going now like storm clouds. There were even moments of pleasure: not to be soaked and frozen was a delightful change. There are ways of finding sanity even in a world of horror. You can do normal everyday things, like paying more attention to the trivial than you would at home, despite the fact that your house might turn upside down at any second. Part of this fantasy were the cabin floor carpets. One of life's pleasures is sinking bare feet into a soft pile carpet when you leave your bed, maybe because as a boy it was always cold boards. Carpets can be used as a barometer, to gauge the weather and your own feelings. When they are warm and dry you are in trade winds and spirits are high. When they are damp you have the miseries. When they have six inches of water over them you are scared silly. With six feet of water your worries are over.

At present there are two pieces of carpet on the cabin floor. One I can do nothing about since it is beneath the water containers. The aft carpet I decide to wring into the bilges, at the same time taking up the inspection cover to see how much water we have taken in the last four or five hours. *Solitaire*'s capacity to hold water below her cabin floor consists of a sump at the back of the keel that extends to its bottom, holding approximately 20 gallons. In normal conditions I pump it out once or twice a week if only to remove smells and any gas that might have leaked from the stove. There is room for around another 40 gallons on top of the lead keel, bringing the water level to about five inches below the floor. With this 60 gallons on board the bilges require pumping in any bad weather or it will splash through the inspection panels.

If in the Southern Ocean we took no more than 120 gallons a day we could manage quite well; pumping first thing in the morning and last thing at night would be sufficient. When I checked the bilges I thought we could last another two hours before going on deck. Later I would fibreglass in the lockers, but that task I wanted to leave until as late in the voyage as possible. With both lockers sealed it would be difficult to dismantle the bilge pump to clear the blockages as I was unable to reach the sea cock on the exhaust outlet.

For the first time since the storm I started to think of food and decided on a tin of stew with peas, and grapefruit for afters. I used to show my friends the logs of previous voyages, some of whom remarked how strange it was that in storms my writing became so much neater. I think this is similar to wringing out carpets; I try to hide my true feelings even from myself. If I write clearly I'm unafraid.

My log for that day read, 'managed to start sailing at 0500 hours GMT this morning. Working jib. Seas quite high and breaking. Self-steering holding reasonable course. Badly need sights for navigation. I don't want to go too far south because of ice. At the same time am concerned about the Agulhas current.'

After another stormy night the next day's log contained even fewer words. 'Still storm conditions. Rain, high seas. Not very nice.' During the night the winds dropped and dawn saw us becalmed in a massive swell, the sky still hazily grey and suspect. I started to clean up the mess and dry the carpet when I received a kick in the stomach. The ship's log records, 'now for the bad news. Sea water from the exhaust pipe has flooded back into the motor. I have drained the oil from the sump and turned over the motor by hand to try to clear the pistons. No spare engine oil. So in a day or two will use the old oil when it has settled and try to start the engine. This voyage is not going too well at the moment.'

In fact I took off the side plate of the motor, first removing the starter. The day was spent turning the engine by hand to wash out the pistons with diesel fuel. As it worked its way through to the sump I cleaned it with toilet paper. And I had counted on the engine to carry us at least 100 miles if the rigging gave way! I checked the seacock on the exhaust pipe but it seemed to be tightly closed. By afternoon I felt I had done all I could; so I re-assembled everything hoping that my first voyage experience of having to make do without the motor was not to be repeated.

Soon after I had finished drying the carpet strong, gusting winds returned to confuse us all: the sea, *Solitaire*, and the self-steering. Finally they settled to their old habits and direction, like some monster that had dropped off to sleep for a few hours and had wakened irritably, roaring its displeasure. The heaving seas took fright and ran before it with spray flying. Within a few hours we were back in the same old conditions, chased by white cliffs, surging forward on rolling surf; and I was back to kneeling on the bunks, my head hard against the cabin roof, trying to see the mad outside world. The one consolation was that my constipation was a thing of the past. Now my only concern was that there would be enough plastic bags to last the voyage.

On Tuesday, October 7, 1980 we had been in the storm for nearly a week and *Solitaire* wallowed in high, breaking seas. However there were a few gaps in the clouds and I managed to log our position, 40°42′S, 23°55′E, 42 miles into the roaring forties, 360 miles below Cape Agulhas. The winds had backed from north to west and now before *Solitaire* stretched the Indian Ocean, a pencil mark showing that we had rounded our first cape. For some days the thought of opening Rome's second parcel had tantalised me, not just for the goodies inside but for the friendship it represented. Its opening would record another milestone on our journey. I would not cheat, no matter how much I wanted to look inside because that would mean I was giving way, and as that was not on I spent the day on my bunk with the present, looking at it, touching it. In the afternoon I managed to get a further sight which proved that we were indeed well past the Cape; so I opened the parcel and used its contents for a special meal, finishing with two squares from a block of chocolate. The card enclosed I pinned above my chart table, the start of a new

163

practice. Henceforward each card or letter stayed on show until replaced by a new one whereupon the old went into the ship's log.

Our thirteenth week at sea had proved to be our worst. *Solitaire* had been in conditions I would have said no ship, let alone a yacht, could survive. Looking at the chart *Solitaire* had been in the worst possible position when the storm started with hurricane force winds from the north whose speed increased as they swept down the western coast of South Africa. Off the Cape of Good Hope they would hit the Agulhas current moving at up to five knots in a contrary direction. *Solitaire* had been lying in a massive east-flowing swell when the storm reached her. I can't see what more ingredients could have been added to make a storm worse. Our survival inspired confidence that we really were going to make the voyage nonstop, that we had learned from my mistakes. The old book of rules for sailing a yacht around the world had been ripped to shreds and tossed over the side, old loyalties being replaced by new. The depression I had felt since leaving home I could at least understand. *Solitaire* and I were not making this voyage with the help of England, but in spite of its laws and bureaucracy.

Week 13 ended with our easing into the Indian Ocean. Our latitude dropped to 40°S, on the very edge of the roaring forties, the log showing that we had covered 8,099 miles with no major damage. The log for Thursday, October 9 read, 'three calendar months at sea. A good day, in fact one of the best.' We had continued to work our way slowly north trying to find calmer conditions so that I could work on the motor, dry out *Solitaire* and take a deep breath before the next stage of our voyage.

Our prayers for calmer seas must have been a bit too strong since we spent the day with virtually no wind in a temperature shooting up to the mid-seventies. *Solitaire* rolled half asleep, her decks decorated by carpets, sleeping bags and wet weather gear. Our spirits went through the roof when, having replaced the sump oil, the motor burst into life. I ran it for an hour, then turned off the engine water intake and allowed it to tick over for a minute to clear the sea water from the block and exhaust pipe. I felt that most of the water had found its way into the cylinders not through the seacock but because the exhaust pipe had not been drained.

All in all it was a red-letter day. One great pleasure at sea is listening to music: the BBC and American Overseas Services play a few hours a day. However once you are within a few hundred miles of a coast you can pick up local stations. I now had the South African

Capital station flooding some old favourites into *Solitaire*. That night another special dinner. I baked bread and covered the crusts with pâté from Rome's parcel, finishing off the menu with sliced onions. They had lasted for three months and I now had only two left, the last of my fresh vegetables.

I lay on top of a dry sleeping bag, wearing dry trousers topped by a dry shirt and sweater . . . listening to music from another world! We had retreated from the roaring forties and were now 84 miles beyond their reach. Tomorrow, refreshed and rested, we would drop south again not to do battle but to assuage the sea's anger. Never again would *Solitaire* lie helpless without sails or self-steering.

The next cape was Cape Leeuwin on the west coast of Australia, 4,500 miles away. Above latitude 40° the chart indicated westerlies (over our stern) around force five to six, with 17% gales indicated. Below 40° gales went up to 20% although it was not this that decided my sailing above the roaring forties; it was that the extreme limit for icebergs during October-November was just below this latitude. I already had experience of sailing in cold seas rounding the Cape of Good Hope and was not keen to repeat that misery.

The man who made the chart must have smuggled it out of a sewer or the Houses of Parliament; had I completely reversed his wild claims for the next 2,000 miles they would have been closer to being right. The projected stern winds of force five to six came on our nose gusting three to four. No calm periods for this area were indicated, yet at least once a week we spent a day bouncing up and down in a 30ft swell completely devoid of wind. The game the charts were about to play started with an innocent log entry, 'grand morning, warm 60°F, clear blue sky. Light winds from the east, (the way we want to go). Smashing music still from South Africa and making the most of it before it fades. Some sail repair work this morning. Reading Annegret's book from the parcel, James Michener's *The Source*. Winds increased to force four. Full main and working jib. Would use number two genoa but must save it for later. Now for spam and tomatoes from parcel, bread from yesterday.'

Next day a short entry read, 'no sights. Back to beating into steep seas. High wind squalls. Two reefs in the mainsail. Grey sky, raining.' And for week after week that's how it continued. Winds increased to gale force and always from the direction in which we were trying to point. *Solitaire* sailed under grey skies through drizzle and breaking seas. Now and again she would find a smooth patch

165

of ocean and gather speed only to drop off the top of the next wave, mast and rigging a-shudder.

For days I was unable to get a sun sight. The winds were pushing us north, but with all the Indian Ocean to play in there was no danger from bad navigation. Lack of progress was the main worry. Despite my shortage of sails I had expected to make 100-120 miles a day in following winds, whereas our best run was 80 miles and that not in the right direction. I dare not go too far north as, apart from extending the distance, we could lose a helping current.

Fear was not part of the reason. The waves that came towards us were normal if high marching, the only problem was dropping down the other side as they went through. We started with full main and working jib heading east-north-east against a wind from east-south-east! After three or four days it would increase from force three to four, which caused us to reef. On the sixth day it would veer for a few hours; and when in the perfect direction for us it would drop altogether, leaving us becalmed in a confused sea. Then, surprise, surprise, it would hit us as a gale from the north-east! Although angry and confused, the seas had no time to attack *Solitaire* in force.

We have three reef points on the mainsail, the third of which I do not use as it turns the canvas into a minute trisail. The slab reefing boom has only two reefing ropes through the boom, so if you want to put in a third reef point you have to release and use one of the other ropes, and standing on deck at night in a gale is not the right time to attempt this operation. Having been caught out once, whenever we became becalmed I would put in the third reef and nine times out of ten it paid off. The self-steering with its small wind vane was always in use and *Solitaire* was happy pointing into waves. The odd one might push over her nose causing seas to break over her deck, but few entered her cockpit. The temperature was back in the sixties and the cabin, if damp with so much rain, fog and drizzle, was not unbearable. And I no longer had to wear sea boots.

I was back to reading my books and baking bread every third day. Wet weather gear was unnecessary apart from when I went on deck. Most of the time I lay on my bunk, a sleeping bag covering my legs. For hours I would look out of the main hatch watching a variety of sea birds; soaring albatrosses, with their 10ft wing span, I could enjoy all day. Despite my moans and groans I was satisfied with the voyage so far. I would have liked the wind to have been from over our stern, and I wished we had more sails, and more food . . . but

166

we were progressing slowly. Life could have been worse.

Week 14 passed like the hands on a faulty clock: *Solitaire* trying to reach 12 o'clock while winds from two o'clock meant we could only make 11 o'clock. The hands stuck for four days with winds gusting between force three and six, then they moved slowly to six o'clock and over our stern. Just as *Solitaire* was about to say, 'thank-you-very-much' they died, leaving us bouncing around in a confused sea after a run of 556 miles. We would curse their sense of humour, to which they would reply angrily from ten o'clock with racing clouds and screaming breath.

In week 15 time passed by like the seas cascading down our decks. The course adjustment on the self-steering broke, and was mended while the clock ticked on. On Friday, October 17 its fingers registered our hundredth day at sea.

Week 16 saw 565 miles logged and on Friday, October 24, 1980 the heart that ticked away the seconds of my life celebrated its 55th birthday, sometimes faint, sometimes strong, now it beat with *Solitaire*'s. It slowed and raced and would stop with hers. Some 1,200 miles from South Africa, in winds gusting up to force seven, the south-easterlies pushed us further and further north. *Solitaire*, a lonely speck 360 miles above the roaring forties, forced her way to Australia, trying to edge back south to pass under its west coast. It was time for Rome's third parcel and I prepared a special dinner on a dancing stove, eating it with a birthday card propped on my knee, dreaming about those at home.

Week 17 saw us pass the 10,000 miles' mark with 746 miles logged, the best for some time. For a few days the winds behaved as the charts indicated, gusting force six to seven from the west, showing how badly I needed a big headsail. I had up the double-reefed mainsail as long as I could, but when strong stern winds arrived they over-rode the self-steering luffing *Solitaire* off course into them. We slipped back to 517 miles in week 18, often becalmed, and the winds, when they came, were more from the west. I started to appreciate the height of the Southern Ocean swell. I had regretted not having a new number two genoa but from now on there would be few days when its absence would not be mentioned in the log as we passed our fourth month at sea. Then I discovered our first crop of gooseneck barnacles under the stern and found pimples on our white-painted topsides, doubly annoying because I had spent good money I could ill afford repainting *Solitaire*. I could have saved time and labour by buying more sails or food instead. We sailed 200 miles north of the small, uninhabited Amsterdam Islands which lie just above the roaring forties although I had intended to sail below them. The south-easterlies decided otherwise. Australia was now 1,800 miles away and we started to pick up their broadcasts. On Monday, November 10, I heard that Ronald Reagan was the new US President. More importantly I found we had used half of the 80 gallons of water with which I had set out.

In week 19 we clocked 746 miles, surpassing the 120 mile mark on a couple of days. For the most part the winds obeyed the charts and came from astern, which meant we could pick our course; so I started to slip south to pass under Cape Leeuwin. The end of the week saw us just 150 miles above latitude 40° where I changed our first gas bottle which meant we had two left. One worry, now that I was down to my last spinner, were the albatrosses chasing it, trying to take a bite. I threw them some stale bread which they spat out, screeching that I had tried to poison them, and went back to spinner chasing. The last thing I really wanted was to drive them away, as they were one of my main sources of entertainment. Cape Leeuwin was now some 800 miles away; it was time for another parcel.

As I had no chart of Australia I thought I should do something about it, especially after Rome's concern about my lack of navigational aids when I left England. I had said it was something to worry about tomorrow; and tomorrow was now today. So I used the chart of the Indian Ocean, changing the figures of longitude to suit Australia, plotting all the main D/F stations and joining them up to make the coast-line. If week 19 was good, week 20 was bad. At the end of it we had been at sea for 140 days logged 12,616 miles since leaving England and were just about to drop under Australia's western coast. But it was the week in which I found that we had used up more than half of our flour; and that 45 of our 80 gallons of water had gone, although I tried catching water off the mainsail in one downpour with some success. All the good books had been read but I started to re-read them for the second time around; what with my marriages and voyages it was something I was making a habit of.

I started to pick up Perth radio station, including their weather forecasts but they gave little help. Their temperature was in the mid-sixties, whereas ours dropped as *Solitaire* was about to enter the roaring forties again.

Then we began to pass through areas shown with nine percent gales on the chart. They were right about the storms if not about their direction (as when we were about to round the Cape of Good

168

Hope), for we had gale force winds from the wrong direction, this time the south-east, at the wrong time.

We were still about 360 miles from Cape Leeuwin which lay to our north-east. For the last three days we had sailed in rain without sun sights, relying on dead reckoning. At one time I thought the wind was veering and reduced to storm jib and headed directly towards Cape Leeuwin, the best course *Solitaire* could hold. It was a bad storm and we took on a good deal of water from starboard. The cockpit started filling again for the first time since leaving South African waters. There was no panic as only the odd wave broke over us and it was far from freezing; indeed on deck I did not even bother to wear sea boots. It was more a case of annoyance than fear.

Weeks earlier I had traced a course to sail under Australia, to re-enter the forties; and since the middle of the Indian Ocean we had made good this track. Now, at the last minute, we were being pushed north towards land. After two days the storm dropped and we were becalmed 250 miles below the Australian coast with 80 miles to go before I could open my Cape Leeuwin parcel.

Week 21 started with a good heart, force two to three winds coming back from the north-west. A warm day with a flat sea and ideal for fibreglassing the cockpit lockers and the bottom board in the main hatch, it was a job I had put off for a variety of reasons. The first and deciding factor was that all across the Indian Ocean I had only to pump out the bilges once or twice in good weather, perhaps three or four times in storms. When I had glassed in the rear locker permanently it would be difficult to open the exhaust seacock. True, it could be reached from inside the boat, but only with a tight squeeze and wasted time.

The main locker that ran down the side of the cockpit was immediately below where the bilge pump was fitted. To clean the pump the locker cover had to be removed in order to hold a spanner on the inside nuts and turn the screws on the outside at the same time. The pump had jammed often; even a piece of matchstick would do the trick! It could be serviced through a small door by the engine compartment but then you had to clamp vice grips onto the nuts and make your way back to the cockpit, with screwdriver, at least three times. Not something I wanted to try on a roller coaster. I was thankful it had not jammed during the Cape of Good Hope storm. The hatch bottom board could have been screwed in place and then fibreglassed. With a following sea both boards had to be left in place but one of my pleasures was that on a good day I could

169

remove the two boards and watch the birds perform – in fresh air.

On Thursday, November 27, 1980 I started to turn *Solitaire* into a submarine by spending the day fibreglassing-in the cockpit locker. In future it would be hard to repair the bilge pump, but with the mouth closed of the biggest intaker of sea water there would be less cause to use it.

At 0100 GMT that Friday we were scheduled to be due south of Cape Leeuwin in 38°39'S, 260 miles below the Cape and 81 miles above the roaring forties, 12,656 miles and 142 days out of Lymington, time to open my next parcel and enjoy a special treat of steak and kidney pie, peas and powdered potato. My friend's letter was ceremoniously pinned above the chart table, replacing the birthday card which went into the ship's log. The final entry in the log that day read, 'Rome, Annegret. Thank you – God bless'.

Solitaire now dropped south to sail under our next cape, off Tasmania. I wanted to pass approximately 120 miles below the island at latitude 46°S, putting us 360 miles into the roaring forties. If yachtsmen had been surprised to see *Solitaire* rounding the Cape of Good Hope on a piece of writing paper they would have been even more confused to see her sailing past a red ink drawing of Australia set in the middle of the Indian Ocean!

My pilot charts were unsuitable for navigation as a notice at the top of each stated and a further few words stopped my putting too much trust in them: 'Founded upon the researches made in the early part of the 19th century by Matthew Fontaine Maury, while serving as a lieutenant in the United States Navy'. I felt I owed Matthew an apology for thinking he was a member of parliament. I must have had him turning in his grave even if he had been buried for a century or more.

Using such charts is like playing a game of chess with a crooked gambler while blindfolded. They are made up of little squares similar to those on a chessboard, each square containing the percentage of gales and calms, and the force and direction of winds to be expected. Although you know full well there's not a hope in hell of winning the game it's the only one in town to play, jumping from square to square trying to avoid the storms and areas of calm. We started to pick up local radio stations and became part of small communities, sharing their pleasures and tragedies. We sneaked into towns like ghosts, unheard and unseen, and leaving without the occupants ever knowing that we had visited.

Sunday, November 30. No sights, wind increased last night and moved to south bloody east, right on our nose. Finished up with the storm jib and three reefs in the main, slamming into rough seas. Albany Radio, 300 miles to the north, reported winds of 30-40 knots but at sea the gusts are much higher than that. A man and a woman have been swept off a yacht and lost during a race from Perth. *Solitaire* and I felt their sorrow but our bowed heads went unnoticed. On the morning of Tuesday, December 2, 1980 we had our first visitor. People often ask me how I keep my mind occupied at sea. 'Do you talk to yourself? What is there to think about?' In fact mind and brain work harder as a storm can present a dozen problems at once. Even a small incident can set you thinking for days. Ideas shoot in all directions like an egg splattering on concrete. On this particular morning I was reading in my bunk when there was a crash at the top of the mast, followed by a squarking and clattering as something fell inside the rigging. The largest and most confused albatross I had ever seen filled the cockpit. We eyed one another cautiously until I realised the bird's wing was trapped in the mainsheet.

'Me friend' I said as I released it. Then I remembered that Christmas was only 23 days away and this bird was ten times larger than any turkey I had ever seen. But there was no way I could kill it. In any case, as every seaman knows, it is bad luck to kill an albatross, and seamen have starved rather than harm one feather of their heads. The creatures of the sea were part of my family. We lived and died together. They entertained me with their beauty and grace. There was nothing on God's earth that would make me kill this bird and eat it. But if it was injured I could make a lead for it and turn it into a pet, taking it for walkies around the deck every morning. Should it die of its injuries I could then eat it for there's nothing in the rules that says you can't eat an albatross that dies from natural causes. Suddenly I became aware how lovely this bird was with its half-frightened eyes and panting chest. I remembered then how many months it was since I had last seen, let alone spoken to, a woman. If it was bad luck to kill an albatross what would happen if you merely tried to seduce one? Was it a criminal offence? I could see the headline, 'Round-the-world yachtsman accused of screwing albatross'. I would make millions. Newspapers would queue up to buy my story and I might even be able to afford some decent charts. This line of thinking came to an abrupt end when I realised that I hadn't the foggiest idea whether this particular albatross was male or female. A seducer of birds, maybe, gay never.

I went to get a piece of rope so that I could prevent its hurting itself

171

further but he must have misunderstood my intentions and shot over the stern like Concorde. As I watched him circling over *Solitaire* I noticed the yellow superstructure of a ship dropping below the horizon, my first sighting since leaving the Atlantic.

Week 21 saw off 596 miles, my Christmas dinner and what might have turned out to be a long and lasting friendship.

Week 22 went by with old Matthew the crooked gambler up to his tricks. We logged 590 miles through storms where there were supposed to be no storms and calms that should not have been there. The former did not worry me but the latter did as we were making less than 600 miles a week in areas noted for their constant following winds and where I anticipated covering between 700 and 800 miles.

Week 22 started with *Solitaire* entering the roaring forties and ended 240 miles deep into them in latitude 44°S. With a number two genoa we could have made more use of favourable winds; instead we were running out of time and the voyage was taking much too long. Week 22 ended on Wednesday, December 10, 1980, after five months at sea. We were holding a good course with winds gusting from the north-west around force six under clear blue skies and with a cabin temperature of 66°F. But the crew was worried, very worried.

The day before I had made the first check of food stock since leaving England. Until then I had imagined we were reasonably well off for supplies. True, I had exceeded my ration from time to time, not because I was hungry; for hunger was nothing more than an ache in the tummy. It was the side effects that caused concern, the loss of body weight, of sailing instincts and the will to survive. After five months at sea things were starting to go wrong, thanks to an ill-planned diet. Because I was spending long hours on my bunk, I was developing bed sores which I would bathe with salt water. My teeth and gums had given no trouble in the past; now when I cleaned them the gums bled.

Annegret had given me a bottle of multivitamins from which I was taking one a day. Whether it helped I did not know, nor whether washing my back in sea water and cleaning my teeth twice a day did more harm than good. These were small problems that, ashore, would take only a few days to clean up, a few good meals with fresh vegetables, fruit, eggs and milk. A few hot baths. Nevertheless they were problems that gave me a good deal of concern as the log shows. '0000 GMT Tuesday, December 9, 1980. Once more becalmed for 24 hours and concerned by slow progress. Either it is blowing so hard that I have to take down the main to prevent

172

weather helm over-riding the self-steering or there's insufficient wind. Since the Cape of Good Hope I have only been able to use the working and storm jibs. The old number two genoa is far too weak for these gusty, squally seas. We are 600 miles due west of Tasmania with the Australian coast about the same distance north. Have logged 13,601 miles. If we were 1,000 miles further on I should have considered us half-way.

Five months at sea with the worst to come and at our present rate of progress we could be at sea for a further six months. My food list shows that two-thirds of our supplies have been used.

Stews, 15.3 oz tins

Chicken, 12 to start, now	6
Beef, 12, now	4
Steak & kidney, 12, now	1
Minced beef, 12, now	8
Savoury mince, 12, now	6
Started with 60, now	25

Greens, 10 oz tins

String beans, 12, now	4
Peas, 12, now	5
Mixed vegetables, 12, now	5
Started with 36, now	14

Baked beans, 8 oz, 48, now 34	
Spam, 24, now	6
Sardines, 12, now	6
Marmite, 1 lb jars, 2, now	1
Bovril, 1 lb jars, 2, now	1
Jam, small jars, 12, now	2
Flour, 70 lbs, now 15 lbs	
Rice, 60 lbs, now 50 lbs	
Water, 80 gallons, now 30 gallons	

Fruit, small tins

Fruit salad, 12, now	9
Grapefruit, 12, now	5
Started with 24, now	14

Eggs, onions, fresh vegetables and yeast finished.
Tea, coffee, sugar, milk, no problems.
I still have six of the ten parcels Rome and Annegret gave me.'

I'm well into the second time round with my books. Oh well it will soon be Christmas with another parcel to open. Apart from the food I was concerned about my parents, having told them I would be away ten months, fully expecting to take no longer than nine. Over the years I'd caused them quite a few sleepless nights what with my broken marriages and forever chasing off to strange lands. For the first time at sea I wished I had a transmitter aboard.

Week 23 saw the start of some of the voyage's hardest time en route to Tasmania. Christmas was approaching and every time I turned on the radio they were singing about it, the first Christmas I had ever spent alone; and not just alone, but ignored. The log reveals some of the problems of sailing close to a friendly shore, hearing a woman's voice and longing to be in the same room with her sharing the same music, breathing the same air, to be close to another human being.

'*Thursday, December 11, 1980.* No sights possible, sea very rough. A good run of 120 miles in 24 hours on a broad reach under storm jib in westerly winds.

Friday, December 12. Latitude 46°19'S. Storms dropped during the night and the day now bright with a few scattered clouds. Swell large and winds light with mini gusts still from the west, was soaked when a wave smashed through the main hatch boards to find me without storm gear on, about to eat my only meal of the day (rice with two squares of melted chocolate on top). We both got soaked and the meal was ruined. Bilge pump packed up so spent the morning repairing it with some difficulty as main locker cover was now glassed in. Lucky it isn't Friday the 13th!

Saturday, December 13. Rain squalls so no sights. Little wind during night. The lights of two ships sighted on horizon. Could have been fishing as they stayed in sight for a long time. Winds from north-east this morning, anything from force three to seven, ending with one hell of a squall. After which they started gusting from south-west. Good show. Now on course with working jib only as gusts too strong for main. Temperature still in the low 50s. Nights are a bit cold and seas chilly. Able to go on deck without sea boots and socks but feet slowly turning blue.

0830 GMT. Large white fishing boat cuts across *Solitaire*'s bow giving me a few grey hairs. I had watched his approach for some time waving my red ensign. I thought he was going astern of me when he suddenly turned and nearly removed *Solitaire*'s bow. I dropped my camera with which I was trying to take pictures and dashed to release the self-steering. When I straightened up he was past us showing his stern. For the first time since leaving England I tried to speak to someone. 'You bloody bastaaard,' I called but I don't think that was his name. On the side of his white hull was HHJE, which was unpronounceable.

0855 Second fishing boat passed astern, JRIU. I think they must be Japanese. A few small dolphins, first for months are around. Ships are coming from the south. Must be returning to Australia from fishing grounds.

2200 Sight shows us 141°38'E. Sunday in Australia. Have just heard

174

Family Favourites with Pete Murray. Makes one a bit homesick.

Sunday, December 14, 1980, 0225 GMT. Noon position, 45°38′S, 142°15′E, 120 miles south of Tasmania.

Monday. Black sky, storm from south-south-east. Hard on the wind under main with three reefs and storm jib. Melbourne Radio reports a low pressure area over Tasmania. Must keep hard on the wind as I don't want to be pushed north. Bit down last night to see my tri-navigation light hanging over the side at the top of the mast; not that I've used it much apart from the odd ship.

Tuesday. Becalmed for eight hours. Slight breeze from the south-east with a high swell inhibiting progress. Charts show no winds from the east or south-east and no calms. They have been useless since Cape Town. Harry Secombe has just been on Hobart Radio now 190 miles to the north of us. Seems he is doing a show there. Very tempting to spend Christmas in Hobart after all this bouncing about but I can't let down *Solitaire* with these thoughts. Have just checked the trailing log, three bloody miles in five hours and Hobart Radio forecasts light bloody winds tomorrow from the south bloody east. Blast, blast, bloody blast. I was hoping to be well past New Zealand by Christmas; now I have no chance and Hobart keeps offering water to a man dying of thirst.

Wednesday, December 17. Hobart's weather report gives temperatures around 50°F with rain to come. At present we have blue skies, scattered clouds and light airs from south bloody east. Full main and working jib as I'm trying to save number two genoa for later. We have now passed under our third cape. *Solitaire* is one of the few to sail so low in this area. Chichester, Alec Rose and Knox-Johnston all sailed above Tasmania. One day we will have to visit this island which seems to have taken the best that England can offer and improved on it. Hobart's radio broadcasts are some of the friendliest I have ever heard. As I write they are talking about a Christmas tree in Hobart Square and asking for tins of dog food to be put under it for the stray dogs' home. The only thing stopping me from going in is the desire to return home to see family and friends. And I can't let down *Solitaire* by a mere tug on the heart strings. This afternoon it's bright and sunny and we have more wind. Strangely although south of Hobart and closer to the icebergs our temperature, 13°C, is higher than theirs. More Japanese fishing boats in sight. Week's run 547 miles, can't even break the 600 mark.'

Week 24 started with high swells and heaving seas as we dropped south to latitude 49° to round our third cape below New Zealand.

The lower reaches of the Tasman Sea have a high percentage of gales. Chichester and my American friend had capsized in the Tasman, both rolled over in hurricane force winds in a sea whose bed alternates between anything from 2,000 to a few hundred fathoms. Our route would take us between Stewart Island and Auckland Island, 200 miles apart, (between them the smaller Snares Island), just below New Zealand. I planned to sail between Snares and Auckland as it seemed the safest way, preferring, as I do, to keep clear of shelving sea beds. Now there was no choice. The waters we would be sailing through drop to 80 fathoms. The chart showed names like Sub Antarctic Slope, Solander Trough, Pukaki Rise, Campbell Plateau . . . If the beautiful names of the South Pacific islands fell from the tongue like poetry, these belonged to a horror story. That we were sailing through the roaring forties, reaching for the screaming fifties, did nothing to stop the hairs on the back of my neck rising. Hobart's friendly radio station gave a final warning, gales from Brisbane down to Tasmania, then a last song from Cilla Black, *Day by Day* from the show Godspell. I have never really liked Miss Black's voice, a bit too high and shrill for my taste, but at that moment everything seemed perfect . . . the fading, friendly island, Christmas shopping, that lovely dogs' food under the tree, the words of the song, 'Day by day dear Lord I pray to see thee more clearly, love thee more dearly'. Someone turned on a tap and tears flooded my eyes, while two rivers ran down my face. When the song ended the tap was turned off.

Solitaire rode the Tasman Sea as on a big dipper. Pushing her way through head-on gales she rolled drunkenly in confused swells that were enormous. Despite those seas we received a small Christmas present: we broke the 600 mile barrier with a run of 617 miles for the week ending December 24 and that Christmas Eve I spent listening to New Zealand's local radio. Tomorrow, with the parcel from Rome and Annegret, would certainly prove my big day.

'Christmas Day, 1980, the start of my 25th week at sea. Food is now a problem. For two weeks I have been cooking rice to last three days, mixing in a tin of soup or mixed vegetables. My yeast has gone but I still try to bake the flour by itself. Yesterday for a change, I tried to fry this hard bread with a tin of beans, and finished having to suck the fried bread as if I were eating a stick of rock. The morning is grey and miserable with a faint breeze on our nose from the east, the sails just about filling and the self-steering struggling to hold a course. We are 260 miles west of Snares Island, drifting to pass below this island

and New Zealand. I have managed to get a few unreliable sun sights through the misty haze but they do tie up with dead reckoning.'

Now for my parcel after a wash and a change of clothes. Just about to open my present, I heard a splash at *Solitaire's* stern and found a seal jumping out of the water to reach a flock of small grey birds that were teasing it. The way it snapped and whirled around with just his head out of the water reminded me of my old dog. Then I opened my present and started crying. It was not that my friends had remembered me on the other side of the world – and Lord knows I needed the things inside – it was the caring and effort, the thought behind their gift. There was a Christmas dinner with all the trimmings, pudding, a cake with a candle to put on top, a cracker, a bottle of wine, chocolate, a lovely tin of salmon and, perhaps best of all, a Christmas card. Rome and Annegret apologised for omitting the traditional Christmas tree. What puzzled me was how they had managed to find all these things in July when I left.

I cried not because I was lonely, or hurt or sad. I was doing something I had wanted to achieve in life but there are times when people show acts of kindness for which words can express no real gratitude. At such times the only way you can show your feeling is with tears. At that moment I would have given anything to wish another human being, 'Merry Christmas'.

I ate only half my dinner, saving the rest for Boxing Day then spent the afternoon listening to the New Zealand parties whom I toasted in wine. For tea I had cake, and for supper a few squares of chocolate. I could not remember the last time I had had so many meals in one day. The salmon was something to look forward to in the future and, with rice, it would last for two days. *Solitaire* had a holiday, too. The wind died completely. As we both slept dreaming of the future and Cape Horn the current carried us three miles in 12 hours.

Boxing Day, 1980. The weatherman gave me a late Christmas present with a clear blue sky for 30 minutes, sufficient to obtain some good sights after three days of fog and drizzle. There are less than 200 miles to Snares and Auckland Islands which lie some 150 miles apart. After months of sailing in open seas I feel *Solitaire* is trying to thread a needle.

We threaded it in week 25, a week when more baby black seals came to play around us, a week when I discovered I had only 22 gallons of fresh water left. I tried to make progress by using the old number two genoa, watching it like a hawk for fear it should split in

177

the breeze. It was also the week in which we picked up a new radio station, Dunedin, our nearest possible port where I heard of the murder of a young girl by five boys. Several weapons had been used including a cricket bat . . . it seemed particularly horrible that something that can give so much pleasure should be used in this way, and to kill at a time when the human race was giving thanks. A tragedy for the victim's parents and for the boys as well. *Solitaire* and I often felt that we were from another planet circling mother earth puzzled by the means of destruction – planes, tanks, rockets, cricket bats.

Week 25 and 1980 ended on Wednesday December 31. I made an entry in the ship's log, 1200 GMT, 2359 New Year's Eve in New Zealand, and spent the night listening to New Zealand welcoming in the New Year. Still 12 hours to go back home. And in large letters I added, 'Happy New Year to Folks Back Home'.

If puzzled by the outside world I tried to bring sanity and order into my own by logging our position and objectives on December 30, 1980.

'Distance by Walker trailing log, 15,300 miles.

Time at sea 175 days.

The four most southerly Capes rounded

1	October 6, 1980,	week 13,	Cape of Good Hope,	South Africa.
2	November 28, 1980,	week 21,	Cape Leeuwin,	Australia.
3	December 17, 1980,	week 23,	Tasmania.	
4	December 30, 1980,	week 25,	Stewart Island,	New Zealand.

Cape Horn, 5,000 miles to the east, will be the fifth and last.

Yacht Solitaire At present in good shape, her hull clean apart from barnacles on her stern and weed trailing from around her propeller and the bottom of her skeg. I can't be sure of the keel's condition. This is better than I could have expected and I'm pleased with Herbert Ochs' anti-foul paint. It is possible the hull will clean when in southern ice.

Rigging Always a worry, but no problems so far.

Sails Very good. Have used only the mainsail, working jib and storm jib since the Cape of Good Hope. Shortage of sails a major problem. My old number two genoa is in reserve for the return trip from Cape Horn.

Self-steering Good at present if a bit noisy. Have not had to waste time at tiller.

Food Have cut down over past weeks. Rome's food parcels have been a godsend. Should be OK.

Water My main worry at present as I have only 22 gallons left out

178

of the original 80 and still 5,500 miles to go to next possible port, Falkland Islands. Hope to catch rainwater off mainsail before then.

Weather so far Surprised by winds from east and south-east. From equator to half-way across the Indian Ocean pilot charts hideously wrong, but pleased with temperature, never much below 50°F. And I'm still not wearing sea boots. Sweaters and trousers worn in sleeping bag.

Crew His worst time was in Cape of Good Hope storm. Feels his slow progress has let down friends. Keenly anticipating rounding Cape Horn to be on the home straight. Worried about mother and father, having had no contact for six months.'

Week 26, Thursday January 1, 1981 found *Solitaire* sailing away from the east coast of New Zealand with only two small islands, Antipodes and Bounty 90 miles apart and some 250 miles dead ahead separating her from her goal, Cape Horn. The islands themselves posed no navigational problems, and at worst I could sail above Bounty Island into the Pacific; but they were the last land before Cape Horn, the point where the shelf that extends around New Zealand with its shallows would end, the seas dropping from a mere 200 to around 2,500 fathoms.

With the start of the New Year we had to change over to our 1981 Almanac which Rome had managed to buy at a reduced price along with my few charts. The parcel he had given me for rounding the bottom of New Zealand was still in reserve. If this was cheating at least it was cheating on the right side. The problem was that it came too close to the Christmas present. Food, or the lack of it, was becoming more and more of a worry. First it had been my bleeding gums, then back sores, now I was noticing more bodily changes. My knee bones and hips were starting to project, and using *Solitaire*'s winches was proving an increasing strain. When I noticed a new symptom I tended to eat more than my official ration and next day would examine my arms, expecting to see developing layers of fat. Alas, it made no difference. All that happened was the loss of another tin of stew or fruit.

The parcel for rounding New Zealand was opened as we passed 35 miles below Bounty Island with one more present, the Cold Weather Parcel, to open before Cape Horn.

The biggest bonus on the voyage so far had been how much warmer it had been than I had anticipated. During the Cape of Good Hope storm I had froze and firmly expected something similar of the Southern Ocean. In fact off South Africa had proved the coldest part of the voyage to date. Now we were sailing at latitude 49°S, well below the iceberg limit although the seas were bitterly cold. To have fallen over the side would have meant death in minutes, but the cabin temperature was still around 50°F, whereas I had anticipated frost on the deck and icicles on the rigging. As it was I was still running around barefoot. *Solitaire* was wet below and a line I had strung to dry my smalls had little effect, but lying under my two sleeping bags was not the teeth-chattering experience I had anticipated.

Soon after passing Bounty Island we crossed longitude 180° and had two Tuesdays in one week. Navigational rules changed again: now the degrees would decrease as we sailed homewards. Entering the deep waters of the Pacific what I had been dreading happened, two bad gales one after the other. Normally they would have given me no concern, coming as they did from the west and over *Solitaire*'s stern. The seas rushing across the shallow banks below New Zealand were neither dangerous nor particularly steep or high, but their speed was phenomenal and the first storm ripped the plastic cover off the self-steering gear. During a brief spell of calm I replaced it and a worn plastic gear selector knob at the same time.

We were thus more or less ready for the second storm which arrived shortly before dark, the breaking waves coming through so fast that *Solitaire* was for ever pushed beam on to them and without help would so have remained during the night. It was one of those situations you find yourself in now and again, when wave speed seems to be twice as fast as wind speed. I changed into storm gear with extra sweaters and prepared to spend a night, black with racing clouds, in the cockpit. I could hear the seas bearing down on us before I could see the flashing phosphorus of breaking waves rushing *Solitaire* forward. I felt I was walking a tight-rope using the tiller as a balancing pole while I tried to hold *Solitaire* atop a knife-edge to stop her falling on her side. As the waves went through there would be a back-wash when the tiller would lose its grip and I would have to work hard to get back in position for the next. I steered by scattered stars flashing on and off as speeding clouds chased the rollers.

By dawn I needed a rest. I was tired but it was a satisfied tiredness. *Solitaire*, the sea and I had spent an almost enjoyable night, each playing his part without taking too many liberties. Politely the seas had kept out of the cockpit and for once *Solitaire* had been glad of my helping hand on her tiller. As for me, well it's always satisfying to feel needed for something more than a sail change or a bilge pump.

180

Week 26 ended on a Tuesday and I struggled to work out how I had managed to lose a day. My navigational figures were still coming out correct so I did not worry too much about it. The week's run was 682 miles.

Week 27 passed with no tragedies although I ruined the film in Rome's camera. I had a choice of keeping the half of film with the whales on or the Japanese fishing boats, and I plumped for the whales rather than the people who give you grey hairs. The sores on my back worsened and I tried washing them with a strong solution of sea water and Dettol. My gums bled even when left uncleaned and new bones I did not even know I had started to develop. I baked golf balls of bread, sawed them into washers and fried them. Spread with a thin film of jam they could be sucked like pebbles and I would enter in the log that I was on the pill. If they provided any nourishment my bones ignored it and stuck out in protest.

On Friday, January 9, 1981 *Solitaire* and I had been alone at sea for six months. The idea of rounding Cape Horn had been born during our stay in Tahiti in 1976. Five years later all that stood between us and our ambition were a few thousand miles of deep water. Thinking of the seas to come I glassed in the lower board of the main hatch, which I hated doing as I was now virtually sealed below. The rear cockpit cover remained to be glassed but that I could leave to the last minute. The week's run was 640 miles, 16,695 in all and 4,000 miles short of Cape Horn.

A week later we were 631 miles closer, still experiencing gales and confused seas which baffled *Solitaire* and crew. During a heavy rainfall I managed to collect seven gallons of water via the mainsail. Mostly I complained about my lack of headsails. Often I had to drop the mainsail when the wind increased because of too much weather helm and would have given anything for a strong number two genoa. Time passed quickly, marked only by pencil on a chart. One day a whale surfaced alongside us as I was putting a reef in the main. One minute, birds apart, the sea was empty, the next we had an upside-down supertanker alongside. It took some moments to appreciate that something so large could be alive. Although there is much that scares the living daylights out of me, creatures of the sea manage only to rouse my intense interest in their activities. I dashed below for a camera but by the time I returned the whale had gone. At no time did I feel it threatened *Solitaire* and for long I lingered in the cockpit and felt lonely when it failed to reappear.

We had some vicious storms during one of which *Solitaire* was

181

knocked on her side and the Bosun compass in the rear of the cockpit leapt out of its plastic holder and finished wedged against a gas bottle. I had to make a dash to retrieve it between breaking waves, minus wet weather gear or harness. There were days when we sailed under clear blue skies, the ocean swell hardly noticed below decks. *Solitaire* snoozed along at four knots with no more noise or movement than when sitting in her berth at Lymington.

Then we passed our point of no return, much as jet aircraft do when flying the Atlantic. From now on *Solitaire* would stand a better chance of surviving by rounding Cape Horn rather than returning to New Zealand, and this engendered a great sense of relief. We *would* round it, possibly without mast or instruments, food or water, but dead or alive we would pass Cape Horn.

In week 29 we recorded 630 miles, and the following week 679 more. I ran the engine for the last time and glassed in the rear cockpit locker which meant that from now on I would have to crawl through from the cabin to reach the exhaust pipe seacock. There were a hundred things I wished I could have done for *Solitaire* and I hoped she knew this. If I had had the money, I would have given her the finest headsails spun from the finest silks.

Week 31 was the week in which I opened Rome's parcel, and the first week since the Cape of Good Hope storm that I experienced real fear. It had started well enough. Storms had become routine, a quick dash on deck to change down to the storm jib before the feet iced up. The log shows our lack of concern.

'*Wednesday, February 4, 1981.* No sights thanks to gale conditions with unbelievable squalls. *Solitaire* being thrown on her side. The sky keeps changing colour, blue to black to pink. Fantastic. Sailing under the storm jib only.

Thursday, February 5. No sights thanks to overcast sky with drizzle. Gales died during night but high seas ran until early this morning. Have changed to working jib and mainsail doubly reefed. Sea not too bad now. Water running off the mainsail but not enought to catch for drinking. We are now deep into the loose ice area and the seas are bitterly cold. I have been wearing the quilted trousers Margaret gave me, another present I can't remember saying thank you for. Margaret said they had belonged to a butcher who spent most of his time in a refrigerated store. I doubt if he ever imagined their being used to keep someone warm off Cape Horn, but a magnificent present for which I'm truly grateful. The height of fashion this season in the Southern Ocean is Rex's thermal jacket with a couple of

182

sweaters and pairs of socks under full storm gear and sea boots. At night I doze under two wet sleeping bags with the temperature down to 40°F by night and 50°F on warmer days. The main problem is the damp cabin that allows nothing to dry. I can take off my quilted storm jacket below by day, but on deck full gear is needed as the strong winds bite through sweaters and the seas soon freeze hands. Provided you work quickly there's no real problem. Loss of weight still a major worry and my strength is going as well. Very concerned in case I have to climb the mast as I just don't know how I would manage to pull myself up. My back continues to get worse. Most of my shirts have now been worn and are bloodstained. It seems a terrible thing to do but I sorted out the few that seem reasonably free from filth and intend wearing them again inside out. I tried washing one in salt water but it would not dry properly and seemed to irritate my skin. Oh well, Rome's present tomorrow. We are about 1,400 miles from Cape Horn. I'll get sights when the sun pops out.

Friday, February 6. Still no sights, winds from west increasing to force six to seven as a few fierce squalls came through. Visibility down to a few hundred yards. Drizzling with some heavy rain during squalls. Have considered sitting in the cockpit and putting up the main, trebly reefed, to catch fresh water. *Solitaire* swinging about with just working jib so have given the idea a miss. At present I have 20 gallons of fresh water left. No worry as far as drinking is concerned but it would have helped hygiene to have washed a few clothes. Opened the parcel from Rome and Annegret marked 'for cold weather sailing'. Everything inside is perfect . . . and so welcome. The conditions are better than I could have hoped for although below they are pretty foul and the cabin smell must be terrible but I have to keep the hatch completely closed with these following seas. As I don't expect visitors I'm not worrying too much about spraying air fresheners. Once or twice a week I treat myself to a throat and cheek shave and the lingering smell of soap in my beard gives pleasure for hours. I've now read all my best books through twice but with this parcel Rome has included a new book. The food and chocolate will give me special treats for a week. Without my friends back home I would have still made this voyage but oh how much I owe them. I just hope we can make it back to thank them properly for all their kindness.

Saturday, February 7. Sights put us at latitude 50°18′S but it's a bit of a guess as the horizon is so hazy thanks to the drizzle but I'm pleased to have anything after five days' sailing on dead reckoning.

Becalmed during night in fog, winds are now gusting from the west about force five to six so working jib only.

Sunday, February 8. Solitaire suffered her worst knockdown since leaving England. For the past few days I have been frightened, not when the wind was screaming but when it suddenly stopped. Without the background of its noise the sound of the breaking seas seemed to increase; and without the wind's controlling hand on the self-steering *Solitaire* ran like a child into thundering traffic. If I had to wait too long for the rogue waves and cross seas to start slamming into *Solitaire* I would sit on the bunk and cover my ears with my hands, singing to drown the silence. The knockdown came early as the log records. 'Problems at dawn this morning. Very bad knockdown, working jib damaged. All the piston hanks are broken and the luff wire has pulled out, halyard parted. I think I can save the sail but regret the loss of the halyard as I have only one left and if that goes it means climbing the mast. *Solitaire* is in a mess with bilge water all over the place. At present winds gusting from the west at gale force with cross seas from the south. Broad reaching with storm jib under a sunny sky which makes no sense. I will have to be more careful until past Cape Horn. Port Stanley is now our nearest harbour 1,600 miles away even if I cut in close to the Cape. The bilge pump is U/S so I've plenty of work for next two days. Longitude sight puts us 102°52'W, 25 miles behind our dead reckoning position. The seas have been too bad for sights over past few days. Pleased to get anything. Worked all day on sail which might shape up tomorrow. At least it will make a good spare.

Monday, February 9. Seven months at sea. Rain or drizzle and no visibility. Winds from west. Had spare working jib up until this morning, then changed to storm jib when rogue waves started breaking over *Solitaire*. Cape Horn lies on latitude 56°S, approximately 1,260 miles to the east. I intend to go down to 58°S, putting us 120 miles below and well into the icebergs, much lower than other singlehander. With only one halyard left and my weakening condition I think it's the safest thing to do. I don't want *Solitaire* driven onto a lee shore without the use of her sails to claw her way off. I've cut down further on food: now I boil two cups of rice to last three days but I still believe we can make this voyage non-stop. Working jib not yet mended. I can't be sure how far *Solitaire* went over in her knockdown. It happened so quickly that I didn't wake up until she had started to come up again. When I went on deck the jib was over the side held only by its sheets and down-haul. Whether the hanks and

184

halyard were broken when the waves hit or as she came up is any-one's guess. The jib is covered with anti-fouling paint but the seams are OK and I have spare piston hanks.

Tuesday, February 10. Week 31's run 614 miles, total 19,249 miles. Good sights in a clear blue sky. Sea is flat with high swell. Winds three to four from west. A perfect spring day. Temperature up to 51°F so able to dry out. Noon position, 53°51′S, 99°34′W with Cape Horn 1,200 miles to the east, only 129 miles south of our latitude.'

In week 32 we covered 643 miles, 45 miles below Cape Horn at 56°45′W. Should we now lose our mast we could jury rig a headsail and run past the Cape. We would even give the Islands of Diego Ramirez a wide berth passing 15 miles to their south. *Solitaire* was in good shape again. I had fixed her bilge pump and mended her second working jib and she even looked tidier below. All the water containers that had covered her cabin floor when we left Lymington, 224 days ago, were now empty and all but four stored in the forward compartment with the spare sails. My disco dancing could be extended with the extra floor space, not that I felt too much like dancing. No signs of depression in the log although constant complaints about the lack of headsails, particularly a strong number two genoa. Food was a constant worry. The problems I had faced with my bleeding back and gums had been only the beginning of many problems caused by a lack of fresh food and vitamins. *Solitaire*'s movement did more than irritate the sores; it seemed to wear away the flesh. First I noticed my thighs, elbows and knees starting to stand out, then the fat disappeared. I still had muscles but no body weight with which to use them. Side effects included headaches, blurred vision and blackened toe nails. I had enough food aboard to gorge myself silly for a few weeks and often would take some of Rome's chocolate and suck it as long as I could make it last, then I would spend the rest of the night with the remains of the bar lying only inches away from my watering mouth, trying to keep my mind on other things, particularly Cape Horn, now only 500 miles ahead.

Week 32 saw my dreams of rounding Cape Horn come true, six years after hitting the reef off Brazil, five-and-a-half years after the birth of the idea in Tahiti.

'*Wednesday, February 18, 1981.* Noon position, 57°30′S, 80°23′W. Sights are not good as sky changes every few seconds. Sun shoots through scurrying grey clouds. Changed up from storm to working jib this morning although winds very strong at times. We don't want to go much further south as we are well into the extreme limit for

185

icebergs. If we could pass Ramirez Island at this latitude all would be fine, 90 miles south of Cape Horn with 2,000 fathoms or more below our keel. Approximately 360 miles to go; very, very cold on deck. It will be good to sail north into warmer seas.

Thursday, February 19. Noon position 56°48'S, 77°41'W, some 290 miles from the Cape and 18 miles south of the Diego Ramirez islands. Log shows 20,061 miles sailed non-stop. Light winds from the south so we have up a full main for the first time in days. Spent last night without my wet weather jacket. Hard to believe we are so close to the desolate Cape Horn in such conditions, with no winds howling in the rigging and the seas flat apart from a constant high swell. Temperatures up to 45°F so we have spent the morning with the carpets drying in the cockpit.

Friday, February 20. Latitude 57°01'S, 60 miles further south than Cape Horn and we have just spent the night becalmed! I left up the main to stop our swaying in the swells. The chart shows that we have added only 30 miles in past 24 hours. Now we have gusting southerlies force three to seven under a main with one reef and working jib. Engine turned by hand seems free enough. A look over our stern for the first time in many a day reveals a crop of goose barnacles that could give trouble. The cold seas are not killing them off as expected.

Saturday, February 21. Lovely sailing yesterday afternoon on a bright blue sea under a bright blue sky. Winds went to the west force five. Gorgeous night with a full low moon, the sky covered with a carpet of stars. Two hours before dawn we ran into our present conditions when the winds died for three hours, then came back gusting from the north to north-east, anything from force four to seven. Reaching under a main with two reefs and working jib occasionally luffing into the gusts on top of the waves. No visibility at times thanks to heavy rain so no sights today so far, but dead reckoning shows us 60 miles below Ramirez Island, with about 200 miles to reach Cape Horn's longitude. And Rome's parcel! Good sight for longitude during afternoon which confirms our position. Clouds have cleared away. Should not have said anything: we're back to black squalls!

Sunday, February 22. Strong squalls through the night reduced us to working jib only. Winds perfect this morning, force five to six from west, for doubly reefed main. Have been taking sights all morning which confirm that we are still 60 miles clear of Ramirez Island. No noon sight. Winds have dropped and given way to rain and drizzly fog. Would have liked sights but at least we are well clear of land and

186

lee shores. At one time I had considered closing Cape Horn but decided it was asking too much of our guardian angel. I would have welcomed a few photos to replace those I ruined, but Chichester nearly lost his yacht by cutting in too close so it is much safer to stay in these deep waters rather than risk the Horn's shallows just for a few pictures.

1650 GMT. I believe Diego Ramirez is 90 miles and Cape Horn 150 miles north-east of us. With reasonable winds we should have reached Cape Horn's longitude by tomorrow evening. At present becalmed in heavy rain.

1832 GMT. Our position 57°30′S, 70°55′W with winds again gusting from the west five to six higher in squalls. Only 75 miles to Ramirez' longitude of 151°W. Shallow waters extend for 40 miles below these islands so our present position is fine.

Monday, February 23. Lowered main yesterday evening during fierce gusts. Sea remained quite flat so I had a peaceful night after all and winds dropped to force three to four. Awoke to heavy rain so after hoisting the main with one reef I spent the morning catching rain

● **Just before rounding Cape Horn. A bottle of champagne tied to the pulpit with Rome's letter on the flagstaff. The only time the ensign was flown at sea**

water for drinking and taking photographs of the operation.

1640 GMT. Noon position 57°03'S, 68°19'W. Distance run 20,380 miles. We are about 10 miles beyond Ramirez Island with 35 miles to go to reach Cape Horn's longitude. Good conditions at the moment so with luck we should pass soon after dark. I have opened Rome's parcel after cheating a bit. It's such a glorious day I wanted to take some photographs with their letter attached to the flagstaff. I have included Peter's bottle of champagne by tying it to the pulpit rail.

2100 GMT. Further sight confirms previous position. Now only 16 miles to pass Cape Horn's longitude. *Solitaire* is pointing due east on latitude 57°S, 60 miles below the Cape in a perfect position with 2,000 fathoms below our keel. Black squalls keep building up astern of us and passing through. How about the navigation? Must have improved since Brazil. Wish the cook could do as well. He dished up Bloody Rice again today.

Tuesday, February 24. The end of our 33rd week at sea, 231 days in all. We passed Cape Horn at 0100 GMT this morning, 20,473 miles from home. Yesterday's sunshine has turned into a mixture of gales dying to whispers, rain, fog, drizzle gusting back with squalls then storm force winds again and changing so quickly that I'm leaving up just the storm jib. Below, everything is wet and miserable. I have just taken off my socks for the first time in more than a week. My feet look like two dead cods and surprisingly white.'

I knew something was missing but could not figure out what until I realised that I was minus my black toe nails. When I turned the socks inside out I found them nestling at the bottom. I was now fleshless, toenailless and my gums bled so badly that I would soon be toothless as well. What else I had to give before this voyage ended I shuddered to think. All I wanted now was to head north and sail into warmer seas, opening hatches and washing myself and clothes if only in boiled sea water. The thought of sitting in a sunny cockpit with cooling breezes which soothed my blistered, itching back was a dream of paradise. I could imagine a shrivelled old man with wrinkles around his Chinese slit eyes eating his daily rice with a gummy smile on his face looking like a refugee from Shangri-la. There was no feeling of achievement, only gratitude that the seas had allowed *Solitaire* to pass over them without making too many demands, and relief that the oceans were now open to us. I had my celebration dinner on February 25, 1981 the start of *Solitaire*'s 34th week at sea. We had been becalmed all morning following the previous day's storms. The afternoon was like an English spring day, clear

● Two days after rounding Cape Horn … like an English spring morning

blue skies with a bite in the crystal air. As the carpets dried in the cockpit the temperature went up to 59°F. *Solitaire* started to make her way north with an escort of dolphins to welcome us back into the South Atlantic.

For that night's dinner I reckoned on half a tin of meat balls accompanied by beans and finishing with a third of a tin of sponge cake. Between courses the instructions on the champagne were adhered to: not to be opened until Cape Horn is abaft the beam although I wasn't too sure what that meant.

The second part of the instructions – 'for internal use only, contents to be consumed in one sitting' – gave no problem. Following these orders I realised how warm and cosy the cabin had become: the saucepan's water had boiled away and my tin of sponge was virtually glowing! In my inebriated condition I forgot about saving some of the sponge for the following day and scoffed the lot, and for a few hours drifted warmly in sleep until a screeching night wakened me. I staggered on deck into biting spume flying from the tops of freezing breaking seas. After reducing to the storm jib I returned to my damp, stinking prison, and lay shivering under sodden sleeping bags.

With the broad Atlantic stretching ahead navigation was less important. Should I lose the last spinner on my trailing log, or the portable radio pack up it would not now be too serious. We still had 8,000 miles to go before we reached Lymington, if the charts proved correct and we did not have too many calms; and provided the anti-fouling prevented our hull from turning into a wet sponge, we would make it home non-stop. All rather iffy.

Two days after rounding Cape Horn we were becalmed again. To sit for hours without movement watching my scant food supplies dwindle was stressful and only partially relieved by my remarks in the log. 'It seems hard to believe but we are once more becalmed. *Solitaire* is lying with just her mainsail and one reef. For the second day we have waves and a high swell but we don't have the most important ingredient, WIND. The red telltales are hanging straight down from the backstays like a girl's skirts, our sails slamming back and forth with frustration. I wonder what the price of property is around here. Might pay us to rent a house while we're sculling about. The log line is visible only for a few feet, dropping out of sight into the sea's black depths. There must be some forward movement as we have progressed two miles in three-and-a-half hours. The Falkland Islands are 230 miles due north so at this speed we could be there next Christmas. After our celebration meal we are back to skipper's choice: half a cup of rice, a third of a tin of peas with curry powder. Sounds bloody delicious. Bet you any money the cook serves up the dish again tomorrow. If we have wind – if – we will soon be sailing over the Burwood Bank where the ocean depth shelves from 2,000 fathoms to 40. Let's hope the winds don't about face. I would not fancy these shallow waters during a storm.'

There were good days. On one I was looking over *Solitaire*'s stern when a whale surfaced. A few seconds earlier he would have certainly given us a lift in life. Near the Falklands I picked up some lovely music on the restricted medium wave, probably from Argentina as the announcer appeared to be speaking in Spanish. All my old favourites, played by a string orchestra, came across: *Tales from the Vienna Woods*, *Maria*, and what seemed appropriate at the time, *All the Lonely People*.

We were carried over the Burwood Bank shallows by current and wave rather than by wind, at times the boat's forward speed was faster than the following breeze, the mainsail backing itself so that for a few seconds the wind seemed to come over our bow. As we dropped off the shallows into the 1,000 fathom line we ran into a vicious storm and were thankful it had not arrived a day earlier. The rest of the week passed in a mixture of gales, storms and breaking seas, *Solitaire* dragging herself north to break the Southern Ocean's icy grip.

On Monday, March 2, 1981 *Solitaire* slipped unnoticed past the Falkland Islands 60 miles to the west. Only their local radio playing request music proved their existence. Next day we ran out of the screaming 50s and fell off the end of our last decent chart. Now all we had for navigation was a pilot chart which proved sufficient. The South Atlantic lay before us, its welcoming arms opening wide for a thousand miles.

Week 34 ended with the Falklands 185 miles in our wake, having logged 575 miles despite the calms, 21,117 miles in all, but it would be another week before *Solitaire* cleared the limit of the icebergs and the high storm areas. My log ended with good and bad news. The good news was that the temperature in *Solitaire*'s cabin topped 50°F; the bad was disguised in a few words, 'checked food supply. Not good'. In fact it was serious. As the food had disappeared from under the bunks the space had been filled by other pieces of equipment. My main food supply, the rice, was kept in a sealed bucket adjoining Rome's last two parcels and such other food as remained was stored behind the main bunks.

Sometimes I failed to understand the speed of its disappearance, as if I were spending £5 notes and finding each was worth only twopence. No sooner had I broken into a fresh cache of food than it seemed to vanish, despite cutting down on my rations so that my bones cried out in protest. At one period I found I had more powdered milk than I needed for tea so I started mixing two spoonfuls of powdered milk, sugar, flour and water which turned out like soft toffee when fried. I would have a little of this at night and cut my rice to half a cup a day.

My last checks on the food supply took no time at all as once I had dropped the bunk backs every morsel of food aboard was in full view. Although we could be at sea for a further three months, hunger was not really all that important. There were millions of people who would have been grateful for a tithe of what I had; it was more a case of wanting to play my part in returning home and not lie on my bunk, too weak to help *Solitaire* on this last stage.

Over the months my attitude had changed frequently. As far as nerves were concerned the worst period had been from England down to the storm off the Cape of Good Hope. In a way I was lucky that it happened so early because, once it was over, it served as a reference point; we survived that one and this is not so bad so we'll survive this one, too.

Week 35 started with a storm that brought some of the worst seas of the last stage. On the first day we had northerlies gusting up and down on our nose. *Solitaire* was sailing reasonably into a fairly flat sea with a full main and working jib but just before dark, for no reason that I could explain, I felt uneasy and put two reefs in the main. Much later I awoke to a violent gale which, had I not reefed the mainsail before turning in, would surely have caused us serious damage. Next day the storm increased and I recorded, 'worst conditions since Cape of Good Hope. Severe storm, squalls from the south-west reaching an all-time high. Bad cross seas. *Solitaire* running on broad reach under storm jib'.

My attitude to this storm was shown by the fact that during its worst period I tied myself to the mast and spent an hour taking photographs. Every now and then I found I was standing without *Solitaire*, clinging to the mast. After an hour I gave up, having failed to take a decent picture. Below wet sleeping bags and the usual smell of rancid cabbage, dirty clothes, and unwashed bodies greeted me. All I had to write about that was, 'oh well, things will improve further north'. Although I felt no great achievement in rounding Cape Horn the pressure of passing it before winter set in had disappeared. The worst of the voyage was behind us, the best to come.

By noon next day the gale had dropped and I even wrote about a beautiful afternoon, a clear sky and a sparkling sea with the temperature up to 59°F. For the first time in months I dropped the pram cover from the main hatch and removed stinking sea boots and socks.

Monday, March 9, was probably the best day of the voyage. We had been at sea for eight months covering 21,568 miles. The South American coast was 600 miles to the west. Our latitude was 43°06′S which left us only with 186 miles to go to clear the roaring forties. After opening up the forward hatch to flow fresh air through the cabin, I stripped off my filthy blood-stained clothes, boiled some sea water and washed all over, to the instant relief of my itching back.

All mildewy or dirty clothing was put into a sealed bucket in which was a mixture of washing-up liquid and scented soap for good measure.

With ropes attached I tossed the cabin carpets overboard to be washed in the world's largest laundry, their brown wake joining the brilliant blue and white one left by *Solitaire*.

The log summed up the voyage so far, 'let's hope the worst is over. We have approximately 7,000 miles to go. The best I can expect is to be in Lymington by the end of May, another 80 days at sea. *Solitaire* is not as fast as when she left England. Her hull must be badly fouled and we have the doldrums still to pass through. With just two more strong headsails and the standing rigging reinforced we could have done so much better. The worst part was not, as I had expected, rounding Cape Horn but the storm off the Cape of Good Hope. Rome's parcels have been lifesavers; without them I don't know what I would have done and shall never be able to repay his kindness. I'm just sorry my performance as driver was not up to standard, something like 325 days for the round trip. Might have to emigrate to Brazil to hide my face'.

Tuesday, March 10, 1981 saw the end of our 35th week at sea and another 595 miles. Used the number two genoa for the first time without having to watch it hawk-eyed. The log finished on a cheerful note, 'becalmed at present but having just heard the budget on the BBC, being becalmed isn't so bad after all!' It was the last cheerful entry I made for some time as the calms continued where perfect sailing conditions were indicated.

'*Wednesday, March 11.* Dinner was a Roman orgy – tinned lamb stew! Should last two days but food really is a problem. I must start catching fish soon which should help. No chance for a spinner now that *Solitaire* is hardly moving.

Thursday, March 12. Slow progress. Swell from the west pushes us forward a few feet now and again but a glorious day with a clear blue sky. Temperature 67°F. Water down to 15 gallons but food still the main problem and leftovers from yesterday's stew will have to last two more days. Now have fishing line trailing over the stern, the last thing I want as I hate the thought of killing anything. Unless we make better progress a non-stop voyage will be difficult. Noon latitude 39°58'S. At last we are out of the roaring forties but still becalmed, sails slamming. We haven't had a decent sail for four days.'

Friday, March 13. Becalmed until 0300 but good progress in the last 12 hours. Logged 67 miles.

Saturday, March 14. Becalmed again. I think the idea is to allow me to sail 60 miles a day and no more. Once the daily allowance has been achieved the wind goes on strike. If I don't catch fish I can't see my doing this trip non-stop. Perhaps I can ask a ship for supplies. This morning I inflated the dinghy while becalmed and cleaned the barnacles off *Solitaire*'s hull although swell made it difficult. Will try again further north.

Sunday, March 15. Full gale from the north-east. Reduced to mainsail only with three reefs. Making no headway; we might even be pushed back towards Cape Horn.

Monday, March 16. Yesterday's storm could have been worse as we lost little ground. Now beating into north-north-westerlies, force five to six and risking our number two genoa in an attempt to make up lost time.

Tuesday, March 17. Gale conditions have reduced us to working jib and 329 miles this week, the worst since leaving England. Feeling very depressed. I have 12 gallons of water remaining and 60 days' rice allowing half a cup or so a day. I can cut no further and as it is am slowly turning into something dragged in by the cat. Today's main meal will be rice with baked beans; yesterday's was curry powder mixed with Marmite poured over half a cup of rice. Recently I have tried fishing without any luck. In these storms I've had to stay closed in again which doesn't help. If I could catch more drinking water and a fish or two! I will try to pass through the doldrums to the Azores but must reckon on calling at St Helena or Ascension.'

During week 37 we still progressed slowly and dinners were not quite up to *Queen Elizabeth* standards.

'*Wednesday, March 18.* Skipper's choice: half a cup of rice, half a tin of peas and Marmite mixed with a little flour. Sounds bloody delicious. Bet the cook dishes up the same meal tomorrow. No luck with the fishing.

Thursday, March 19. Worked on damaged toe rail and washed my smalls in boiled sea water as becalmed, which does allow one to do the odd job like building another yacht or celebrating your 100th birthday. I was right about the flaming cook: curried peas again.

Friday, March 20. Another 400 miles should see us coming out of the high gale areas. Dinner today: half a small tin of spam, half a cup of rice with mustard. Yuk.

Saturday, March 21. Dinner, finished the rest of the spam.

Sunday, March 22. Dinner, the human skeleton had baked beans and half a cup of rice but it is a glorious day with temperatures up to 76°F.

194

Gorgeous to sit in the cockpit with the hot sun bleaching your bones. Fishing line out but no luck. Feel content despite shortages. 1500. Nearly caught my first fish, bright green and about three feet long. I had it alongside for around ten minutes trying to get a loop of wire around its tail with a boat hook and pull a sail bag over it but it broke the hook and escaped. At least it proves my spinner and tackle work so maybe better luck tomorrow. Whooopeeee, food!

Monday, March 23. A few squalls during the night, more a whisper on black velvet compared with the screams of the Southern Ocean, forced me to lower the main. No fish so settled for rice, half a tin of sliced green beans, flour and curry powder. Maybe cook will give me fish tomorrow . . . I could use the other half of the sliced beans.

Tuesday, March 24. The end of week 37 with a run of 486 miles and another glorious day in the low 80°s under a clear sky on a flat sea. A faint westerly barely fills main and genoa. If only I had food and water, life would be perfect. *Solitaire* is still the most beautiful lady in the world but her constant movement over the last months has worn down my flesh, leaving only muscle and bone and I have to keep bracing myself against her movement even when asleep. A beautiful lady but she's wearing me out. Dinner: beans, Marmite, curry, flour. And all there is left is hunger!

In week 38 we logged only 299 miles, the worst this voyage despite doing everything I could to increase speed. My old number one genoa I had saved for passing through the doldrums was hoisted but day after day the sail lay useless on deck. We kept up the main merely to reduce pitching and tossing. Thoroughly frustrated I opened up the rear cockpit locker, breaking my fibreglassing, turned on the seacock and started the motor for the first time in many weeks. It ran effortlessly to charge the batteries for a couple of hours then I switched it off to lie ahull, rocking back and forth under a slapping main.

To vary my monotonous rice and curry powder diet I spread some toothpaste on rice and forced it down as my day's ration: thereafter each time I cleaned my teeth I felt sick. Then I remembered that Annegret had given me a box of medicines and sorting through it, found some throat lozenges which I treated myself to at the rate of one a day. Drinking water went down to eight gallons so I cut my tea ration from three cups a day to three half-cups until I managed to catch six gallons during a rain squall which put a stop to any water rationing. Intermittent calms and squalls gave problems with both old genoas and time after time I was caught with long repair jobs.

195

In week 39 the winds became more constant from astern and our daily runs increased from 80 to 125 miles, 668 miles in all by the week's end and my spirits rose. Although my trailing line was now constantly in the water, the nine inch spinner breaking the surface a hundred feet astern, I caught no fish. With the high temperatures and crystal waters you would have thought the ocean would have been alive with flying fish, dolphins and sea birds but it was empty. Lack of wind could have been the reason for the absence of flying fish since a sea without constant wind is a death trap for them but perhaps they realised that if they dropped on deck I'd have 'em instanter.

Week 40 was one of the best as the winds continued to increase when we reached the south-east trades, and daily runs first touched and then surpassed 100 miles.

● **One way of getting a supply of water. Catch it off the mainsail!**

On Thursday, April 9, we recorded our ninth month at sea and 23,638 miles, only another 5,000 to Lymington. On a glorious day with hardly a cloud *Solitaire* stretched her legs as we sailed past another landmark, Ascension Island 900 miles to our east. Provided there were no major problems we would now reach the Azores although we still had the doldrums to pass through. And I still had two of Rome's parcels to look forward to. *Solitaire* was in good shape and my own health was not too bad, at least my skin was starting to tan and the blisters on my back had healed. We were progressing.

Friday, April 10 saw us 600 miles from the equator, and on my last parcel but one. Winds were a little light but *Solitaire* seemed content as flying fish started to appear, lifting in panic to splash back when their wings failed to gain lift in the zephyrs. Seated in the cockpit, two cushions protecting my fleshless posterior, I willed them to fall into our web of rigging and sails, weary flies for a starving spider. The spinner glinted appetisingly in *Solitaire*'s wake but attracted no takers; our radio, however, hauled in its own catch, gorging itself on the BBC's overseas broadcasts. The American space shuttle epic was in progress, reducing *Solitaire*'s efforts to a stroll in the garden but we shared a common aim, we were both reaching for the impossible and yet making it probable. I was content despite settling for a dinner of . . . you guessed it . . . curry powder, peas and rice.

Next day, Saturday April 11 our position was 08°S 28°53'W (480 miles to the equator), having sailed 23,862 miles (112 in the past 24 hours). Winds were force three to four from the east and we were under full main and number one genoa. *Solitaire* made five to six knots on course. Spent morning repairing number two genoa. No luck with fishing so for dinner opened my last tin of sardines and rice, maybe the voyage's last fish dish.

1800. Caught and photographed my first fish, a beauty. Food, bloody food! I was resting on my bunk conserving strength when I heard a scraping sound and lay awhile trying to work out which part of the rigging was causing it before staggering on deck to investigate. The fishing line was sawing back and forth across the top of the pushpit. The shock cord taking the initial strike was stretched to its limit, so grabbing a pair of heavy rubber gloves I started to haul in the line which felt as if I had hooked a junior whale. When I had brought it within 20 feet or so of the stern I could see it was three to four feet long; white and bright emerald green flashed as it twisted and dived, a starving man on one end of the line, a creature fighting for its life on the other. Slowly the hunger of the one overcame the

197

will to live of the other until I had it alongside, holding its massive head out of the rushing water, staring into frightened eyes. How could I kill this beautiful creature which would surely turn me into a cannibal? I would be eating my own kind and I knew I must not.

My fellow traveller metamorphosed from the most beautiful fish I had ever seen into fry pan potential, and my mouth filled with succulent juices which, overflowing, streamed from my lips. Lacking a gaff I feared he might be too heavy for me to pull onboard and that he would escape, but I heaved him out with such force that he shot over my head to the bottom of the cockpit where he flapped and flounced, clinging to life. I grabbed him by the throat to strangle him with hands like claws but in this I failed so dashed below for the biggest hammer I could find, scattering tools in all directions, before

● 'When the choice lay between my hunger and another creature's life I would kill unhesitatingly.' But only once

I killed him with it. Remorseless, I sat back as the beautiful greens faded to lifeless greys and learned something about myself: that when the choice lay between my hunger and another creature's life I would kill unhesitatingly.

Having hung the body on the backstays, I photographed and measured all 46 inches of it. Lord knows what it weighed as it was as thick as the top of one of my legs – before I started dieting. After removing its head and tail, I cut the rest into steaks, dropped them into buckets of fresh sea water, and selected two pieces, one to be left on deck to dry out for later, the other to fill my frying pan. Slowly it turned from grey to heavenly white food and as I watched it saliva streamed down my chin although I managed to resist the compulsion to eat from the pan. Instead I dusted off my best plate and laid the fish upon it, ignoring the protests of my tormented stomach. The fish required a dressing to bring out its flavour so finding the remnants of some sherry I splashed a few drops on the fish course and poured the rest into a glass which I topped with water to make a fine wine. The Queen, God bless her! I lifted the glass to check the wine's colour then smelt and tasted it before declaring it a vintage. Carefully I selected one of the larger flakes of steaming meat, then lay back as it dissolved in my mouth with a flavour never before experienced this side of heaven, the finest banquet, I decided, I would ever have. For the first time in months I purred contentedly, satiated. One more thing would fill my cup: the aroma and taste of coffee. I had run out some time ago but located a jar with some dark stains in, filled it with boiling water and had my last wish, a delicious cup of coffee-coloured liquid.

The fish should have lasted a week but, fearful that it might go off, I gorged myself for three days, frying, baking and boiling it and for the first time since leaving England ate three good meals a day. Had I known I could have made it last longer for after a few days the pieces I had kept in water grew slimy and started to smell whereas the chunk left on deck to dry in the sun slowly turned white, looking for all the world as though it were frozen. Best of all there was no smell. Sliced in the frying pan with a tin of tomatoes my last fish meal proved one of my better recipes. Back on rice and curry powder I regretted I had not dried out more but, starvation apart, I resolved never to catch a fish again, still remembering the fading colours as the fish died. The smell of death lingered in *Solitaire*'s cockpit and fish scales would turn up in the most unlikely places for days to come. *Solitaire*'s main problem now was her passage through the fickle doldrums: if we were lucky enough to make a fast passage there would be no need of further mayhem.

The effect of the three days' feasting was dramatic. Bleeding gums, stomach pains, headaches, sore eyes and foul mouth vanished and if my body were still skeletal at least now it could pull its own weight. With perfect sailing conditions it was bliss to laze in the sunny 80s cooled by spray.

I had bouts of depression, worrying about my parents and my return to England with nothing in the world but the £60 I had left with which would not last long as I owed the VAT on my new Lucas sails. Since I would not have spent a full year outside the country the £60 must be earmarked to clear that debt. Perhaps I would be allowed to see my family, then sail to the Channel Islands to finish out the year there. Also I still had a court case awaiting me, the very thought of which sickened me. My chances of finding work would be slim, for who would want a 56-year-old electrical engineer who had spent the last six years at sea? On the dole it would be hard to look after *Solitaire* and get her back to sailing condition. I looked forward to seeing my friends aboard *Solitaire*, perhaps, if I were lucky, being invited out to dinner, but that would be the limit of my social life. To go with a crowd to a pub for a drink would be out of the question: I could not stand my round.

England had no place for *Solitaire* and me. Had I been sponsored things might have been different, but we had left unknown, without fuss, and were returning similarly. I had no yacht club, *Solitaire* and I were working class misfits, our best hope to settle the court case quickly and sail before debts bogged us down. Some of *Solitaire*'s gear could be sold: I would no longer require two self-steering systems and if the worst came to the worst I could sell the engine. Yes, I certainly had my moments of depression.

In week 40 we covered 772 miles in all but the following week would be the important one; with luck it would see us through the dreaded doldrums across the equator. Luck-less we would spend days becalmed, watching our stores dwindle. We started well.

On Wednesday, April 15, the day's run was 120 miles, then the winds swung from south-east to north-east, a sure sign that we were leaving the constant southerlies to enter an area of uncertainty and confusion; my sextant recorded that we were just 29 miles south of the equator. We must have been passing through one of the main Brazilian shipping lanes for during the day two ships passed down our side. That night one was in sight for hours before slipping astern of us and over the horizon, the *thump thump* of its engines echoing behind. After that I snuggled down in my sleeping bag for what I hoped would be a long rest, but black clouds racing across the sky brought strong winds and heavy rain. My main concern was that for some time we had had two small islands, Sao Pedro and Sao Paulo, dancing on our bows. As they were only a few hundred feet high they were difficult to see but I was unwilling to spend too much time giving them a wide berth. I changed down to working jib, reefed the main and came hard on the wind.

By Thursday morning we were 40 miles due east of the islands. The wind first dropped although there was still a sea running after the night's squalls, then went back to the south-east giving us a broad reach under full main and number two genoa. By noon we were 01°24'N, so despite the squalls we had covered 109 miles and were 84 miles above the equator, *Solitaire*'s sixth crossing.

Friday, April 17 was Good Friday. Although it meant opening two parcels close together I needed to do it and then decide whether to pass through the high pressure area of the Azores in the hope of stopping a small ship for supplies, or sail west taking advantage of current and the lower percentage of calms. I opened Rome's last two parcels, one for crossing the equator, the second for Easter, and indulged in half a tin of faggots and peas. Having read the letter accompanying the food I changed it for the Cape Horn missive pinned above the chart table; had chocolate for supper and watched the sun set while drinking a tin of Coca Cola, totally content. We had sufficient food to get us back to England non-stop, I reckoned. By noon we were well and truly in the doldrums with a hazy grey overcast sky whose light winds died by sunset. We drifted windlessly into Saturday on a flat sea, with the main hard in not just to cut down our oscillation but also to alert passing ships to our presence.

Traffic grew so dense that I gave up thoughts of sleep and stayed on watch that night. Shortly after midnight a ship zigzagged towards us. Normally I show no lights as they seem to attract supertankers like moths to a candle, but on this occasion I had no option. The effect of switching on my deck and running lights was instantaneous as the ship promptly turned towards us like a retriever wagging its tail, two searchlights bathing us in their brilliance. It is difficult to know what to do in these conditions: if you wave too much they may think you need help; if you don't wave at all they may think you are too weak to do so and try to help anyway. Normally I wave until I'm sure they have seen me then go below and watch

201

from the porthole. In this case the light went out and the ship pulled away, whereupon I spent the next 30 minutes trying to close my eyes without seeing stars and flashing lights!

On Saturday when we were 240 miles north of the equator and becalmed I sighted a larger vessel on the horizon. For some days I had been making up a chart of the voyage with messages asking that my family be contacted in England. I had tied these onto weighted pieces of rubber tubing in the hope that if I could get close enough to a ship it might be possible to toss them across.

After starting my engine we were spotted and the ship swung in our direction, passing down our port side 100-150 yards away, throwing up a decent bow wave. I held up my red ensign hoping our name would be reported to Lloyds. When well astern of us she started to turn on to what I assumed was her correct course but, instead, she completed the circle and steamed down our starboard side. When well ahead she swung across our bows and stopped engines. Appropriately enough she was the *Lloyds of Rotterdam*, registered in Rio de Janiero.

She lay dead in the water rolling back and forth in a high swell, her hull offering a good wind break so I started circling, each time closing the ship. Passengers looked down at us from every vantage point. I went within 40 yards of her then, as we were sucked closer to the towering sides of the ship, I realised I could not safely make contact. The spreaders on *Solitaire*'s mast pointed like fingers about to be crushed against steel plates. In panic I pushed the throttle fully open, my heart missing a beat as the engine hesitated . . . before we slowly drew away.

I made a few more passes, showed the flag and pointed to the name on our stern while the sun set in a blaze of colour. With a final wave I resumed course for home, hoping that we would be reported. I would have given much to let my family know I was safe but not at the expense of having *Solitaire* damaged in the process. We motored until dark when, with the ocean to ourselves, I shut down the engine to enjoy a night broken only by the crack of sleeping sails.

Sunday, April 19, was spent going around in circles, sails constantly backing, the air full of vacuums and bad language. To prevent *Solitaire* running over the non-trailing log I hauled it aboard but despite this and the confused conditions we still managed to log 53 miles. Sights gave us a distance of 90 miles with another 300 to go before we cleared the doldrums and sailed into the North Atlantic. With luck we would then have 1,000 miles of easterly trades. That night we surged along under a full main and jenny.

Monday was a great day. With dawn the winds backed to nor-nor-east and dropped, enabling me to hoist the big number one genoa. I thought about spending the day fishing but discarded this when dancing dolphins surrounded us. Two ships came over to take a look at *Solitaire* and her performing circus, clapped briefly and departed. Having nothing better to do than relax contentedly I tried to sum up our present position: the Azores were approximately 2,200 miles away and England another 1,800 miles, say 4,000 miles to Lymington. Provided our guardian angel looked after us for a further few weeks we should make it non-stop. Even if I had to cut down my rations to a mouthful of rice a day we would still carry on, skirting the Azores to the west and leaving their high pressure area to starboard. Temperature hit 92°F. Man, *Solitaire* and sea sighed in luxygence, a harmony of luxury and indulgence.

Tuesday, April 21, 1981 brought week 41 to a close. We had sailed 583 miles through the doldrums with far less trouble than I had dared to hope, the nor-nor-easterlies blowing at anything from force four to six. Still concerned about damage to the worn number two jenny I tried sailing hard on the wind with reefed main and working jib, but clearly I was under-canvassed and would have to use the genoas even if they were sacrificed in the attempt for more speed to overcome the close chopping waves. *Solitaire*'s staccato steps of the Cha, Cha, Cha turned into a graceful, gliding waltz. Now and again a vicious wave would vent its anger; and spray, filled with rainbows of a thousand colours, would shoot up from our bows before cooling the cockpit. At times mast and rigging would vibrate and the leech of the reefed main flutter. *Solitaire* would tremble and shake, match-ing her movements to the rhythm of wind and sea.

For a week she danced the miles away effortlessly, 878 by the end of week 42, our best run yet. Thanks to our speed through the dol-drums I thought I could risk increasing my third of a tin of soup or greens to half a cup and my rice from a half cup a day to two cups over three days. I had 10 gallons of water left; no worry there.

We still had to pass through the Azores high pressure area when I could really start thinking ahead. Could we reach home by the end of May was a question that could be answered only when we had passed Flores, 1,100 miles to the north. Next day, Wednesday, April 29, things worsened. I should have learned my lesson by now, not to take too much for granted. The log reports, 'over the past 24 hours our luck has changed. The seam on the leech of the number two

203

genoa has ripped and the bottom piston hank has broken through its holding eye, cutting the luff rope. Islands of yellow and brown Sargasso weed have started to appear, promptly wrapping themselves around the self-steering rudder and forcing me to pull in the trailing log. The winds are still light from the north-east but the occasional squall prohibits our using the large number one genoa so we ghost through a sea, half blue, half brown, chasing more wind'.

I still felt cheerful. The number two jenny had lasted much longer than expected and, if the problem arose, was still repairable but I would have to cut back to my old food rations for there was no hope of fishing in this expanse of weed. Thursday was spent working on the jenny, and by clearing weed from the self-steering blade we managed to push 80 miles through the jungle of floating Sargasso.

By Friday morning the headsail was repaired and ready to offer a few more hours of its valuable time at which point the wind died to a faint breeze barely giving *Solitaire* steerage way. To make up for the slow progress I had a celebratory 'parcel' dinner, half a tin each of pilchards and coleslaw, the closest thing I had had to fresh vegetables since South Africa. From the BBC I learned that a certain Bobby Sands was deliberately starving himself to death. 'I always thought the Irish were mad,' I wrote in the log.

Saturday was gloriously sunny but we made only 16 miles in 24 frustrating hours.

Sunday, May 3. We still had 600 miles to go before clearing the high pressure area. Although supposed to have only 2% calms we spent hour after hour rocking in great puddles of flat water, rising and falling with the islands of yellow weed. I started the motor which at least charged the batteries as we found a path through the islands, jumping from one puddle to the next, the sails still flapping. Once more I cut my ration to half a cup a day, with a small tin of beans for luck today.

Monday, May 4. In 24 hours *Solitaire* had moved only 10 miles through an oily sea with not a ripple on its surface. I hoisted the sails a dozen times but *Solitaire* was asleep. Dinner was half a tin of mixed vegetables and my rice ration. The entry for the day ended as had so many 'Worried about Mom and Dad. I must get word to them somehow.'

Week 43 ended on Tuesday, May 5 with a mere 395 miles on the clock and with another 670 to the island of Flores in the Azores, plus 1,700 for Lymington. Our chances of being home by the end of the month were fading and food was at a premium. Although I dared not risk losing more weight, I felt reasonably fit and since my fish banquet had no further problems with teeth and eyes. If I did not fancy climbing the mast at least I felt I could at a pinch.

Week 43 was depressing. On Wednesday I heard on the radio that the imprisoned Bobby Sands had died and remembered that I had been in Birmingham on the night that the IRA had killed 22 young people there. I could feel no sympathy for the Irishman. Since the start of my voyage on July 9, 1980 four leaders in their own fields had reached the top of the tree only to find there a pool of blood: John Lennon, ex-Beatle, shot and killed; President Sadat of Egypt, shot and killed; the Pope, shot; President Reagan, shot.

I had watched nine security guards accompany ex-President Ford around a golf course, condemned, as all presidents are, to being watched over for the rest of his life. Millionaires live in secluded fortresses and spend fortunes protecting their families; bank managers work all their lives to be rewarded with a gold watch and a first-class funeral. I wanted no part of their world, my epitaph read.

Dinner consisted of half a tin of beans with rice and while eating it I heard that Bobby Sands had died of starvation. Bloody amateurs!

That Saturday, May 9, 1981, I celebrated our tenth month at sea after sailing 26,368 miles by deciding to wash my shoulder-length hair. I remembered that Annegret had been the last person to cut it before I left England and I hoped she might be the first to cut it on my return. With this in mind I added tomatoes as a treat to the beans and rice before lying on my bunk to hear the Cup Final.

Next day the winds increased at the wrong time from the wrong direction. We were sitting on top of the mid-Atlantic ridge when clouds from the north raced over in evenly spaced banks and as the day wore on the howling in the rigging started to revive old memories of air-raid warnings in the last war. The storm could not have come at a worse time. The seas that had travelled for a thousand miles now hit the shallow banks surrounding the Azores where *Solitaire* lay, burying her bow and running down her decks in gurgling rivers. I reduced sail first to storm jib with two reefs in the main then, just before dark, when I discovered that we were making no forward progress against advancing seas, to just the mainsail with three reefs, pointing into wind and weather but getting nowhere. Here the current flowed south, trying to take us back over hard-fought ground. Had we been 300 miles further north we would have been in the homeward-flowing Gulf Stream. The cook belatedly served up half a tin of chicken soup with rice to a crew close to mutiny. Each wave that slammed the boat was answered by a head thrust out of the hatch and an abusive flow of foul language. When another wave was about to sweep over us I would hurriedly drop below and carry on the diatribe from the safety of my bunk.

The storm continued throughout Monday and Tuesday when I managed a few poor sun sights which indicated that we had been pushed back 31 miles over the last 48 hours. The trailing log for week 44 showed 421 miles covered when in fact we had made good only 390. And the blasted pilot charts showed no gales in our area! That I could live with, but the poor food situation and the beating *Solitaire* was taking, were raw salt in my wounds. Not that I felt endangered or even threatened. There was little chance that *Solitaire* would capsize so late in our passage or that her equipment would let us down. I could make it non-stop, but my growing concern for my mother and father was rubbing my nerves raw.

Wednesday, May 13, 1981 saw the start of week 45. 'The storms have died down. I changed up to full genoa and main, then the winds fell away altogether to leave us rocking and rolling in a high swell. By noon we had logged 60 miles which meant that we were precisely where we had been on Monday, time, food and effort wasted for nothing. One good thing about the high winds is that they have blown away most of the Sargasso weed. If we could start sailing again it would be possible to put out a fishing line.' That morning the first big turtle came drifting down *Solitaire*'s side, unaware of the hungry eyes watching it. I could very easily have reached down and patted him on the head, or slipped a rope around his neck. Turtle meat, I'm told, is delicious but as I looked upon its worried, wrinkled brow, I knew I could never kill it. So for dinner I had half a tin of mixed vegetables with rice, after which I wondered if I could catch the damned thing up.

Thursday, May 14 was no better as we covered only 30 miles in 24 hours. I left up main and number one genoa and sat in the cockpit watching them slam back and forth, oblivious to their wear and tear. What with calms, northerly storms and southerly current we had made hardly any progress in five days and the food position was now dangerous. I had 14 cups of rice left which, if I cooked two cups to last three days, meant I would have rations for 21 days. Apart from rice I had six 15oz tins of mince, soup and goulash; a third of a tin a day would feed me for 18 days. Also I had two small tins of mixed fruit that I desperately tried to ignore; they were for emergencies. And I still had 30 tea bags left with enough sugar and milk.

All in all I felt we could last another 21 days after which I would have to go without. The sensible thing would be to call into Flores but having got this far I put aside the temptation: it had to be England non-stop now, or put up with starvation.

Friday, May 15, 1981. At noon the Azores were 200 miles to the east and in another 80 miles we would pick up the east-flowing Gulf Stream. If becalmed after that we would drift towards home and not back to Cape Horn. Dawn's light winds strengthened to a westerly five and *Solitaire* started to stretch her legs with the smaller genoa. My fishing line found no takers although three or four turtles drifted by, looking so contented that I knew I could not hurt their feelings by catching, let alone eating, them. As we had made good 90 miles in the past 24 hours I celebrated with goulash and rice.

Saturday, May 16. *Solitaire* had covered 121 miles in the last 24 hours in mixed conditions, heavy rain, drizzle and sunshine. Fortunately the winds that gusted up to force seven were from astern and for which I reduced sail to our number two genoa by itself. Flores Island lay 120 miles east of us with Land's End only another 1,500 miles away by crow. Having no wings *Solitaire* would most likely log 1,700 miles but I would pick up BBC local programmes, perhaps Radio Solent with their weather forecasts and lovely, lovely music after another 1,000 miles or so. I finished off the goulash and rice.

During the night I had to change down to working jib as the fronts passing through were too strong for the weakened jenny but *Solitaire* still surfed forward on the top of breaking waves. Temperatures were now in the low 60s and I was back to wearing sweaters and quilted trousers which, once more, were keeping my legs hot-house warm. 'As I am on my last five gallons of water *Solitaire*'s floor is now unnaturally clear after so many months of clutter.' Sunday night's dinner consisted of a third of a tin of mince with rice.

Monday, May 18 was bad. The fronts swept through from nor-nor-east to north and we made only 63 miles. Yesterday's waves which she had rode now buried her bow with sheets of cold salt as she tried to stagger forward, halting, burying her hull and breaking free only to be submerged again. I had to put three reefs in the main and hoist the storm jib as the BBC reported that gales were sweeping England's south coast. Then my rice deliberately jumped off the stove onto the deck, so dinner had to consist of mince, brown rice and gritty carpet.

We passed over Chaucer bank on Tuesday when the winds dropped to five but with only 15 fathoms under our keel the sea ran high accompanied by a heavy swell. Week 45 ended with a run of 572 miles.

Land's End was 1,030 miles away on Wednesday, May 20 but I smelt green fields despite spending the day under a grey overcast trying to place a misty sun on an indifferent horizon. As we cleared the shallows the wind dropped, the sea flattened and *Solitaire* glided through banks of fog, a ghost ship returning from the dead. I started to tidy up, cleaned the cabin and heads and found some yellow cloth with which to make a Q flag for the customs man. Able to spare a little sugar and powdered milk I fried it into a sticky toffee, not my favourite sweet but at least something to suck. For dinner I opened another tin of mince and took out my rationed third. *Solitaire* made 82 miles in silence.

Thursday, May 21 saw us glide 113 miles, drifting in peace more or less in the middle of the Gulf Stream to Land's End, 1,000 miles ahead. Dinner, mince and rice.

Friday, May 22 bit off another 121 miles despite a stormy night when I reduced to working jib only. During the morning the weather cleared leaving a high swell behind, but the winds stayed around six and seven. I left *Solitaire* to do all the work while I sat contentedly below as we rolled along under the smaller jenny, thankful for the luxury of a following wind. For dinner the last of the mince with, you guessed it, rice.

Saturday, May 23 saw us bowling along in rough seas under broken cloud, content to sit below out of the flying spray while *Solitaire* chopped 130 miles off our voyage under working jib. For dinner I had a change, one third of tinned beef and . . .

Sunday, May 24, 1981. Gale force winds and high breaking waves made sights impossible but we made good progress with just the working jib on a broad reach. Log shows 125 miles in the last 24 hours. Dinner: guess.

Monday, May 25. Squally winds from the north as we reached with working jib and three-reefed mainsail. I picked up the BBC last night and for the first time in nearly 11 months actually heard a local English station. Batteries, like the crew, are nearly worn out. By day I can pick up Irish commercial stations which prove we're in the right ocean and manage some sights which confirm yesterday's dead reckoning. Dinner, minced beef, and rice served with curry powder.

Tuesday, May 26 saw the end of week 46 with 124 miles in the past 24 hours, 801 for the week, 27,856 in all which *Solitaire* could have bettered with more help from me. We still have up the working jib with three-reefed main as the winds gust from the north. Were I not so tired we could be tearing along on a reach with a single reef. I'm feeling the cold perhaps because my blood is so thin. Better that I keep what strength I have for sailing up the English Channel with its heavy shipping even if we lose a few miles. Land's End is now only 420 miles away. Soon I'll be with parents and friends. May they please feed me with anything but rice, bloody rice.

Wednesday, May 27. The winds died during the night but still we managed 90 miles turning east for the English Channel. When I tried to start the motor this morning I found the tank had rusted and lost seven gallons of fuel. Luckily I had eight gallons of diesel in plastic containers so I disconnected the fuel line from the tank and fed it directly into one container and after bleeding the system the motor started without fuss. The sky became hazy with a weak sun apologetically trying to force a way through. Warmly wrapped I settled in the cockpit listening to BBC music before starting my last tin of mince after which I would have only rice, the chink in my armour.

Thursday, May 28, 1981. Just before dark the wind strengthened and the main started to slam. Instead of dashing on deck I dithered and the sail's seams ripped open just below a reefing point after 28,026 miles of constant use and only a few hundred miles from home. I replaced it with the mainsail from our first world voyage rather than waste time with a repair. Wednesday had not been one of our better days what with the fuel tank and then the sail. Dinner consisted of curry powder on mince. Land's End now 240 miles away.

Friday, May 29. Becalmed since dawn and all I have left is half a gallon of water, half a tin of mince and less than two cups of rice. And, unable to get them out of my thoughts, I'm worried sick about my family. All morning I have been trying to catch the attention of fishing boats for whom I have made up more messages and charts asking them to contact my family. They come within a few hundred yards but when I start *Solitaire*'s motor and try to close them they pull away. After a few minutes' chase I lose ground, switch off the engine and lie lonely in a world of mist and lifeless sea. Dead reckoning shows Land's End approximately 160 miles away bearing 075° with Bishop Rock in the Scillies on the same bearing 30 miles closer. Had I a good directional radio there would have been no problem pinpointing our position as we were now well within range of British and French stations but mine was playing up. There was a faint chance it might give some indication when close to the station and assist our channel passage. For dinner half a cup of rice with mince-and-curry-powder gravy. Donning my warmest white sweater I sat in the cockpit while the boat idled on an oily sea, the only sound the faint rattle of her rigging caused by my own movements and dis-ease. I was attracted by movement at the bow which at first I thought was a butterfly but, as it neared, I could see was a small land bird, black in colour with bright blue markings. For a while it performed acrobatics then, having sung for its supper, landed on the foredeck and walked towards me hesitantly, bowing shyly as if unsure of its reception. I slipped below for food, trying not to disturb *Solitaire*, for fear of scaring away our visitor. There was little with which to tempt him but a few grains of rice and sugar which I put on a piece of paper, filling a saucer with fresh water. Back in the cockpit I feared it had flown away until its head popped from around the mast as though it had been playing hide and seek. The bird took an age to reach the cockpit, sometimes standing for minutes looking around, ignoring me completely. After gaining a few feet it would scurry back in panic while I sat motionless. Reaching the cockpit it flew directly on to my knee from where it stared at me, head to one side, then ducked under my sweater and worked its way up until it lay above my heart, its own rapid beats demanding care and protection. Nothing could have made me move, neither storm nor tempest. For hour after hour I sat, unmoving, worried about my family but strangely comforted. For the first time in nearly 11 months *Solitaire* and I were no longer alone.

Shortly before dark it came out of its hiding place and flew into the cabin. I put on the kettle and worried when the bird settled on its handle, as if still deprived of warmth. I made a nest of cotton wool and placed the food and water beside it. Then a faint wind sprang up and as I hoisted main and genoa *Solitaire* started moving, trying to hold a heading for home. With thoughts of more fishing boats in the area I switched on our running light, lay on my bunk and to the faint accompaniment of passing waters slipped into a restful sleep. I awoke to find *Solitaire*'s cabin pitch black. The wind strengthened and we were moving quickly but the sea was flat so nothing was straining. I checked our course and looked around for shipping before remembering my new shipmate. Finding a torch I searched the cabin only to discover a fluffy mound on the chart table, head to one side, its eyes finally closed.

Saturday, May 30, 1981. No noon sights possible. Since raising sail yesterday we have been beating hard on a force five south-easterly through drizzle and fog trying to head eastwards but slowly being pushed too far north. Despite being becalmed in the early stages we have managed to log 100 miles in the past 24 hours and have also picked up faint RDF signals putting us 20 miles north-west of Bishop Rock which means *Solitaire* will now have to sail 40 miles south in poorish conditions to round the Scillies. The winds are gusting and swinging a good deal with mist and rain so visibility is minimal. Instead of cutting through the shipping lanes at right angles we will be sailing down them. It's going to be a bad night. To prove it I dine on half a cup of rice and the last of the mince-with-curry-powder. All I have left now is half a cup of rice.

Sunday, May 31. Some 87 miles logged in the past 24 hours but thanks to tacking back and forth our forward progress has been only 40 miles. At noon we are 30 miles south of the Scilly Isles, becalmed and bewildered, sails sagging under a blanket of drizzle. For dinner a quarter cup of rice mixed with sugar and powdered milk which makes two mouthfuls. Thank goodness I can still enjoy a cup of tea.

Monday, June 1. Logged 81 miles with more tacking into strong gusting winds from the east-south-east accompanied by heavy rain. *Solitaire* is sailing as close to the wind as possible but a short, choppy sea sends up sheets of spray. Water is now very short but unless I turn and run with the wind there's no way I can catch any. Noon position by faint RDF and dead reckoning shows us 10 miles beyond and 30 miles below Lizard Point, with Lymington less than 150 miles away. Both RDF and portable radio have heavy background noise which suggests there's a storm about. For dinner another quarter cup of rice mixed with curry powder to make a weak soup, a terrible recipe! Wind is still increasing as I try to round Prawle Point, but without tide tables find it impossible to calculate the current. With luck I'll be with friends and talking on the phone to Mom and Dad very soon. I propose lying alongside Lymington Town quay until I have talked to Customs about the money I owe them.

Tuesday, June 2. At 0400 GMT Prawle Point light is flashing five miles due north and with dawn the outline of land appears, the first I have seen for 326 days. Since noon yesterday conditions have been ghastly and the radio is reporting the worst storms for 20 years with lightning turning night into day. Strong winds have died only to allow heavy downpours of rain. Our deck and running lights vanish as a blinding zig-zag flashes across a black sky destroying my night vision. I imagine *Solitaire* being found at dawn, her mast struck by lightning, a burned, shrivelled figure at the tiller. My trailing log line was cut during the night and I had no spare, but we were only 90 miles from Lymington and once past the Portland Bill tide race we could move inshore and follow the coastline.

Scenting she was nearly home *Solitaire* moved effortlessly over a flat sea and as the wind fell the mist lifted. Then Lyme Bay fell away from us and we could no longer see the land. As we neared Portland the Royal Navy started to appear and a couple of submarines swept down our side. By noon we were 20 miles from Portland Bill but land was still invisible. Late that afternoon the wind dropped completely, the sun emerged and the mist lifted. For the first and only time in the English Channel I took a sun sight which put us east of Portland, time to come on course for Lymington.

No matter what happened I wanted to be home the following day. For dinner I had eaten a spoonful of rice with powdered milk and sugar; now there was nothing. As the sun set we picked up a faint breeze from the west and *Solitaire* crept home like a runaway child, uncertain of its reception.

My own feelings, too, were confused. I dreaded my return to bureaucracy with the problem of deciding how *Solitaire* and I should spend each day. Once alongside, and after phoning my parents, my every move would be controlled by strangers. Customs officials would see a battered salt-encrusted yacht with a skeleton trying to form words for the first time in nearly a year, trying to explain that he had no money with which to pay the duty on torn sails. They might feel sympathetic but, responsible to higher authority and books of rules and regulations, what could they do? After that I would have to phone the solicitor. Had there been any way of avoiding courts I would have taken it, but I was in too deep. The best I could hope for now was that since I had sailed non-stop around the world and proved my point about the rejected sails the manufacturer might wish to settle out of court. If I could get back my money speedily and sell my spare self-steering gear I could leave England for America in two to three months' time. By August *Solitaire* and I might be free. For some time I had decided that for my next voyage I would sail to Newport, Rhode Island following the course Rome had taken on his transatlantic trip. After that I would sail down the inland waterway and cruise in Chesapeake bay before setting out for Cape Town and the Christmas tree in Hobart Square.

I started the motor, reduced the throttle until it throbbed in a contented tick-over and held a close-hauled course for the Needles 25 miles away. The three knots we were making meant a dawn arrival, perfect. I spent the night in the cockpit watching the shore lights to port and ships' navigation lights to starboard. I was tired and the slow beat of the engine made me feel sufficiently secure to nod off from time to time, only to jerk upright. Just before the dawn I must have drifted into deep slumber for on awakening all signs of life had disappeared. *Solitaire*'s engine still held its constant beat as she pushed through banks of fog but our course had changed slightly, taking us farther south into the shipping lanes. Without a trailing log I had no idea how far we had travelled, but when I tried the RDF I heard a weak signal from St Catherine's Point, half-way down the Isle of Wight, and decided to home in on it.

With dawn the sky lightened and the fog eased. When we broke out of one bank the white cliffs of St Catherine's lay off our bow, and the greens and golds of patchwork fields greeted me for the first time in 329 days. In the small box-like homes ashore well-fed people drank water that flowed from taps, talking together with faces that showed love and kindness and caring. After so long with only the background noise of wind and sea and the expressionless front of a portable radio we were close to the old sounds, of a footstep, the bark of a dog. When the wind blew it would no longer start the blood racing; we would hear only the rustle of leaves in bending trees.

I turned *Solitaire* north-west, following the island's shoreline to the Needles channel 10 miles away. Tipping the last of my water into the kettle I washed my face with some and boiled the rest to make a final cup of tea with my last tea bag. Now we had neither food nor water, just half a cup of sugar and a quarter tin of condensed milk.

From the Needles I turned into the channel past Hurst Castle where I dropped the mainsail and put on its sail cover, then stowed the headsail and sheets, making ready the berthing lines and fenders.

At 0915 on Wednesday, June 3, 1981 *Solitaire* nodded to the line of buoys she had last seen on July 9, 1980. I intended carrying on to the Town Quay with its public mooring but the thought of the people in Lymington Yacht Haven proved too tempting. As I neared the entrance I weakened, pushing over the tiller and *Solitaire* swept down the lines of moored yachts towards the visitors' berth.

A solitary figure awaited us. Keith Parris had been the last person I had spoken to when I left: it was appropriate he should be the first to welcome me home.

'Where the hell have you been?' was his greeting.

People were lining the upstairs' balcony, many of them old friends. When I arrived in the office they had already phoned the Customs. The good news was that the VAT I had been worrying about since rounding Cape Horn was payable only on the sails' value and after a voyage around the world that was nil.

213

As soon as practicable I rang my family. My father, over the moon, spoke first, having long since given me up for lost. Then I asked to speak to my mother only to learn that she had died eight weeks earlier.

Keith gently wondered if there was anything my friends could do. They had all known about Mom, but not how to break the news to me. So I returned to *Solitaire* and made my last entry in the log, '*Wednesday, June 3, 1981.* 0915 GMT. The end of week 47 after 329 days and 28,496 miles at sea. Arrived Lymington Yacht Haven and learned that my mother has died'.

Solitaire had shown me the world. Now I was lost.

● **Snug alongside again**

2

WHEN BOUND FOR SEA, or immediately after returning from it, there is a period of transition between the known hazards of life ashore and the less predictable problems of those afloat. For me the process had reversed; I accepted the solitary life of single-handedness that posed questions without always providing answers, an existence that for me could mean a shortage of food and fresh water, the rancid smell of unwashed clothes, with a circling albatross or a dancing dolphin my only companions. I was less certain of existence back ashore.

On the day I returned from my circumnavigation Keith Parris was the first to greet me. He followed me into the marina toilets, where I was anticipating my first hot shower in a year, still questioning me about the voyage. Without thinking I undressed and heard a gasp. Turning, I caught his disbelieving eyes and a quick glimpse in the mirror revealed a Belsen horror of skin and bone. I apologised for my thoughtlessness, at which he made a joke about my appearance, said he would fetch his camera and returned instead with a saucepan of vegetable soup. It was the last time I would take off my shirt in public for two weeks, by which time flesh had started to cover the bones and my weight had increased from less than nine stones towards its normal 13–14 stones.

After an initial hunger for fresh fruit and vegetables I slipped back naturally into my old life of food and conversation and at a welcome home party that first night ashore I found my verbal diarrhoea had returned with a vengeance. But fresh water I still used sparingly, reluctant even to wash *Solitaire*'s decks with it; to see a running hose untended filled me with a sense of panic.

Next day I phoned my solicitor thinking that I had proved beyond

215

doubt my knowledge of what was required in the way of sails for a non-stop voyage. In the hope that I would soon be off again I contacted George and his wife Antje Fisher whose yacht had lain in the next berth to *Solitaire*'s before we set off. Among their many acts of kindness they had made copies of my first voyage's log. Now I asked if they would make ten copies of the second. Later I put them into folders, together with photographs, for family and friends in the belief that this would be all I could offer as a memento of our voyage.

Then a visit was made first to the local Job Centre where shrugging shoulders greeted me, followed by the dole office and the searching questions of a girl not yet old enough to vote. For one triumphant moment I brought confusion to calm.

'When did you leave the UK?' she asked. 'And by what means?'

'By sea eleven months ago,' I replied.

'What countries did you visit?'

'None,' I replied and brought the system to a grinding halt.

My voyage had attracted little publicity. For anyone seeking fame and fortune from the sea the first thing you need is a good public relations man who, if he is good at his job, will find the second requisite, a wealthy sponsor. The third essential is a powerful transmitter to keep in touch with the first two. If you progress this far then it's time to find a suitable craft . . . Bob Fisher had interviewed me on TV before the voyage and a BBC TV crew had followed me down into the Solent although, to be honest, I have no idea how they discovered I was leaving.

A couple of days after my return Des Sleightholme, editor of *Yachting Monthly*, turned up personally and asked for a couple of articles. *The Observer* newspaper made me Sports Personality of the Week and sent enough champagne to enable me to give a party for the people in the marina. My hometown newspaper kept the story going for a few days and arranged for me to meet the Lord Mayor. Accounts were published in the USA, South Africa and Australia, and within a couple of days I had congratulatory telegrams from friends who had read the story, one of the first from my American pal, Webb Chiles, who had spotted the news in a local paper while sitting in a cafe in Darwin, Australia. One lasting friendship emerged from this attention. Dennis Skillicorn had interviewed me for the BBC before my departure and soon after my return arrived on board where I nearly strangled him. After settling in *Solitaire*'s cabin the first thing he did was to insult her. Only the twinkle in his eye saved him! Since then I have spent many happy hours with him, his

216

wife Marie and his family. Dennis is one of the very few people allowed to insult *Solitaire*. There was talk between us of a book but this costs time, effort and money, and my real interest was to sail first to America then to the Christmas tree in Hobart Square, Tasmania.

As so few people knew about the recent voyage, I was surprised to receive a visit that Christmas from Errol Bruce who said I had been nominated by The Yachting Journalists Association for the *Yachtsman of the Year Trophy*. Had it been anyone but Errol I would have suspected that I was on Candid Camera. I had not even heard of the trophy and when I discovered that the previous holders read like a yachtsman's *Who's Who* and included Chichester, Knox-

● **Yachtsman of the year with his trophy**

Johnston and Alec Rose, I had even more doubts. Later I was to learn that the choice lay between Chay Blyth and myself. I was selected by a single deciding vote because Chay had won it on a previous occasion. Had this not been the case I would have been a nonstarter. The award gave me a great deal of satisfaction if only because so many had said I had been foolhardy and had given sailing a bad name. Like the chappie released from a mental home I now had a certificate saying I was not completely bonkers.

My departure for America was delayed on three counts, the first sickening. My solicitor reported that the sailmaker had been unimpressed by my voyage and although the duff sails had been left in England they were available for use and therefore had been accepted as satisfactory. The firm also claimed that the time allowed for their return had been exceeded. It was to take until early 1982 to have a court hearing, when I was promptly awarded the return of the purchase price with costs which by now were higher than allowed at this court level, the difference to be borne by L Powles Esq. The case had lasted nearly three years and cost lord knows how much time and money. What really hurt was that if I had left on schedule I would have been with my mother before she died.

The second reason for the delay was an act of generosity. The Lymington Yacht Haven, learning of my financial problems and in recognition of *Solitaire*'s voyage, gave us a year's free berthing. The third pleased me most. By waiting until the following March Rome and I could leave together. He had sold *Solitaire*'s sister vessel and bought the hull of a 13-metre Colin Archer sloop. By now Annegret had given up her work as an air hostess and had returned to Germany, but before leaving she had helped to fit out Rome's new boat, *Aroha*, which now lay only yards away from *Solitaire*. The plan was that *Aroha* would cruise in the Mediterranean before setting off for Cape Town where I would join Rome.

He left on time with a young Australian nurse and Ian Large as crew. *Solitaire* sailed a week later on April 3, 1982 just ten months after her circumnavigation. Apart from a new number two genoa from Peter Lucas and an 18-gallon fuel tank made by Brian Gibbons to replace the old seven-gallon container little had changed. We still had blistered topsides and the worrying rigging connections. Having sold my back-up self-steering gear and been paid for my *Yachting Monthly* articles I had about £600 in the kitty.

My first stop was Dartmouth to visit Richard and Anne Hayworth and to anti-foul alongside the harbour wall. A week later I sailed for

218

Newport, skirting the Azores to pick up warmer weather, which I reached on May 20, 1982, logging 3,775 miles in 39 days. We hit a storm on entering the Gulf Stream and as there was no sense in beating into it with our weak rigging we lay hove-to for three days.

Peter Dunning, who ran the Goat Island Marina in Newport, and was largely responsible for the success of the transatlantic races, gave me a free berth for the night to allow me to clear customs and then let me use his own mooring which lay within a stone's throw of the marina facilities.

Reluctantly *Solitaire* left this hospitable harbour some five weeks later to cruise down Long Island Sound through the centre of New York itself, her ensign waving at taxi drivers and joggers alike. After passing under the Brooklyn and Manhattan bridges and circling the Statue of Liberty we made our way to Cape May at the southern tip of New Jersey and turned into Delaware Bay. At its northern end we entered the canal which links Delaware with Chesapeake Bay and then joined the intra coast waterway at Norfolk in Virginia to leave it at Beaufort in North Carolina on September 27, 1982. The hospitality

- **Solitaire sets off for Newport and Goat Island Marina**

I received throughout was beyond belief. Part of my time was spent giving lectures, the first a few days after my arrival at Goat Island. I had been to a barbecue at the yacht club in time to hear that some interesting character was giving a talk that weekend. Turning to my companion I said I would really like to be there.

'You'd better be, you're giving it!' was his reply.

My last talk was at the Museum in Beaufort. I arrived to find I could not get in and struggled through the crowds trying to explain that it could not start without me! My cruise down the American east coast had lasted three months.

From Gibraltar Rome wrote me suggesting we met in Antigua for Christmas and with this in mind I set sail on October 6 for Bermuda, some 600 miles to the east, and arrived on October 15. The Sports and Dinghy Club gave me a splendid berth on their pontoon and I received a letter from Rome's mother dated October 24 (my birthday) saying Rome had made a radio link call reporting he was 50 miles off Cape Town where he would arrive the following day. On November 3 Keith Parris rang me from Lymington to say Rome had been missing for eight days. Next day my golf partner in South Africa, Frank Minnitt, sent a telegram from Cape Town to say wreckage had been found but no life raft, so there was still hope. On November 5 I phoned Rex Wardman to learn the search had been abandoned.

Grace's daughter Terry had died of cancer within a month of my circumnavigation. Now she had lost Rome. I thought I could be with her over Christmas and set sail next day but Atlantic winters are always bad and after a week out *Solitaire* was pounding though head-on storms. During the night I heard what sounded like guitar strings breaking but despite searching by torchlight I could find nothing amiss. Early next morning I found that one of the Talurit connections I had worried about for so long had given way. The forestay in use had shredded at the top of the mast, the strands wrapping around its twin which I cleared by using a halyard to pull up loops of rope. My worry now was how long the twin forestay would last. There was no way I could reach England before the spring so reluctantly I turned *Solitaire* before the wind to run to St Martin's in the Caribbean, arriving there on November 29, 1982.

During the winter I worked on local charter boats before sailing for England on April 6 to arrive non-stop on May 16, 1983 after logging 3,636 miles.

Rome's body was never found. In his last letter to his mother, sent from the Canary Islands, he sounded confused and undecided, and

220

even talked of sailing to Recife in Brazil. At this stage he was single-handed in a boat designed to carry a crew. A vicious storm had hit the South African coast just after his last broadcast but what went wrong we shall never know.

On my return to England a large envelope greeted me. On it Rome had written, 'these are all your letters from the first voyage. They might be of use in writing a book . . .'

This is it and why it has to be dedicated to Rome Ryott, friend.

● **Rome**

SOLITAIRE
OF
HAMELE